ENCYCLOPEDIA OF MAMMALS

VOLUME 12
Por–Rac

MARSHALL CAVENDISH
NEW YORK • LONDON • TORONTO • SYDNEY

PORCUPINES

RELATIONS

The porcupines are members of the superfamily of cavylike rodents, or Hystricomorpha, which also includes:

GUINEA PIG

CAPYBARA

COYPU

PACAS

HUTIAS

Stephen Krasemann/Bruce Coleman Ltd.

Porcupines belong to the order Rodentia, which is divided into squirrel-like rodents, mouselike rodents, and cavylike rodents. Porcupines are cavylike rodents, a suborder named from the South American guinea pig, more correctly known as the cavy. Cavylike rodents have the largest number of families within the order Rodentia but the smallest number of species.

ORDER
Rodentia
(rodents)

SUBORDER
Hystricomorpha
(cavylike rodents)

FAMILY
Erethizontidae
(New World porcupines)

FAMILY
Hystricidae
(Old World porcupines)

GENERA
four

SPECIES
eleven

SPINY DEFENDERS

THEY MAY BE COMIC IN APPEARANCE, BUT THESE BUMBLING RODENTS POSSESS THE ULTIMATE DEFENSE: AN ARMORY OF NEEDLE-SHARP, BARBED QUILLS THAT FEW PREDATORS WILL DARE TO TACKLE

In a wooded area of Canada, a coyote approaches an animal only half its size, ready for an easy meal. In seconds, the smaller animal has whirled around to present its rump to its attacker. It raises a large ruff of spines and thrashes its tail—also bristling with quills—from side to side. Quickly, the coyote backs away; if those quills stab its nose, they will snap off and imbed themselves in the flesh. If the points stick in its throat, it could die of starvation.

The little animal is the North American porcupine. In South America, it has some nine or ten prickly relatives. In the Old World, extending through most of Africa and across central and southern Asia, there are eleven more porcupine species.

The various porcupines have many common features, but the most obvious of all, their armory of quills, differ little among species. All species have quite large heads in relation to their robust bodies, and their legs are fairly short. The jaws and dentition, too, are similar throughout. But just how closely the porcupines of these different areas are related to one another is uncertain.

BEGINNINGS

The first rodents appeared more than 55 million years ago. The New World porcupines evolved from the cavylike rodents in South America some 38–26 million years ago. The porcupine appeared in North America much later, from 7 to 2 million years ago. The North American porcupine is the only cavylike rodent to have successfully settled in North America. The Old World porcupines are younger still, in evolutionary terms: The oldest known species appeared in Pakistan about 15 million years ago. This prickly animal, known as *Sivacanthion*, had a big, blunt head and broad feet.

The principal difference between the New and Old World porcupines is that the former live mainly in trees, whereas the latter keep to the ground. Both groups are chiefly nocturnal and walk rather clumsily on the soles of their feet, like bears.

The most widely spread New World porcupine is the North American porcupine, which is found across most of Canada and the United States. It has a large, heavy body, a fairly small head, and short legs. The barbed quills—there are some 30,000 of

Alan Root/Survival Anglia

The tree porcupine or coendou (above) *has special gripping foot pads for climbing trees.*

The Malayan porcupine's boldly patterned spines serve as a warning to would-be attackers (below).

Kenneth W. Fink/Ardea

them in all—are dense over the upper body and are intermingled with long, stiff guard hairs. The short, thick tail bristles with quills on the upper surface and stiff hairs on the underside.

The other six New World species occur mainly in South America. These, and the two prehensile-tailed species, are well suited to life in the trees. Their upper parts bear short, fairly thick quills. In the tree porcupines, the spines are mixed with long, thick hairs, and each species has a long, spineless tail, with a tough-skinned, upward-curling tip that it can wrap around branches as an extra limb. These species vary widely in color.

The Upper Amazon porcupine is a smaller, more thickset animal. Its pale brown to black hair is mingled with spines; these are sparse on the forequarters, but increase in density and strength along the back, although the short, hairy tail is spineless. The rare, thin-spined porcupine sports most of its sharp quills on the tip of its head and neck.

Old World porcupines

There are five species of crested porcupines across Africa, India, and southern Asia. The African porcupine is dark in color, and the quills on its back and rump are banded in black or brown and white. Up to 20 in (51 cm) long, these can be erected like hackles to deter enemies. A crest of hairs on the forequarters can also be raised. The broad head ends in a snub snout, and the clawed feet have naked soles. The short tail has a battery of hollow, open-ended quills, which the porcupine rattles when annoyed.

Heather Angel/Biofotos

The North American porcupine (left) *is treated with caution by humans and animals alike.*

CONVERGENT EVOLUTION

Mammals that are wholly unrelated to one another and that have evolved in different areas can acquire similar adaptations. This is called convergent evolution.

Echidnas, found in Australia and New Guinea; the hedgehog, an inhabitant of Europe; and the porcupines all have prickly spines. However, they are in no way related; in fact, each is contained in a separate order. The two species of echidnas belong to the order of monotremes, along with the duckbilled platypus, whereas the hedgehog is a member of the insectivores. Echidnas and hedgehogs use their spines in defense quite differently from most porcupines; they both roll themselves up into a ball, presenting an attacker with an impenetrable orb of spines.

The crested porcupines of Southeast Asia and the Indonesian islands have shorter spines and lack the mane of long hairs. The short tail bears small spines that can also be rattled. The upper parts are usually dark, and the underbelly is pale. The spines are white at the base and tip, and the head is large. These three species are referred to by some experts as the Indonesian porcupines.

The two species of brush-tailed porcupines are found in central Africa and parts of Asia. Slighter than many other species, they also have a more pointed snout. The body spines are at their longest in the center of the back. These porcupines have short, thickset limbs, and their partially webbed feet have straight, fairly blunt claws.

The long-tailed porcupine looks similar to a rat. In place of spines it has a coat of stiff, brown bristles, which are flexible and grooved. Beyond them are some longer, stiff, almost spinelike hairs. Its tail is also longer than in many species—up to 9 in (23 cm) long—and for most of its length it is scaly. The tip has an oval tuft of stiff bristles. ■

Color illustrations Simon Turvey/Wildlife Art Agency

NORTH AMERICAN PORCUPINE

Erethizon dorsatum

(eh-REH-thiz-on dor-SAH-tum)

This is the only porcupine in its genus and the only one to have colonized North America, where its range is extremely extensive, owing to its ability to adapt to a wide variety of habitats.

SOUTH AMERICAN TREE PORCUPINE

Sphiggurus spinosa

(svig-YOUR-us spin-O-sah)

The six species of tree porcupines in this genus occur mostly in northern and western South America.

Together with the prehensile-tailed porcupines, they are the most arboreal of all porcupines.

OTHER SPECIES OF NEW WORLD PORCUPINES:

PREHENSILE-TAILED PORCUPINES
UPPER AMAZON PORCUPINE
THIN-SPINED PORCUPINE

SQUIRREL-LIKE RODENTS

MOUSE-LIKE RODENTS

THE PORCUPINES' FAMILY TREE

The cavylike rodents of the suborder Hystricomorpha, to which all porcupines belong, has nearly 200 species in 60 genera distributed among 19 families. Among the best known are the cavies of South America. Cavylike rodents are found mainly in North and South America, Africa, and across Southeast Asia; they are completely absent from most of Europe, Russia, Mongolia, northern China, Japan, and Australia.

OTHER SPECIES OF OLD WORLD PORCUPINES:

BORNEAN LONG-TAILED PORCUPINE
BRUSH-TAILED PORCUPINES
INDONESIAN PORCUPINES

AFRICAN PORCUPINE

Hystrix cristata (*HISS-tricks criss-TAH-tah*)

This is one of the five species of crested porcupines found in Africa, India, and Southeast Asia, including some of the Indonesian islands. The long black-and-white banded quills that grow over the back and rump, and the crest of erectile hairs that extends from the top of the head over the neck and shoulder region, give it one of the most bizarre appearances of any animal.

COYPU

B/W illustrations Ruth Grewcock

OTHER CAVYLIKE RODENTS INCLUDE:

CAVIES
GUINEA PIGS
CAPYBARA
HUTIAS
PACARANA
AGOUTIS
CHINCHILLAS
VISCACHAS
PACAS

CAVYLIKE RODENTS

ALL RODENTS

ANATOMY: THE PORCUPINE

The North American porcupine (below center) is the largest of the New World porcupines, up to 47 in (120 cm) long including the tail. The crested porcupine (below left) has a head-and-body length of about 33 in (85 cm). Smallest of all is the long-tailed porcupine (below right), which measures a maximum of 19 in (48 cm) and weighs up to 5 lb (2.2 kg).

THE HEAD

is small but thickset. Although the small ears are mainly lost in the fur, hearing is one of the best developed of the senses.

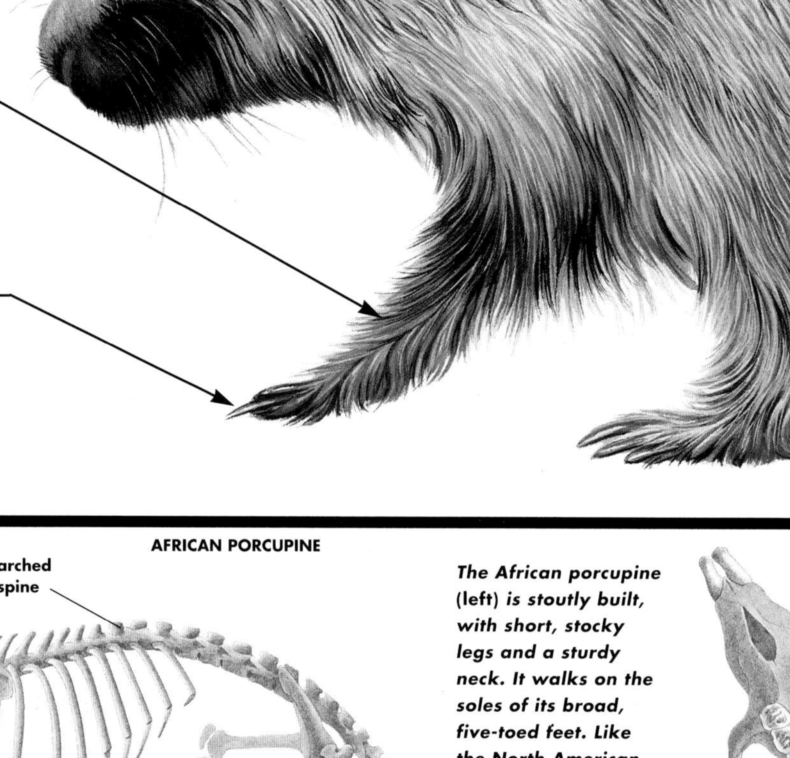

THE EYES

are small and round; this animal tends to be very nearsighted and often fails to notice the approach of other animals when on the ground.

THE LEGS

are short and stocky, giving a short stride and a waddling gait. This animal moves at a faster, but still clumsy, trot or gallop when alarmed.

THE FEET

are broad and heavy. The naked soles have small, fleshy ridges that improve grip. Four toes on the forefeet and five on the hind feet all have long claws.

X-RAY

AFRICAN PORCUPINE

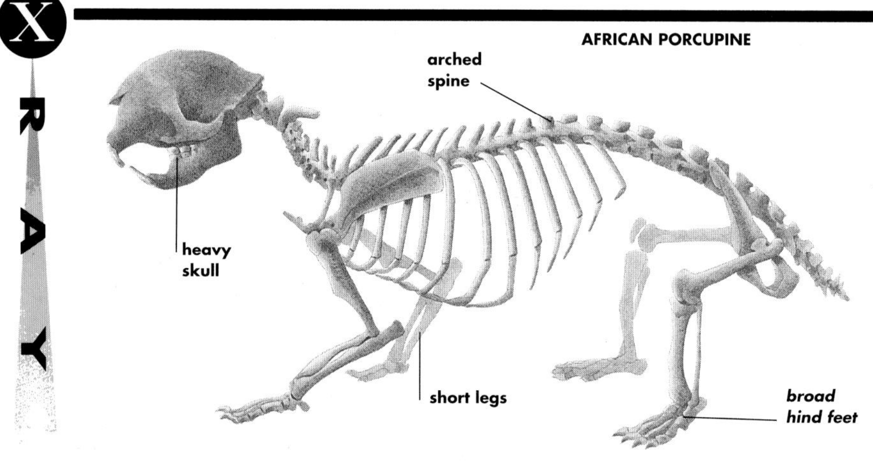

The African porcupine (left) is stoutly built, with short, stocky legs and a sturdy neck. It walks on the soles of its broad, five-toed feet. Like the North American species, it has a noticeably arched spine. The tail is shorter than in the other Old World porcupines.

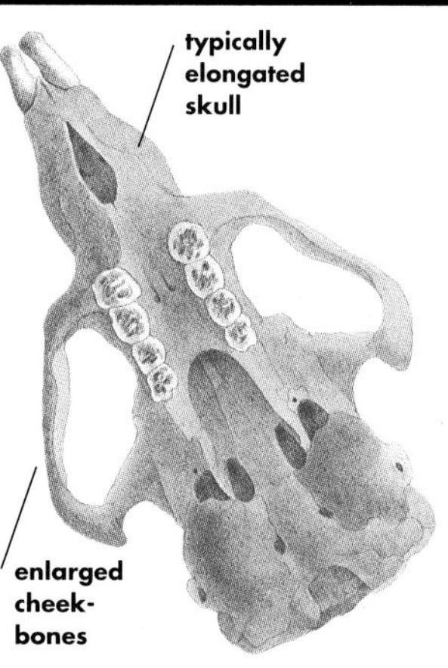

X-ray illustrations Elisabeth Smith

THE QUILLS

grow most densely on the back and rump, giving the animal an almost impregnable defense.

EACH QUILL

is sharply pointed and armed with barbs. Once a quill is fixed in an animal's skin, the victim's muscular action works upon the barbs to draw the quill in deeper.

THE BODY

is large and robust, with an arching back. The quills on the upper parts are intermingled with long, stiff guard hairs. Beneath these lies a softer underfur. The belly lacks quills but has a thick coat of stiff hairs.

FACT FILE:

NORTH AMERICAN PORCUPINE

CLASSIFICATION

Genus: *Erethizon*

Species: *dorsatum*

SIZE

Head-body length: **25–35** in **(64–89** cm)

Tail: **6–12** in **(15–30** cm)

Length of quills: up to **3** in **(7.6** cm)

Weight at birth: **12–22** oz **(340–624** g)

Weight: **8–40** lbs **(3.6–18** kg)

COLORATION

Upper parts of body are usually black or brown in eastern part of range, but more yellow in western areas. Quills have a cream-colored base, darkening toward t he tip. The overall effect is quite pale on top, due to light guard hairs, and much darker underneath

FEATURES

Small, rounded, dark eyes. Small ears are almost hidden in the fur

Quills can be erected as a defense mechanism, and the tail is swung violently from side to side at the same time

Broad, hairless, and slightly ridged soles of the feet give good grip on branches

Fairly poor eyesight, but good senses of smell, touch, and hearing

THE TAIL

is short and thick, heavily armored with quills on the upper surface and stiff hairs below.

NORTH AMERICAN PORCUPINE

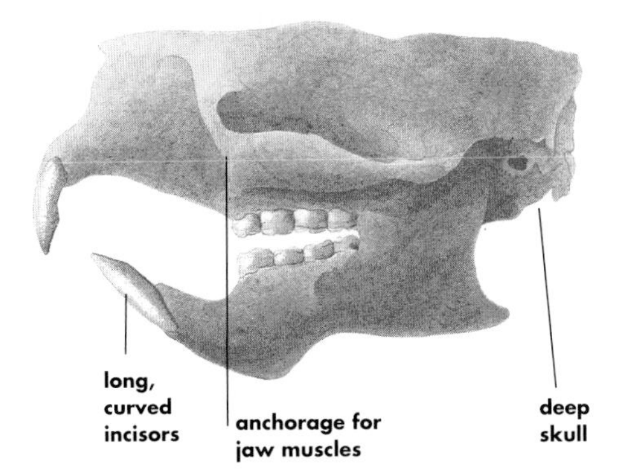

The differences between porcupines' skulls are highly important, as they enable zoologists to classify the various species. The African porcupine has a heavy skull (right); the back of the head supports powerful neck muscles. The North American porcupine (left) has an elongated skull, with lighter bone and a flatter top.

AFRICAN PORCUPINE

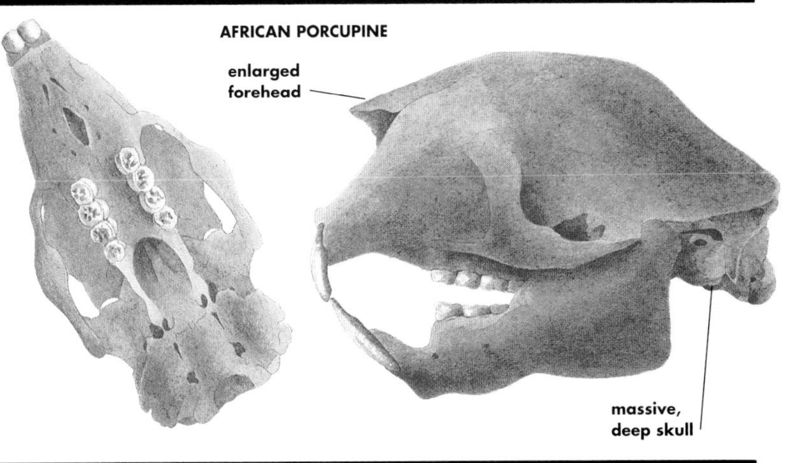

Main illustration Rachel Lockwood/Wildlife Art Agency

NIGHT FORAGERS

OLD AND NEW WORLD PORCUPINES NOT ONLY LOOK QUITE DIFFERENT, BUT MANY FEATURES OF THEIR LIFESTYLE ARE ALSO DISSIMILAR. HOWEVER, THEY HAVE IN COMMON A NOCTURNAL HABIT

The principal difference between the Old and New World porcupines is that those of the New World are primarily arboreal while those of the Old World are terrestrial and seldom, if ever, climb trees. Many of the New World porcupines actually make their homes in trees—the prehensile-tailed species, for example, rests by day curled up high in the treetops, often among a dense tangle of vegetation and twisted branches.

The North American porcupine is perhaps the least arboreal of the New World species, although, depending on its location and the time of year, it may spend a considerable amount of time in trees, climbing slowly to heights of at least 60 ft (18 m) and balancing on thin branches that scarcely seem heavy enough to hold its weight. By day, it generally finds shelter from predators or harsh weather in a cave, a crevice among a rocky outcrop, or a hollow log. Sometimes it takes over a burrow abandoned by some other animal or digs its way into a snowbank. Usually, its dens are at ground level, but occasionally it makes a simple nest in a tree up to about 19 ft (5.8 m) off the ground.

MANY NEW WORLD PORCUPINES BOTH REST AND SHELTER AMID THE TWISTED BRANCHES, HIGH IN THE TREETOPS

Like most other species, the North American porcupine uses a number of regular paths and tracks around its home range to reach feeding places. The home range varies in size, but is markedly smaller in winter, when the animals do not stray far from shelter—sometimes no more than 26 ft (8 m) compared to about 426 ft (130 m) in summer. Although a porcupine will mark the paths it uses around its home range, as well as den entrances and the area at the base of feeding trees, with urine, it does not actually defend a territory.

The crested porcupines of the Old World also use a system of regular runways around their home range, shuffling along them noisily and stopping to feed on plant roots and bulbs exposed in the often sandy soil. Daytime shelters are strictly terrestrial—caves and rocky crevices are used, but usually these porcupines have a well-established burrow, which may be used for several years. Sometimes they take over the burrow of another

Jeff Foott/Survival Anglia

Rod Williams/Bruce Coleman Ltd.

An African brush-tailed porcupine (above) *lives on the ground, but it also climbs and swims well.*

The prehensile-tailed porcupine (below) *lives in forests from southern Panama to northern Argentina.*

Luiz Claudio Marigo/Bruce Coleman Ltd.

animal—an aardvark, for example; sometimes they dig their own. Either way, the burrow gets enlarged progressively as the porcupines dig ever farther to modify it to suit their requirements, often turning it into an extensive warren.

Although several porcupines may share one shelter, they are still basically solitary by nature and pursue their nighttime forays alone. They will often make use of temporary dens or shelters close to a good food source. It is not known if these porcupines have a recognized and regular home range; they will, however, travel as much as 10 mi (16 km) from their burrows at night. Those that inhabit areas of Europe, although not true hibernators, may stay in their burrows for days on end during the harshest winter weeks.

The nocturnal brush-tailed porcupines are also basically terrestrial, but they are unusual among Old World species in that not only can they climb well when they need to, but they can also jump over 3 ft (1 m) into the air. For their ground-level dens, they make use of cavities among tree roots, rocky crevices, and caves, or, since they are good swimmers, a hole in a stream bank. ■

Although arboreal, the North American porcupine (left) *usually shelters and dens at ground level.*

HABITATS

In their various areas, porcupines have proved themselves to be enormously adaptable to different countryside, and they can be found in a wide variety of different habitats.

FOREST DWELLERS

The North American porcupine is the most widespread of all the New World species, ranging across most of Canada and the United States and extending south to New England, New York, and parts of Pennsylvania, Michigan, and Wisconsin in the east. It is primarily a forest dweller, but it is not fussy about the type of woodland it inhabits and may be found in both evergreen and deciduous forests.

The type of woodland, however, often dictates where this porcupine spends most of its time. Deciduous trees provide more food than coniferous

Heather Angel/Biofotos

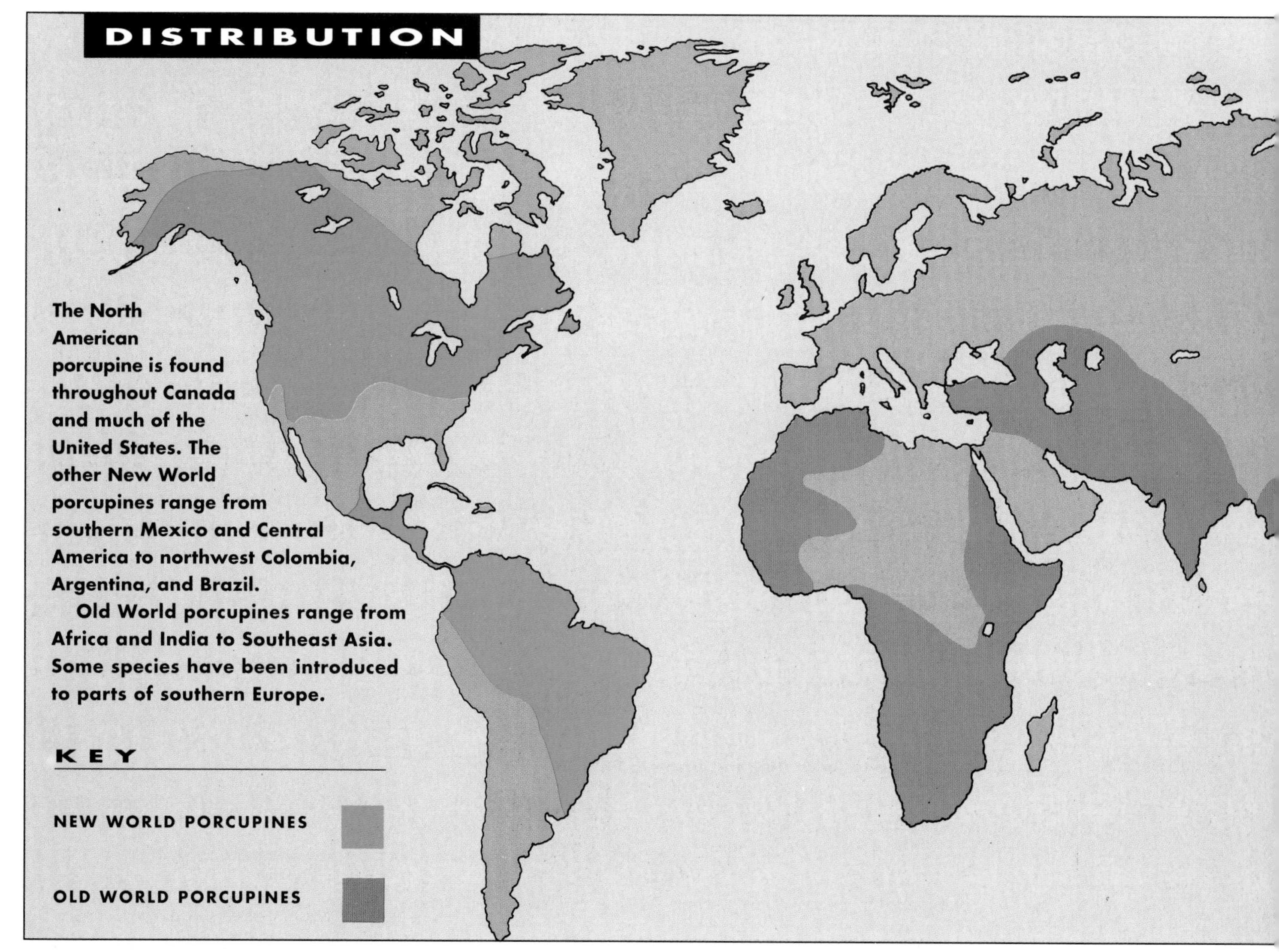

A North American porcupine (left) *has poor eyesight and moves slowly and awkwardly. Yet in its forest home, it can climb to great heights in search of food.*

The Cape porcupine (right) *is one of five species of crested porcupines found in Africa, India, and Southeast Asia.*

Clem Haagner/Ardea

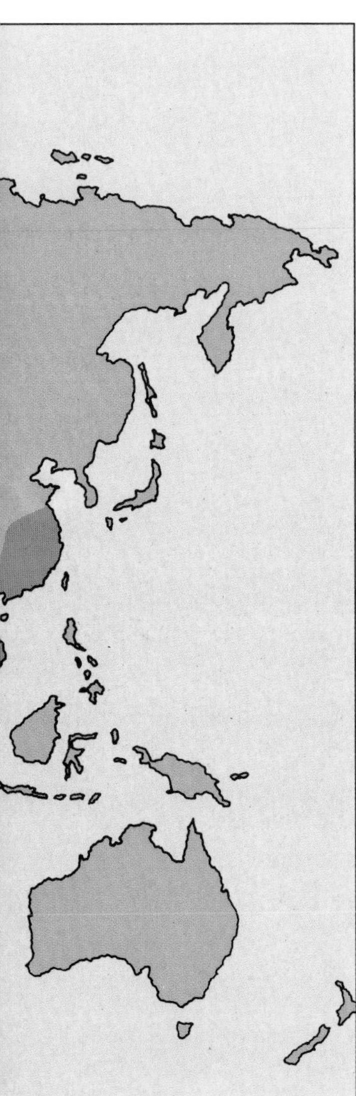

ones; consequently, in woodlands of the former, the porcupine is generally found up among the branches, while in coniferous forests it tends to spend more time foraging on the ground in spring and summer, then climbing into the trees to eat the conifer needles and chip away at the bark during the autumn and winter.

Although woodland is undoubtedly the preferred habitat, the North American porcupine is also found in open tundra and plains and even semidesert environments. Different seasons will often bring a change of habitat; in winter it most often inhabits woodland, seeking the shelter given by tall trees and sheltered den sites. Come spring and summer, however, it tends to wander farther afield, often into open parks and agricultural areas. Whatever the time of year, though, it is usually not too far away from a water source.

The Upper Amazon porcupine of central Colombia is a true forest dweller, being extremely arboreal in habit. The equally arboreal prehensile-tailed porcupines that occur from southern Panama along the range of the Andes from northwestern Colombia to northern Argentina are also necessarily inhabitants of forests, and they are sometimes found in cultivated woodland plantations. Occurring from the coast to tropical jungles well into the interior, they are at home at elevations of 500–8,200 ft (150–2,500 m), and they rarely descend from the trees. The South American tree porcupines occur in very similar situations, spending the great majority of their time high in the tallest trees.

THE UPPER AMAZONIAN PORCUPINE ENJOYS THE HIGH LIFE AT ELEVATIONS OF 2,600–4,000 FT (792–1,220 M)

in SIGHT

TELLTALE SIGNS

Around its habitat, the North American porcupine leaves lots of evidence of its presence. Large, irregular patches of bark will often be stripped from tree trunks, while branches are neatly gnawed, bearing numbers of toothmarks. Around shelters used as dens or at the bases of trees, there are often little accumulations of feces. If the ground along its well-worn tracks is soft, the porcupine leaves distinctive footprints. Those of the forefeet are about 2.5 in (6.4 cm) long, with the hind prints a little longer and usually placed just ahead of the foreprints. The stride is short—prints are generally no more than about 6 in (15 cm) apart—and the tubercles on the soles of the feet are often clearly visible in the print.

OLD WORLD ADAPTABILITY

The Old World crested porcupines are among the most adaptable of all porcupines. Across their range—southern Italy, Africa, India, Southeast Asia, and the Indonesian islands—they may be found in all sorts of different country, from natural woodland and cultivated plantations to rocky, shrubby areas, steppeland, and even sandy deserts. They occur at all altitudes, from sea level to as high as 11,500 ft (3,500 m). The Indian porcupine, *Hystrix indica*, is said to favor rocky hillsides, but may still be found in a wide variety of terrain.

In spite of their essentially terrestrial nature, the brush-tailed porcupines and the long-tailed porcupines of central Africa and parts of Asia, and Borneo, Malaysia, and Sumatra, respectively, are all forest dwellers. Brush-tailed porcupines are found at elevations of up to about 10,000 ft (3,000 m). In fact, these little porcupines are among the most agile of all on the ground—considerably more so than the larger, much heavier crested species.

Solitary and Vocal

Although they are essentially solitary, porcupines are extremely vocal animals and make a variety of noises ranging from high-pitched whistles to whines, grunts, and snuffles as they forage around their well-worn tracks.

While frequently these noises are made for no apparent reasons, they also make a chattering noise with their incisor teeth by grinding the top and bottom pair together, which seems to be both a sign of recognition and a challenge between males.

Temperature and Rainfall

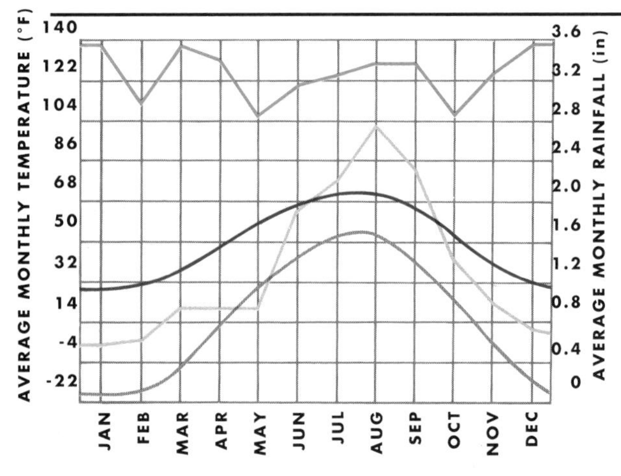

DECIDUOUS FOREST
RAINFALL
TEMPERATURE

BOREAL FOREST
RAINFALL
TEMPERATURE

Oak, maple, ash, and chestnut need a temperate climate in order to develop a full leaf canopy. The needle-shaped leaves of evergreens can withstand cold and drought.

Young North American porcupines are said to make a noise like someone singing an ascending scale, note by note.

Who Nose Where?

As porcupines emerge from their shelter, they sit up and sniff the air, like a bear does. But in spite of their excellent sense of smell, this action gives them little information about their surroundings, and they still shuffle along a track unaware of anything in their way until they are right up against it! ■

Focus On

The North American Woodlands

Because of its wide distribution across the United States, the North American porcupine has adapted to a number of different woodlands. The forests in the northern part of its range are the boreal forests—woodland that stretches across Alaska and Canada and dips into the northern United States. The climate varies extensively, with hot summers and very cold winters. Usually the rainfall is quite low, and in the winter it falls as snow—conditions to which the North American porcupine has learned to adapt.

Besides the boreal forests of the north, the North American porcupine also inhabits the country's temperate forests, a habitat that has suffered extensive destruction. At one stage, temperate forest extended down the northwest American Pacific coast from southern Alaska to California. More than 90 percent of temperate forest found in the southern states has been felled to make way for some of the most densely populated areas in the world.

Temperate forests vary in composition. Around the region of the Great Lakes, they tend to have coniferous and deciduous trees, such as oak, birch, pine, and maple. Farther to the east, they are mainly broad-leaved deciduous with varieties of oak, as well as beech, ash, and chestnut.

Kenneth W. Fink/Ardea

Neighbors

Covering such a large range means the porcupine has a huge variety of neighbors. The forest is able to provide for them all, since different species feed and sleep at varying times.

COMMON GOLDENEYE

This duck is found on the bogs and lakes of the woodland inhabited by porcupines.

LYNX

This inhabitant of the deep forest ranges across the northern part of the American continent.

Illustrations Peter Bull

ENEMIES

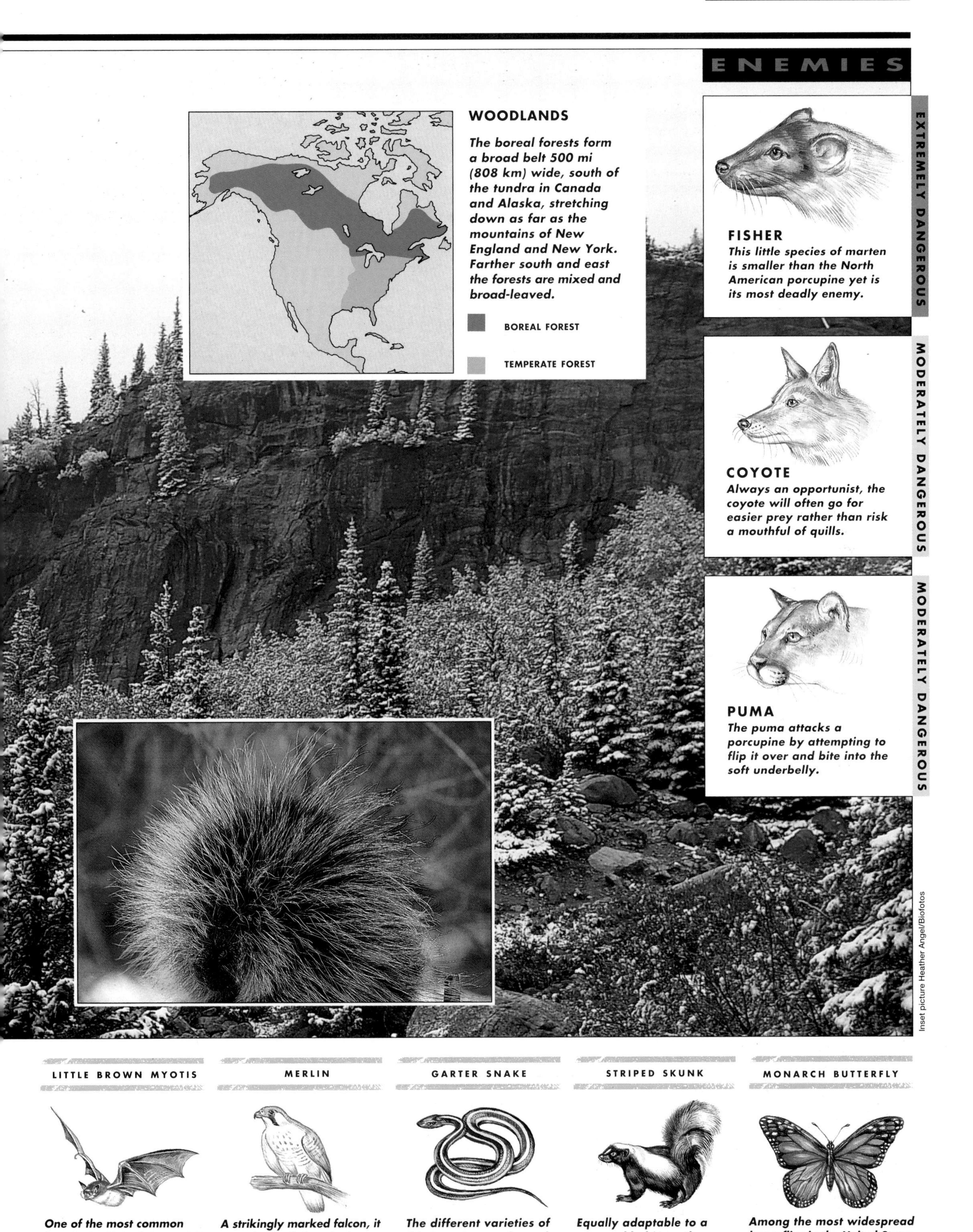

WOODLANDS

The boreal forests form a broad belt 500 mi (808 km) wide, south of the tundra in Canada and Alaska, stretching down as far as the mountains of New England and New York. Farther south and east the forests are mixed and broad-leaved.

FISHER

This little species of marten is smaller than the North American porcupine yet is its most deadly enemy.

COYOTE

Always an opportunist, the coyote will often go for easier prey rather than risk a mouthful of quills.

PUMA

The puma attacks a porcupine by attempting to flip it over and bite into the soft underbelly.

LITTLE BROWN MYOTIS

One of the most common bats in the United States, it is found right across the North American porcupine's range.

MERLIN

A strikingly marked falcon, it nests in North America's boreal forest, from coast to coast. It winters farther south.

GARTER SNAKE

The different varieties of this harmless snake make it one of the most common —and most colorful.

STRIPED SKUNK

Equally adaptable to a range of habitats, the striped skunk lives alongside the porcupine.

MONARCH BUTTERFLY

Among the most widespread butterflies in the United States, it is found from Canada south across the country.

ADAPTATIONS

Each porcupine species is perfectly adapted to its individual lifestyle and environment. The crested porcupines of the Old World, unable—or unwilling—to climb trees to escape predators, are probably the most heavily armored of all species. They burrow readily and possess stout claws to move the soil. Their forefeet are broad and the soles of their feet are smooth, making it easy to shuffle over any type of terrain.

THE NORTH AMERICAN PORCUPINE CAN SWIM VERY WELL; THE HOLLOW QUILLS MAKE IT REMARKABLY BUOYANT

The brush-tailed porcupines are much faster movers than the crested species, and their bodies are relatively longer and sleeker. Being lighter, they can also climb well, although they are still basically ground dwellers. They are capable swimmers, even having partially webbed feet. Their claws, not needed for digging or burrowing, are blunt and straight.

LIVING THE HIGH LIFE

The porcupines of the New World are all suited to life in the trees. The North American porcupine is the largest and heaviest; a slow but steady climber, it relies on its excellent balance and surefootedness as much as its inherent agility. The naked soles of its broad feet are patterned with creases or tubercles. These give a greater tread for a superb grip when balancing on branches and increased traction when moving along them. Well-developed big toes on the hind feet also help it grip. All digits have strong, curved claws, which are used in climbing up and down trees and in clinging to branches while feeding or resting.

These porcupines climb trees by hanging on to the trunk with the forefeet and claws, and then

KEY FACTS

- **The Old World crested porcupines are the longest lived of all rodents. The greatest recorded age is 27 years 3 months, for a Malayan porcupine kept in the National Zoological Park in Washington, D.C.**
- **The muscles in the skin that enable porcupines to erect their hairs and quills are present in other animals, such as cats, making their fur bristle when they are angry or alarmed. In a crude form, they are also present in humans.**

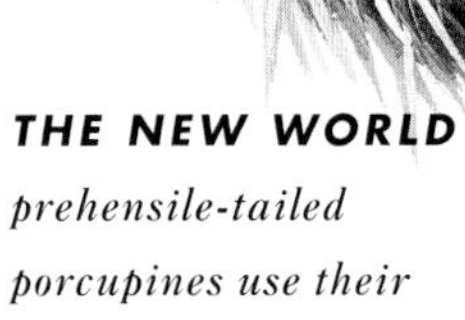

THE NEW WORLD *prehensile-tailed porcupines use their curling tail as a fifth limb to support them in the trees* (above).

THE FOREPAWS (right) *of these species have naked palms and long, sharp claws to provide a sure grip on trunks and branches.*

J. L. Mason/Ardea

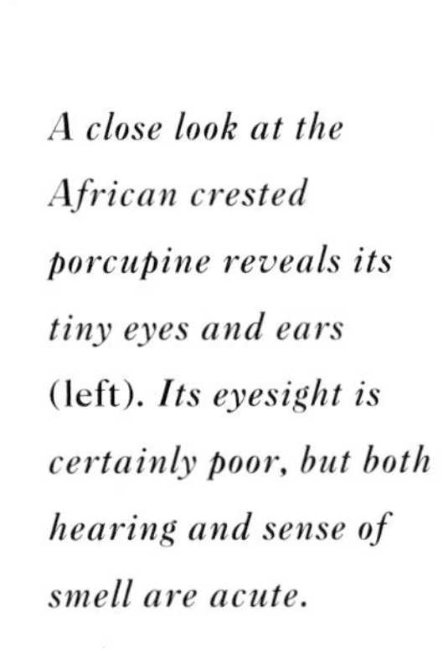

A close look at the African crested porcupine reveals its tiny eyes and ears (left). *Its eyesight is certainly poor, but both hearing and sense of smell are acute.*

Illustrations John Morris/Wildlife Art Agency

TREE-LIVING *porcupines have an ungainly gait on land but excellent balance in the treetops* (above right).

bringing the hind feet up together. They swing up over a branch and balance on thin tree limbs that look far too flimsy to carry their weight. They descend a tree rear first.

The prehensile-tailed and the South American tree porcupines are entirely at home in the trees, and are much lighter in build than the North American species. The long tail of the prehensile-tailed porcupines acts not only as a fifth limb when climbing, but it can support the full weight of the animal as it hangs from a branch. Stiff bristles at the tail's root help it grip the trunk as the animal climbs and, together with the foreclaws, supports the animal during an ascent. The upper surface of the tail is naked with a callus pad near the tip; this gives a firm grip. The tip coils upward—the opposite way from most prehensile-tailed mammals—and wraps easily around branches. Unlike most other porcupines, the tail of the prehensile-tailed porcupines lacks any spines; not a weapon of defense in any way, it is wholly modified for climbing.

The feet of these porcupines are similarly adapted. As in the North American species, they are relatively wide, and the hind feet possess a broad, fleshy pad that widens them still further. This is opposable to the toes and acts like a thumb to grip the branches. The toes are well developed and extremely mobile. ■

DEFENSES

The New World porcupine's battery of 30,000 quills are distributed among stiff guard hairs on the upper parts of its body, particularly over the rump. Its short, thick tail is similarly well armed with quills on the upper surface. Up to 3 in (7.6 cm) long and about 0.08 in (2 mm) in diameter, the quills are hollow and feel slightly rough to the touch. This roughness comes from thousands of microscopic, overlapping scales, which act like barbs on a fishhook, making them almost impossible to remove once they are embedded in flesh.

American defense

When under threat, the North American porcupine's first instinct is to climb a tree. It may also try to run away, but it knows that speed is not one of its great attributes. It is much more likely to face away from the attacker, erect its quills, and lash its tail furiously. Each quill is attached singly, and fairly loosely, into the skin muscles, so that it readily detaches. Because of their sharpness, the quills enter the flesh of the attacker with ease.

THE GENERIC NAME OF THE NORTH AMERICAN PORCUPINE MEANS "ONE WHO RISES IN ANGER"

In fact, the quills themselves rarely cause lasting damage; they seldom fester, although the victim's reflex muscle action slowly draws them ever deeper into its flesh. Carnivores have been found with quills embedded deep into vital internal organs, such as the stomach wall, the liver, and the kidneys, but these have not been the cause of death. It seems that an animal's body fluids eventually soften and erode the quills, or they simply work their way back out. They can cause death if they enter the attacker's throat and tongue, making it impossible for it to eat, and it eventually starves. It may also be blinded if a quill pierces the eye.

The North American porcupine will turn around and lash its tail even when cornered on the tip of a high branch, but it will always try to pull away rather than bite.

Old World aggression

The crested porcupines of the Old World use their defense mechanism even more aggressively, but they will first give plenty of warning. The quills on the back are considerably longer than those of the North American species, measuring up to 20 in

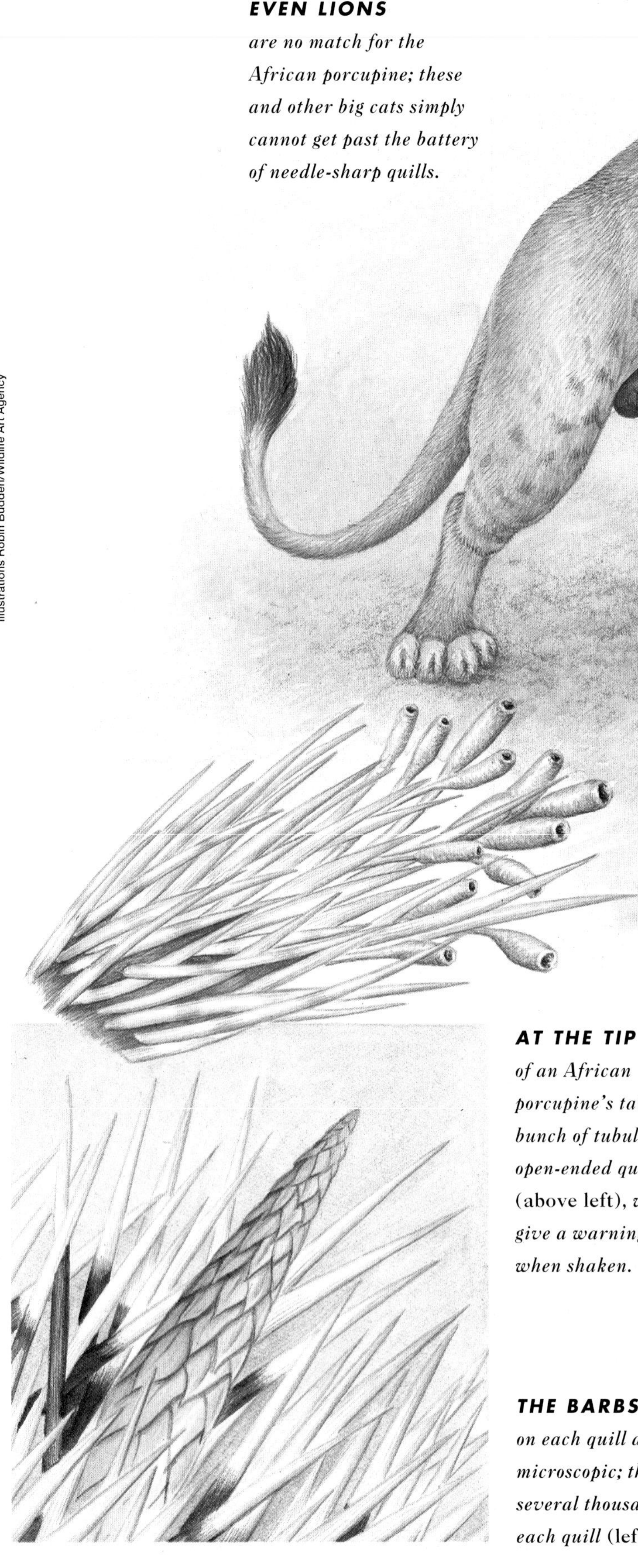

Illustrations Robin Budden/Wildlife Art Agency

EVEN LIONS *are no match for the African porcupine; these and other big cats simply cannot get past the battery of needle-sharp quills.*

AT THE TIP *of an African porcupine's tail is a bunch of tubular, open-ended quills* (above left), *which give a warning rattle when shaken.*

THE BARBS *on each quill are microscopic; there are several thousand on each quill* (left).

(50 cm). They are also often boldly banded in black or dark brown and white—a warning signal which ought to deter predators from the start. The tail is tipped with a bunch of tubular, open-ended quills that rattle loudly when the porcupine shakes its tail —yet another warning signal.

The quills are normally held flat against the body, but when danger threatens, these porcupines erect the quills on the back, together with the crest of bristles on the head and neck. They also stamp their feet, rattle their tail, and utter menacing growls and grunts. If the attacker perseveres, the porcupine will charge backward rapidly, its tail shaking, to point its weaponry toward the aggressor. Although they grow from the skin in groups of four to six, the quills nevertheless detach easily—and are similarly barbed. The fact that these spines and quills detach and penetrate flesh so easily gave rise to the myth that porcupines can actually "fire" their quills when threatened. Although widely believed for many years, this is completely untrue.

The prehensile-tailed porcupine is unusual in that it will often protect itself by rolling up into a spiky ball, in the manner of a hedgehog. However, it seems to enjoy a fight, so it will first stamp its feet, gnash its teeth, and strike at an attacker with its spines. By using powerful muscles in the skin, it can make its spines move.

In some species of South American tree porcupines, the quills are so interspersed with long hairs that they are said to resemble tufts of moss. This gives a natural camouflage when the animal is resting on a high-up branch of a tree. ■

THE DEADLY FISHER

The porcupine is vulnerable in very few areas. A sharp, timely blow to the head can cause death, and so, too, can an attack to the unprotected underbelly. The fisher, a species of marten that shares much of the North American porcupine's range and has a great liking for its flesh, exploits both of these vulnerable spots and is probably this porcupine's deadliest enemy.

The fisher is actually smaller than its prey, but it uses its low profile to its advantage. Circling adroitly, it seizes any opportunity to land a vicious bite on the porcupine's face. As ever in times of trouble, the porcupine tries to thrust its flailing tail at the fisher, but the nimble little predator whips quickly around, avoiding the mass of quills. If it manages to deliver enough bites, or just terrifying jaw snaps, to the porcupine's face, the prickly quarry enters a state of shock; in an instant the fisher flips it over and begins to rip into the soft underbelly. It may take the fisher a full thirty minutes or more to subdue and kill a porcupine, but the rewards are great: One porcupine provides this little marten with sufficient food for two weeks.

Ken Cole/Natural Science Photos

FOOD AND FEEDING

All porcupines are primarily plant-eaters, living on leaves, buds, fruit, twigs, shoots, roots, and tubers, as well as the bark of a number of trees.

Porcupines have ideal teeth for this diet. The four orange incisors of the North American porcupine are veritable wood chisels, some 1 in (2.5 cm) or more in length. They need to be used constantly, both to keep them sharp and clean and to stop them from growing too long. As with all rodents, the teeth grow constantly throughout the animal's life. The cheek teeth are flat crowned, making them suitable for grinding vegetation.

New World diet

The diet of the North American porcupine varies a little throughout the year. In spring and summer, the menu is at its most varied, including all manner of vegetation—seeds, nuts, berries, stems, and leaves—from both the trees and the ground. This animal is particularly fond of lupine, clover, and a wild plant known as skunk cabbage. It often takes advantage of the fresh growth of spring grass and may be seen grazing in the meadows in the evening light. As winter approaches, the porcupine spends more time in the trees, eating mainly evergreen needles and chewing through the bark to get to the tree's juicy inner cambium layer. When the snow lies thick on the ground, a porcupine may stay in the same tree for weeks on end, moving around it, alternately feeding and resting.

AFRICAN PORCUPINES IN SEARCH OF CARRION HAVE BEEN FOUND IN TRAPS BAITED WITH MEAT TO TRAP CARNIVORES

The North American porcupine eats 1 lb (454 g) of vegetation a day, excreting about one-fifth of it. It makes small work of the bulk of fiber and cellulose contained in the diet; nearly half of its immensely long digestive tract is small intestine, which contains bacteria that can break down cellulose. It is a very wasteful feeder; while perched

STRIPPING BARK *enables the North American porcupine to feast upon the juicy tree growth and also to keep its teeth clean. Other food favorites of this species are shown below.*

Food illustrations Ruth Grewcock

SALT CRAZY

The North American porcupine has a great craving in its diet for salt. It will chew on wooden tools impregnated with sweat from human hands, and has been known to enter homes and chew on such "salty spots" as furniture and windowsills. Where grease and salt have been spilled, porcupines will chew at the floorboards, reducing some old houses and forest shacks to matchwood.

The Old World porcupines satisfy their mineral cravings mainly by gnawing on scavenged bones, from which they obtain calcium. This also cleans and sharpens the teeth keeping growth in check.

in the trees, it may drop as much vegetation to the ground as it eats, and often deer and rabbits may be seen scavenging on the easy pickings that shower to the ground.

The prehensile-tailed and South American tree porcupines have a similar diet, although they feed mainly on leaves from the trees. They also eat insects and, possibly, small reptiles when the opportunity arises.

Old World nibblers

The crested porcupines of the Old World find all their food on the ground, feasting off a variety of roots, bulbs, tubers, fruit, and berries. African porcupines reputedly feed on a species of plant that is poisonous to cattle and occasionally steal cultivated crops. Windfalls from fruit trees are great favorites with these species, and they grip each fruit tightly between the forepaws, steadying it against the ground while they gnaw into it. Although vegetable matter undoubtedly makes up the greater proportion of the diet, crested porcupines are also known to feed on carrion from time to time.

Mineral meals

On the island of Sumatra in Indonesia, crested porcupines have a beneficial relationship with elephants. The elephants visit certain caves where they use their tusks to gouge lumps of rock from the roofs and sides. These they break up still further to get to minerals, such as sodium and potassium, in the rock. Porcupines later visit the caves to feast on the mineral-rich debris. ■

Main illustration Kim Thompson

LIFE CYCLE

The autumn mating season is one of the few times of the year when the solitary North American porcupine seeks company. Its acute sense of smell probably helps it locate a female in estrus.

Courtship between North American porcupines can be rowdy. Grunting and wailing, the male dances about energetically, then finally stands up on his hind legs and soaks the female in a shower of urine. Mating generally follows shortly after this; when the female is sufficiently aroused she relaxes her quills and raises her tail over her back, presenting herself to her mate.

Gestation is remarkably long for such a small animal—nearly seven months—at the end of which a single young is born, usually between April and June. A gestation period of this length ensures that the newborn is well developed; it weighs up to 22.5 oz (638 g), its eyes are open, and it is able to walk almost immediately. Covered in long, black hair, it already possesses short, soft quills. To avoid injury to the mother, the young is born headfirst in an amniotic sac. Within half an hour, the quills have hardened.

PRECOCIOUS PORCUPINES

The newborn porcupine seems to have an instinctive knowledge of its defense reaction. Before even witnessing a parental demonstration, within fifteen minutes of its birth it will whirl around and wave its tail in the direction of any unusual noise or movement. In just a few days, it starts to climb trees—not without a few false starts, particularly when the youngster tries to descend headfirst! Generally it

MATING
is one of the few times that the solitary porcupines come together. Courtship can be dramatic and noisy but, needless to say, mating itself is a more cautious affair.

INDEPENDENCE
is reached by the time the porcupine is two months old. The time has come for it to leave the parent and begin establishing its own feeding areas and dens.

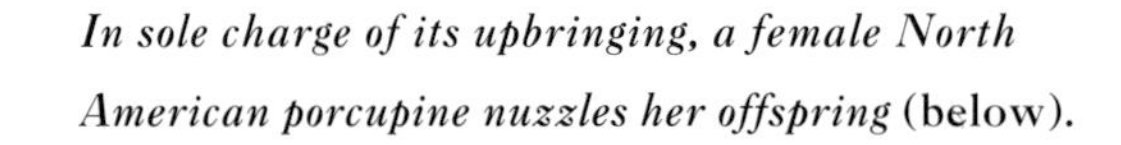

In sole charge of its upbringing, a female North American porcupine nuzzles her offspring (below).

Dr. Robert Franz/Planet Earth Pictures

in SIGHT

THE SOCIAL SCALE

Most porcupines are loners, even though the crested porcupines of the Old World may share the same burrow and even forage together. The most overt exceptions are the brush-tailed porcupines of Africa and Asia. These small animals seem to live in family colonies—six to eight individuals sharing a burrow and feeding together. The colony comprises a mated pair with young from a few litters. They occupy a small territory in the forest, which they mark with deposits of dung.

GROWING UP

The life of a young North American porcupine

AFTER MATING, *the female drives away the male. He has no further involvement with the rearing of his offspring.*

Illustrations Joanne Cowne

AT TWO WEEKS *of age, the young porcupine has started to nibble at vegetation and puts on weight rapidly. It continues to suckle, however, for a few more weeks.*

takes a few tumbles before it discovers that the way to descend is by leading with the rear end.

Within two weeks of birth, the young porcupine is nibbling away at soft vegetation and puts on weight at a rate of 1 lb (454 g) a day. It generally continues suckling for up to about seven weeks; it becomes fully independent shortly after this. Females can begin breeding from the time they are about eighteen months old; although males can also mate from this time, they generally do not do so for another year.

Other New World species also give birth to well-developed young after a relatively long gestation period. The prehensile-tailed species produce a single offspring weighing some 14 oz (397 g), which is able to climb right away. It becomes totally independent by the time it is ten weeks old, and at eleven months is fully grown. The newborn young of the South American tree porcupines are also well developed, although the soft quills that cover them at birth take longer to harden than those of the North American porcupine's young—usually about one week.

BORN IN THE BURROW

The Old World's crested porcupines produce their young after a gestation period that is only about half that of their New World counterparts—usually 100–112 days. There may be up to four in a litter, although there are usually only one or two. The young are well developed at birth, although they weigh only 3.5–10.5 oz (100–300 g). Birth takes place in a grass-lined chamber within the burrow, and the young porcupines are able to move around in the warren in just a few hours. They are born with soft spines that harden and resemble those of the adult by the time the young are ten days old. They suckle for at least three months and become fully grown at one year. At this time, they are also sexually mature, although they are unlikely to breed for at least another six months. Some species, such as the brush-tailed porcupines, produce two or even three litters a year. ■

FROM BIRTH TO DEATH

NORTH AMERICAN PORCUPINE

MATING SEASON: SEPTEMBER TO NOVEMBER
GESTATION: 205–217 DAYS
LITTER SIZE: 1
FIRST SOLID FOOD: 14 DAYS
WEANED: 50 DAYS
LONGEVITY: 18 YEARS IN THE WILD

CRESTED PORCUPINE

MATING SEASON: ALL YEAR
GESTATION: 93–112 DAYS
LITTER SIZE: 1–4, USUALLY 1–2
WEIGHT AT BIRTH: 12 oz (340 g)
WEANED: 90–100 DAYS
SEXUAL MATURITY: 8–18 MONTHS
LONGEVITY: AT LEAST 15 YEARS IN THE WILD

TROUBLE IN THE TREES

LIKE MANY MAMMALS, PORCUPINES ENJOY A RELATIONSHIP OF VARYING FORTUNES WITH HUMANS. TO SOME THEY ARE A THREAT TO TREES AND CROPS; TO OTHERS THEY ARE AN IMPORTANT SOURCE OF FOOD

The North American porcupine can cause extensive damage to forestry, particularly in the winter when heavy snows restrict its source of food to only what it can find high up in the trees, where it spends its time.

The evergreen needles provide it with a certain amount of nourishment, but, in addition to these, it feeds on the tree's cambium layer—the section just inside the bark that carries the starches and sugars that are vital to the tree's survival. To get to the cambium, the porcupine chisels away at the bark with its strong incisors. Generally, feeding from the comfort of a perch in a high-up branch, the porcupine attacks the bark on the upper surfaces of branches and those parts around the trunk that are within easy reach. The tree will die only if and when the bark has been chipped away all around the trunk; it then dies above this point. Before it reaches this stage, however, calluses are formed where porcupines have irreversibly damaged the bark. Clearly certain trees are known by porcupines to be good for feeding, for they will return year after year to the same trees, chipping away still further around those areas already damaged.

A PORCUPINE CAN WREAK SPECTACULAR DAMAGE ON A SINGLE TREE, BUT THE FOREST SUFFERS LITTLE OVERALL HARM

If the porcupine damages the cambium layer all the way around the tree, it effectively creates a dam, stopping the flow of nourishment up and down the tree. The tree's roots extract minerals and moisture from the soil, and these travel up the inside of the tree. The leaves, using sunlight, make starch and sugar that travel back down through the tree to the roots through the cambium—and it is this sweet layer that attracts the porcupines. When this inner layer becomes damaged, sugar and starch accumulate above the wound.

Some studies suggest that the porcupine is aware of its effect on timber. Selected trees in a forest in Maine were ringed by being cut all around the bark with an ax and left to die slowly. It seems that porcupines in this area actively chose to feed

Jeff Foott/Survival Anglia

Trees in Grand Teton, Wyoming, bear the scars of a porcupine's feeding bout (above).

THEN & NOW

This map shows the former and present range of the North American porcupine.

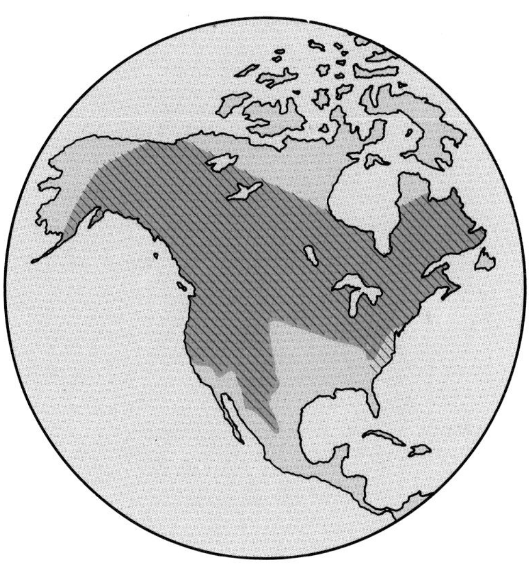

FORMER DISTRIBUTION
PRESENT DISTRIBUTION

The North American porcupine is widely distributed in many habitats across Canada and the United States, excluding a few of the southern and eastern states. In the 18th and 19th centuries its range included Maryland and Virginia, but it is now absent from these states—as a result of climatic changes or direct persecution. However, despite being hunted as a pest and a source of food, it is still common over most of its range.

on these trees, chipping at the bark above the cut, where they would find a buildup of sugars and starches. Analysis of the inner bark found that the ringed trees contained 20–300 times more sugar above the cut than below. This amounted to about treble the amount normally found in the inner layer along the length of an undamaged tree.

It was the North American porcupine's taste for cambium that prompted the official introduction of the predatory fisher marten (see page 1709) to the worst-hit forest areas. This has had a marked effect on porcupine numbers.

Foresters argue as to the extent of the damage caused by porcupines and thus how much of a pest they really are. It seems, in fact, that although they

The long incisors of the North American porcupine (left) *are the scourge of American foresters.*

ALONGSIDE MAN

A SOURCE OF ARTIFACTS

The porcupine was of special significance to the early North American Indians. They recognized its potential as a source of food, particularly in the winter, when many supplies that were readily available in the spring and summer were scarce.

They also found a decorative use for the quills, capitalizing on their natural luster and smoothness. First they would soften the quills in water, then dye them various colors before flattening them. After this, they used them in sewing or wove them into intricate and attractive patterns. Boxes, blankets, and all manner of clothing—from elaborate robes and shirts to moccasins—were decorated with porcupine quills. Today this craftwork is rare and has been mainly replaced by beading.

Before the invention of plastic, porcupine quills were also used extensively in the production of fishing floats, their hollow construction making them naturally buoyant.

characteristically strip the bark from very large spot areas, it is unusual for them to chip the bark away all around a tree trunk. Many people feel that the damage they do has actually been greatly exaggerated; in fact, they are frequently considered more of a nuisance around encampments in woodland, where they will gnaw on any woodwork that contains salt deposits from human sweat, often causing considerable damage to property (see Salt Crazy, page 1711).

Quite apart from their tree-stripping activities, the New World porcupines are certainly viewed as pests by crop farmers. Many have a liking for sweet corn, and just a few of these animals can lay waste to an entire crop field. The South American tree porcupines also have a fondness for bananas and other soft fruit.

In some areas, the damage that porcupines do to forestry and food crops is considered to be outweighed by the fact that they are an easy source of food to anyone lost or stranded in the woods. Indeed, they are said to be one of the few wild animals that can be easily killed without a gun. First of all, they do not try to escape when cornered, and they can be easily captured by grabbing the tail—albeit carefully so as to avoid a handful of quills. A sharp, stunning blow to the nose—a vulnerable spot—kills them quickly, and they are apparently very tasty. To the trappers and natives of North America, porcupines were once considered most important in this regard. They would cook them by throwing them into a fire to burn off the quills and hair before skinning and roasting them. In a few places, the North American porcupine was given protection because it was easy meat for anyone wandering lost in forest areas.

PORCUPINES IN DANGER

BY AND LARGE, PORCUPINES ARE NOT GREATLY ENDANGERED. THE SPECIES THAT IS PROBABLY MOST AT RISK IS THE THIN-SPINED PORCUPINE. IT IS CLASSIFIED AS INDETERMINATE IN THE INTERNATIONAL UNION FOR THE CONSERVATION OF NATURE (IUCN) *RED DATA BOOK*. FOUND ONLY IN THE ATLANTIC FORESTS OF SOUTHEASTERN BRAZIL, IT IS RENDERED EVEN MORE VULNERABLE BY THE NATURE OF ITS PREFERRED HABITAT: THE FOREST EDGES, WHICH ARE MOST AT RISK FROM FOREST CLEARANCE.

***INDETERMINATE* REFERS TO SPECIES KNOWN TO BE ENDANGERED, VULNERABLE, OR RARE, FOR WHICH THERE IS NOT ENOUGH INFORMATION TO STATE WHICH OF THE THREE CATEGORIES IS APPROPRIATE.**

A Cape porcupine of southern Africa raises its spiny hackles in threat (below).

ZEFA

Rod Williams/Bruce Coleman Ltd.

TROUBLE IN THE OLD WORLD

The situation of porcupines in the Old World is similar. In many parts of its range, the crested porcupine is considered a pest, but it has also been valued since early times as a source of food. Farmers dislike it because it ruins their fruit, vegetable, and cotton crops. It also gnaws at the bark of trees, in the manner of the North American porcupine. In some parts of its range, it has been destroyed as a pest, and in other parts, it is widely hunted as a source of easily caught and tasty food. Its attractive quills have been valued by local tribespeople for ornamental purposes and also as lucky charms. ■

INTO THE FUTURE

It seems unlikely that any of the porcupine species are facing any great threat of extinction. The North American porcupine has become scarce, or disappeared completely, from a few parts of its range, notably in some parts of southeastern areas. However, it is thought that this might be because of climatic changes rather than through persecution by humans, and it is both widespread and common over the greater part of its range.

The crested porcupines of the genus *Hystrix* have similarly become scarce in a few areas. They have been exterminated from parts of Uganda, are rare in much of Egypt, and have not been sighted in Singapore for some time. The subspecies *H. brachyura yunnanensis*, confined to the forested areas of Yunnan in China, is considered vulnerable. However, the species as a whole is still widespread and comparatively common, particularly in Africa where it has flourished—thanks, in many areas, to the food available to it from increased agricultural cultivation. Although farmers will kill it as a pest, it seems to survive regardless.

The most endangered of all the porcupines is the thin-spined porcupine, *Chaetomys subspinosus*. Found only in a restricted area of Atlantic forests in southeastern Brazil, it is known to occur in one national park and one preserve in Bahia, and three reserves in Espirito Santo farther to the north. Through the protection of their forest habitats, these porcupines will also automatically receive protection, but it has been suggested that there is also an urgent need to initiate captive-breeding programs to ensure long-term survival.

It is not easy to promote the conservation of rare species in South America. So little is known about wildlife; furthermore, there is little incentive to preserve animals in countries where the human population is often struggling to reach the standards of living enjoyed by developed nations. ■

PREDICTION

SPINED SURVIVORS

Although porcupines are still killed for sport and money, or as pests, the losses are not significant. More worrying is the steady loss of the world's wilderness; for some species, preservation of suitable habitat is essential to their survival.

HARDSHIP IN EUROPE

Although not endangered in any way across most of its range, there is a question mark over the status of the crested African porcupine, *Hystrix cristata*, in those parts of Europe to which it has been introduced. This includes the island of Sicily and the southern part of Italy, extending no farther north than Lucca. It is thought to have been introduced to these parts by the Romans. It has also been introduced to Albania and northern Greece. This nocturnal species prefers arid, rocky uplands with ground vegetation, where it spends the day holed up in rock crevices or burrows.

Within Europe, it has had to contend with being hunted, and also with habitat destruction. Although it was given protection in 1974, it is still apparently illegally hunted. Many authorities list it as officially rare, and it is also placed at number four on the list of the top ten endangered rodents in Europe, with an exceedingly restricted range. In Egypt, it appears to be on the brink of extinction, with sightings confirmed only along a single stretch of cliffs.

TREE PORCUPINES

The porcupines of South America, while remaining fairly numerous, are victims of habitat destruction in many parts of their range. They are hunted for sport and, like their relatives the cavies or guinea pigs, they have also been used fairly widely for biomedical research. The South American or spiny tree porcupine, Sphiggurus spinosus, *is recognized to be rare in Uruguay.*

Unfortunately for the tree porcupines, the special adaptations that have helped them thrive up in the trees may finally work against them; if the forests are degraded or destroyed, the porcupines will be left with no suitable habitat.

Illustration Evi Antoniou

POSSUMS

RELATIONS

The possums belong to a marsupial suborder known as the Diprotodonta. Other diprotodonts include:

KANGAROOS

KOALA

WOMBATS

WALLAROOS

RAT KANGAROOS

WALLABIES

Kathie Atkinson/Oxford Scientific Films

Possums are marsupials, or pouched mammals. There are fifty species within three families; these should not be confused with the opossums of the Americas.

ORDER

Marsupialia (marsupials)

SUBORDER

Diprotodonta

FAMILY

Phalangeridae (cuscuses and brush-tailed possums)

twenty species in six genera

FAMILY

Petauridae (gliders)

twenty-three species in six genera

FAMILY

Burramyidae (pygmy possums)

seven species in four genera

HIGH TAILS DOWN UNDER

POSSUMS ARE POUCHED MAMMALS WITH A HEAD FOR HEIGHTS, AND THEY HAVE DIVERSIFIED TO FILL EVERY AVAILABLE ECOLOGICAL NICHE IN THE TREES OF AUSTRALIA AND NEW GUINEA

The fifty species of possums form one of the largest and most diverse groups of marsupials. Just how long they have flourished in Australia, New Guinea, and various islands we cannot say for sure, but their ancestry is certainly a long one. Marsupials differ from other mammals in that their young do not experience prolonged development inside the mother's body, though most of them do spend a part of their infancy inside a pouch on the mother's abdomen.

Primitive marsupials were well established in Australia by the time the landmass drifted away from Antarctica and South America, with which it was once joined, about 45 million years ago. Moving north in isolation, Australia sidestepped the spread of placental mammals, which invaded almost all the other landmasses, rapidly became dominant, and drove most of the world's marsupials out of existence. Few reached Australia, and marsupials continue to flourish there to this day.

Not all possums can glide; those that cannot have a tail with naked gripping surfaces (below).

Hans and Judy Beaste/Ardea

In the absence of competition, Australian marsupials diversified to fit every sort of environment on the continent. For much of its history, Australia has been heavily wooded, and it is not surprising that some of the more successful groups were those that took to the trees for food and for shelter. Possums evolved to become the dominant plant-eaters in the trees; some of them developed broad diets, while others specialized in leaves, fruit, nectar, or sap, and a few in the group came to rely heavily on insects.

In adapting to their particular niches, many of the possums evolved characteristics that strikingly resemble those of tree-dwelling placental mammals on the other continents. Features of squirrels, flying

The spotted cuscus lives the high life in the forests of New Guinea and Queensland, Australia.

Gerald Cubitt/Bruce Coleman Ltd.

in SIGHT

FELLOW GLIDERS

Tree-dwelling marsupials are by no means the only forest animals that have evolved a gliding habit as a means of traveling from tree to tree. Some of the squirrels of Eurasia, Africa, and North America have developed along remarkably similar lines, so much so that species like the southern flying squirrel and the giant flying squirrel look and behave much like marsupial gliders. All possess a similar form of flight membrane, called a patagium, that stretches between the limbs. In the flying lemurs of the islands of Southeast Asia, the patagium is so extensive that, when gliding, these animals resemble toy kites. The Southeast Asian forests are also home to frogs, lizards, and even snakes with broad membranes or flattened surfaces that help them sail through the air when leaping.

squirrels, bush babies, lemurs, and monkeys all have their equivalents among the possums.

About 15 million years ago, Australia's climate began to dry out. The forests shrank toward their present limited distribution in the east, and much of the remaining country became bush with a thin cover of trees. Though most possum species continued to depend on the reduced forest habitat, some adapted to the drier, sparsely wooded alternative.

At about the same time, the Australian landmass was colliding with a continental plate to the north. Mountainous New Guinea was thrust into existence, and possums migrated and further flourished there. Much later, cuscuses—possums that appear to have originated on the island—spread out to smaller islands in the region, such as Sulawesi and the Solomon Islands. They probably did so by accidentally rafting on floating vegetation when sea levels were low, and the same chance events may account for their colonization of northeastern Australia across the narrow Torres Strait.

POSSUMS TODAY

Today possums have the widest distribution of any Australasian marsupials. Varying in size from that of a mouse to a monkey, they all have long, flexible tails and bulging eyes adapted for nighttime vision. Though a few of them live on the ground, most spend all their lives in the trees and possess various adaptations that help them climb. The first digit of each foot, and in the cuscuses and ring-tails also the second digit of the forefoot, is opposable to the other digits—like our thumb and forefinger—allowing the animals to grasp narrow branches. Sharp claws give a firm grip on large branches and trunks. In most species, but not the brush-tails and gliders, the tail is prehensile, able to curl around and grip branches.

Plenty of differences

For all their common features, though, the possums are also a very diverse group. Cuscuses differ greatly from the brush-tails in their slow gait, their often colorful coat, their tiny ears, and their largely naked tails. Ring-tails might resemble brush-tails in their appearance and agile habits, but their tails are also lightly furred, and, when not used for gripping, they are held in a tight coil. Pygmy possums are less inclined to coil their tails, and their chief distinction is their mouselike form and high rate of activity. Because of their small size and high energy consumption, both cold weather and food shortages present survival problems that pygmy possums overcome by entering states of torpor—a kind of hibernation.

The most remarkable of the possums, however, are those species that can glide. Representatives of three families have evolved gliding ability in the same basic manner. Gliders, the greater glider, and the feathertail glider all have thin, furred membranes attached to each flank between the hind and forelimbs. Called the patagium, this flap is held against the body when at rest; but when the animal leaps into the air and extends its legs, the patagium is stretched out to form a flat flight surface that greatly increases the distance the animal can travel before it hits the ground or alights on another tree. ■

DENTAL DISTINCTIONS

Teeth are often studied to distinguish groups of mammals, and two main kinds of tooth arrangement are recognized in marsupials. Those groups with at least four incisor teeth in the lower jaw are classed as polyprotodonts. They include most of the insectivorous or carnivorous marsupials, such as the bandicoots, dunnarts, and Tasmanian devil.

Other marsupials, including the mostly plant-eating possums, koala, and kangaroos, are classed as diprotodonts. They have just two lower incisors, but these are generally large and forward-pointing. It may well be that these enlarged tools originally evolved as a means of snatching insects, but today they are used very effectively for nipping off choice leaves and other delicacies.

THE POSSUMS' FAMILY TREE

The classification of marsupials is continually being debated. One scheme divides them into two suborders, the polyprotodonts and the diprotodonts. The latter are further split into at least three lines, leading to the koala and wombats on one branch, the honey possum as another branch, and the possum families and kangaroo families on a third branch.

Ring-tailed possums

Pseudocheiridae
(soo-doo-KAY-rid-ie)

These are medium-sized possums with long tails that are either partly naked and held in a tight curl or well-furred and straight, as in the greater glider. Mainly leaf-eaters, they are nocturnal and chiefly confined to high forest levels. There are seventeen species in Australia and New Guinea.

Wombat and kangaroo Ruth Grewcock. Koala and honey possum Alan Male/Linden Artists

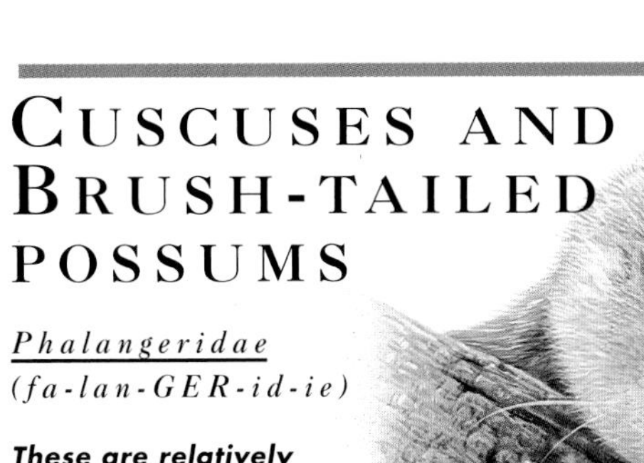

Cuscuses and Brush-tailed possums

Phalangeridae
(fa-lan-GER-id-ie)

These are relatively large possums with dense, often patterned fur and long furry or partly naked tails. Active by night, they are mostly arboreal and rather generalized in diet, although many rely heavily on leaves. There are twenty-two species in Australia, New Guinea, and adjacent islands.

Gliders

Petauridae
(pet-OW-rid-ie)

These possums have long furry tails and often have dark eye patches and stripes. Folds of skin along the flanks can be stretched out to form flight surfaces in the gliding species. They are nocturnal tree-dwellers that feed mainly on plant exudates or, in the striped possums, on insects. There are eleven species in Australia and New Guinea.

Pygmy possums

Burramyidae *(bur-ah-MIE-id-ie)*

Pygmy possums have long thin or flattened tails. They are highly active at night, with all but one species living in trees. These tiny creatures eat mainly insects, but some species rely on nectar and pollen or seeds. There are seven species in Australia and New Guinea.

Honey possum

Kangaroo

Color illustrations Steve Kingston

ANATOMY: THE SUGAR GLIDER

From left to right: ***The black-spotted cuscus and lesser Sulawesi cuscus show the range in size of the cuscuses and brush-tailed possums. Representing the size span of the other possums are the little pygmy possum and the rock ring-tailed possum.***

Gliders put their long, sharp claws to good effect when they land on trunks—the extra grip helps the animals cope with the recoil of the landing impact without falling. Opposable digits on both the forefeet and hind feet also enable these and other possums to grasp objects, just as we would use our forefingers and thumbs to do the same.

The fourth digit of the striped possum's forefoot is about twice as long as the other digits. This sharp-clawed probe is used to dig out insects from deep inside tree-bark crevices.

X-RAY

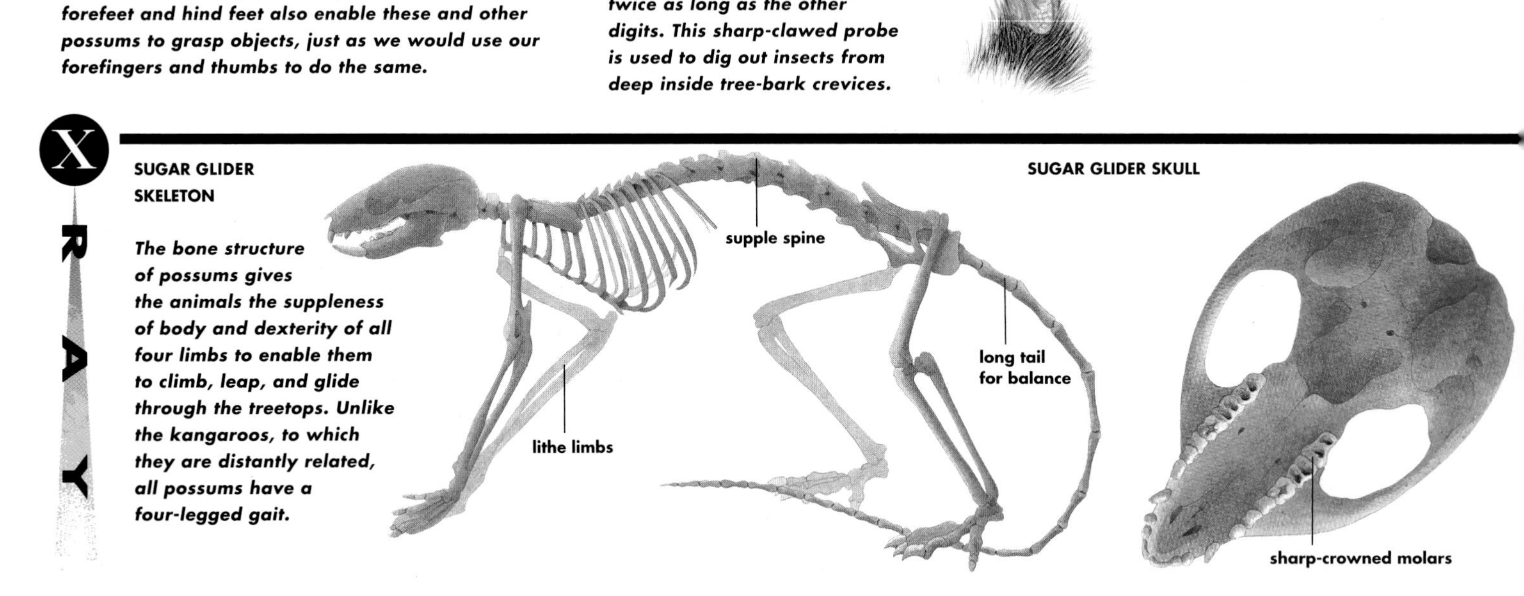

SUGAR GLIDER SKELETON

The bone structure of possums gives the animals the suppleness of body and dexterity of all four limbs to enable them to climb, leap, and glide through the treetops. Unlike the kangaroos, to which they are distantly related, all possums have a four-legged gait.

X-ray illustrations Elisabeth Smith

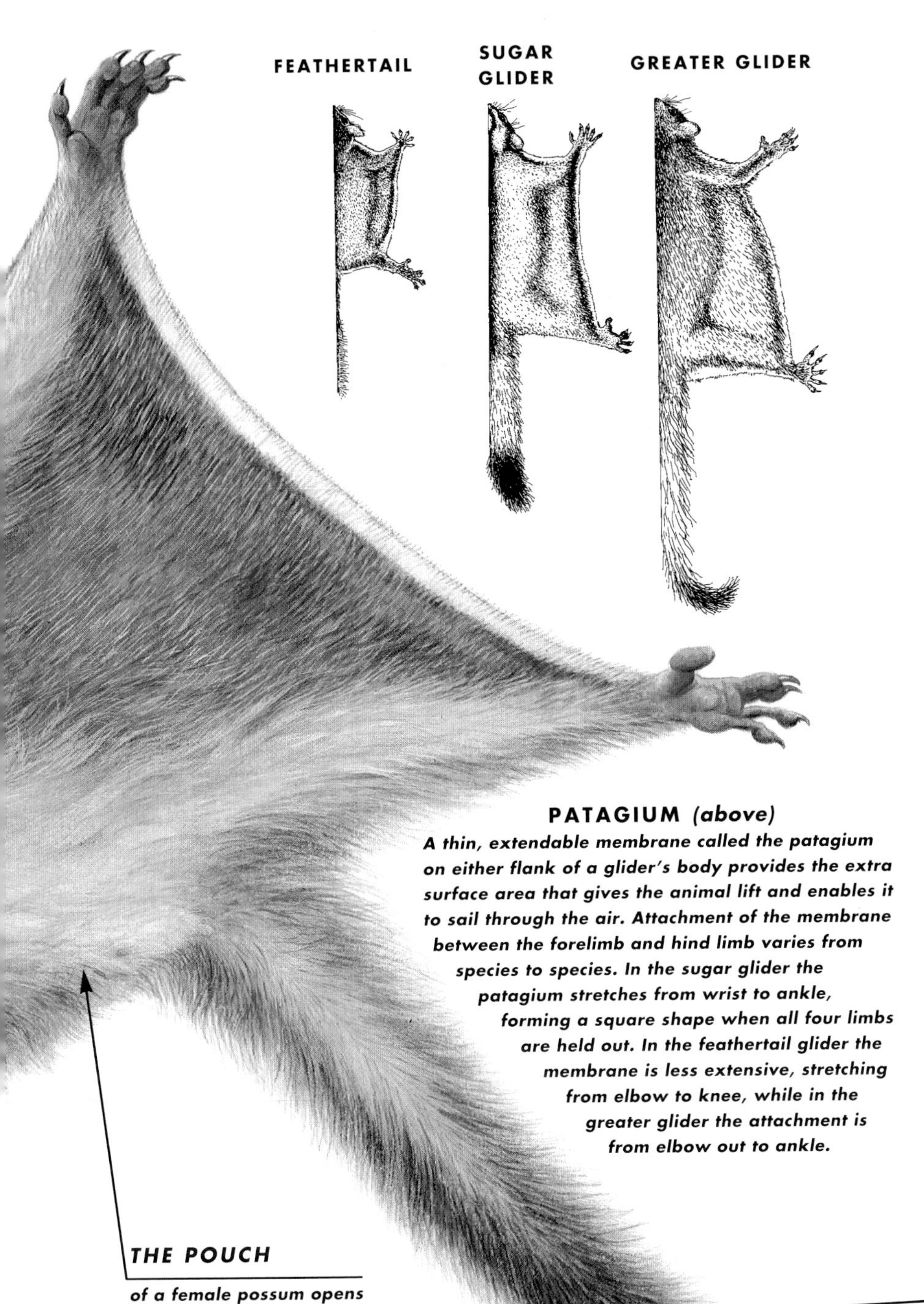

PATAGIUM *(above)*

A thin, extendable membrane called the patagium on either flank of a glider's body provides the extra surface area that gives the animal lift and enables it to sail through the air. Attachment of the membrane between the forelimb and hind limb varies from species to species. In the sugar glider the patagium stretches from wrist to ankle, forming a square shape when all four limbs are held out. In the feathertail glider the membrane is less extensive, stretching from elbow to knee, while in the greater glider the attachment is from elbow out to ankle.

THE POUCH

of a female possum opens forward (it opens backward in marsupial carnivores like the dunnarts and the Tasmanian devil). The pouch is basically a fold of skin that encloses the mother's teats and the newborn infants that attach themselves to them.

FACT FILE:

SUGAR GLIDER

CLASSIFICATION

GENUS: *PETAURUS*

SPECIES: *BREVICEPS*

SIZE

HEAD–BODY LENGTH: 6.3–8.3 IN (16–21 CM)

TAIL LENGTH: 6.5–8.3 IN (16.5–21 CM)

WEIGHT: 3.4–5.6 OZ (95–160 G)

COLORATION

PALE GRAY ABOVE, CREAM TO PALE GRAY BELOW; DARK STRIPE FROM FOREHEAD TO BACK AND SOMETIMES WHITE NOSE TO TAIL

FEATURES

LARGE EYES

LARGE POINTED EARS

SUPPLE BODY

EXTENDABLE GLIDING MEMBRANES ON FLANKS

OPPOSING FIRST OR FIRST AND SECOND DIGITS

LONG BUSHY TAIL

DARK DORSAL STRIPE AND PATCHES BEHIND EARS

THE TAIL

is long and well furred. It tends to be held straight when the animal is gliding, and, along with the curvature of the gliding membranes, it probably helps control the direction of flight.

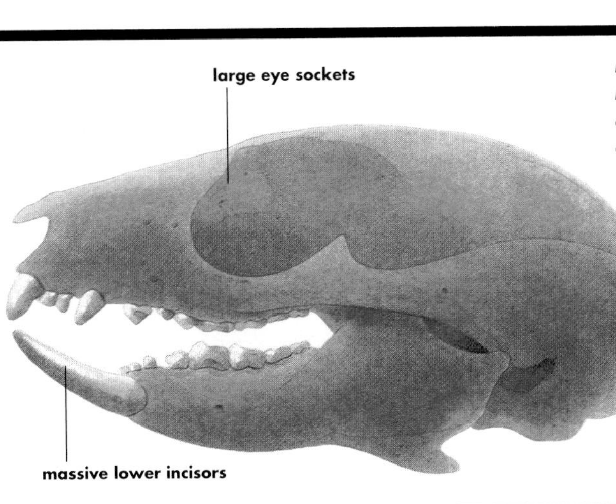

Possums typically have a rather broad, flattened skull, with large eye sockets to house the prominent eyes. The foremost incisors in the lower jawbone are large, stout, and forward-pointing.

TEETH OF A LEAF-EATER

The molar teeth of leaf-eating possums are well suited for grinding fibrous food. Sharp ridges on the crowns of these teeth break the food down into a more readily digestible form.

BRUSH-TAILED POSSUM SKULL

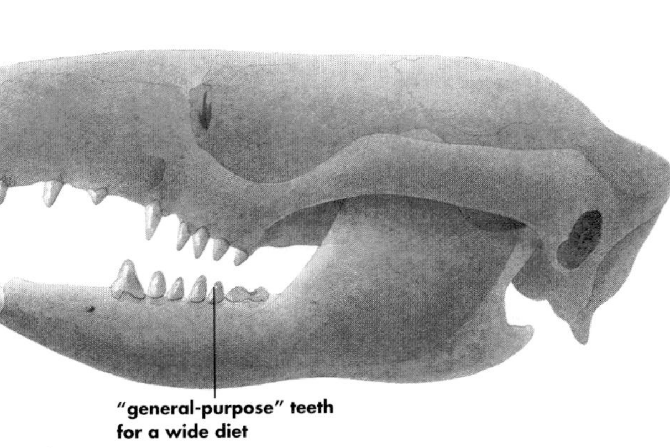

Main illustration Peter David Scott/Wildlife Art Agency. Color detail illustrations Wayne Ford/Wildlife Art Agency

NIGHTLY FORAGERS

THEY MAY BE COMMON, BUT MOST POSSUMS ARE SELDOM SEEN BY HUMANS, FOR THEY GO ABOUT THEIR BUSINESS OF CLAMBERING OR GLIDING THROUGH THE TREES UNDER THE CLOAK OF DARKNESS

Possums are creatures of the night. By day, they lie concealed in tree or rock hollows, disused birds' nests, and old burrows. At dusk or nightfall they stir from hiding and, with climbing, running, leaping, and gliding movements, head off to find food. As a result, most possums are rarely seen in their bush, eucalyptus, and forest habitats. Many live high in the trees or are solitary in habit and, though they use a range of gurgles, chatters, yaps, and screams, are generally rather quiet animals. Adult green ring-tails have never been known to utter a sound.

The spotted cuscus is common in New Guinea; yet, because of its nocturnal and secretive habits, casual visitors to the rain forest are unlikely to spot one. Like other cuscuses, it moves slowly through the branches, keeping a firm grip with feet or tail as it reaches out with a forepaw. Though it travels with the cautious action of a sloth, it actually has much in common with monkeys. Its diet is broad, its hands can exert a powerful clench, and it has a prehensile tail very similar to that of many South American monkeys, even down to the hairless tip with its roughened, textured underside, which improves grip.

GETTING AROUND

Most possums can make use of a prehensile tail, but they also move in a less deliberate fashion. Pygmy possums climb nervously but nimbly around twigs, foliage, and flowers, often hanging by their tails as they swing into feeding position. The feather-tailed possum makes agile leaps, and the striped possum races along branches with a flowing gait, often hurling itself to the next tree. This possum walks in an odd, rowinglike style, in which diagonally opposite limbs are swung in unison.

It is easy to imagine how the leaps performed by so many possums evolved into gliding ability. An animal with even small folds of skin between the limbs would be able to extend its leaps. The limited patagium of the feathertail glider is enough to give the animal an advantage when moving through lightly wooded habitats. And having extra skin flaps seems to confer little disadvantage: The champion of gliders, the yellow-tailed glider, can also climb and run fast in the canopy.

One possum defies all generalizations. The common brush-tail, though nocturnal, is one of the better-known marsupials in Australia mainly because its adaptable, opportunist nature has brought it into close proximity with humans. It is widespread wherever there are trees, and, with its broad tastes both for food and shelter, it has successfully colonized new environments, including suburbs. An agile climber, it also readily travels over the ground. ■

The feathertail glider (right) *uses its tail both as a rudder and as an anchor for flight maneuvers.*

ANT/NHPA

ANT/NHPA

The spotted cuscus (above) *in the forests of New Guinea and Queensland uses its tail as a fifth limb.*

AMAZING FACTS

RECORD BREAKERS

Many of the possums are accomplished acrobats, with even some small species renowned for their leaping prowess. Both the long-tailed pygmy possum and Leadbeater's possum make sudden horizontal leaps of over 3 feet (1 meter) or more between branches. The lemuroid ring-tail flings itself with limbs outstretched across gaps of 6.5–10 feet (2–3 meters).

But among the gliders, acrobatics turn to aerobatics. The little feathertail glider can sail across gaps of 66 ft (20 m), and it has even been known to make spiraling glides around trunks, steering by altering the shape of each patagium and the position of its flattened, fringed tail. It lands with an upward swoop; the bulbous, ridged pads on its digits help it cling to the smoothest vertical surface. The sugar glider and squirrel glider can remain airborne for 165 ft (50 m), and the greater glider can double this distance. But the horizontal-distance record presently lies with the yellow-bellied glider, whose glides have been measured at up to 380 ft (115 m).

Rod Williams/Bruce Coleman Ltd.

The sugar glider's "wings" fold neatly into its flanks when they are not in use (above).

HABITATS

The greatest diversity of possum species, area for area, lies in the lush rain forest of New Guinea, one of the largest islands in the world. Cloaking the dramatic mountain slopes and deep valleys of the island's Central Range and extending into the lowlands sweeping from its feet, this is the largest remaining stretch of tropical rain forest outside Africa and South America. The limestone peaks are clad with huge trees entangled in stout liana vines, and laced with raging torrents and deep cataracts in narrow ravines. In contrast to its breath taking beauty and rich natural treasures, it is unforgivingly hostile to human intrusion and, as such, retains pockets of unspoiled wilderness.

Possums are particularly abundant in the dripping montane forest between 3,300 ft (1,000 m) and 10,000 ft (3,000 m) up—among them cuscuses, ringtails, striped possums, and the feather-tailed possum. In some cases, different species tend to occupy

The dwarf cuscus lives on the island of Sulawesi, far from its ancestral origins in New Guinea.

Gerald Cubitt/Bruce Coleman Ltd.

FOCUS ON

THE VICTORIA HIGHLANDS

In the cold, misty central highlands of Victoria, Australia, huge yet slender-trunked trees soar to heights of 330 ft (100 m) and more. They are mountain ash, a eucalyptus that predominates in this small area of Australia. Every century or so, natural fires clear part of the forest, and most of the trees are destroyed. The seeds, however, are more hardy and the heat actually stimulates them to sprout in the charred soil. As new trees develop, their crowns form a dense network with those of acacias. This low ash canopy is an ideal habitat for one of Australia's rarest animals, Leadbeater's possum *(right)*.

Fredy Mercry/ANT/NHPA

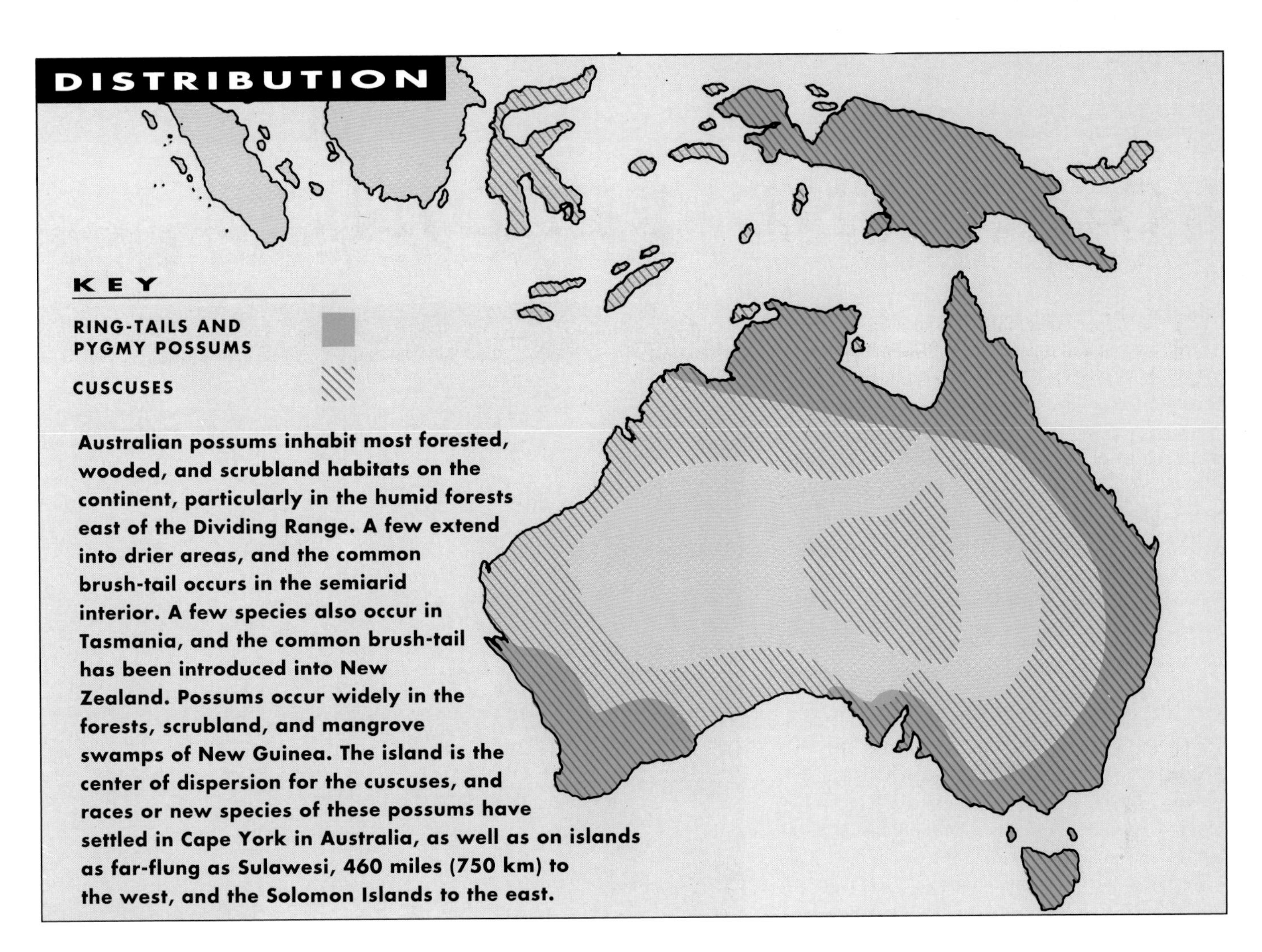

different ranges according to altitude. A journey up into the mountains progresses through ever cooler and moister forest types; these are associated first with the gray cuscus, then Stein's cuscus, then the mountain cuscus, and finally the silky cuscus, which has the longest, densest fur of all to ward off nighttime cold. The ground cuscus is unusual in that it spends much of the time on the forest floor. It has also colonized other islands close to New Guinea, on some of which it even lives in caves.

Australian Possums

Pockets of tropical rain forest also exist in northeast Australia, populated by gray and spotted cuscuses and several ring-tailed species; but for millions of years such habitats have been receding as the continent has become steadily drier. In its place eucalyptus forests and woodlands have filled those parts of Australia still moist enough to retain extensive trees, while more hardy gum trees, acacias, and scrub dot the interior savanna. These more open habitats have spurred the evolution of new possum forms. Most gliders live in the eucalyptus forests, where the spaces between trees have prompted even greater leaping ability.

The spreading eucalypts also required inhabitants that did not rely on foliage or fruit like most ring-tails and cuscuses—eucalypts are a poor source of these foods—but were capable of feeding instead on gums and saps or the nectar and insects more abundant in the sunbathed habitats. Today the woods and bush are populated both by dietary specialists like the pygmy possums and gliders, which eat nectar, gum, and sap, and by generalist feeders like the brush-tails.

Possums on the Rocks

Possums on the whole spend as much of their time as possible in trees and shrubs, but there is one Australian species that completely defies the norm. The mountain pygmy possum is the only Australian mammal restricted to habitats above the tree line. It lives in upland heaths in the Snowy Mountain range of southeastern New South Wales, where it searches for food over the rocky ground. Thick fur protects it from the cold of winter, and it continues to forage under blankets of snow.

Some other possums, though they climb into vegetation to feed, take their shelter on the ground in burrows or among rocks. In the Kimberleys and neighboring rugged zones of northern Australia, both the scaly-tailed and the rock ring-tailed possums find their daylight hours' refuge in rock crevices. This compares with the tree hollows and other arboreal shelters utilized by most possums. The common brush-tailed possum, in its spread into artificial habitats, has found shelter around buildings, especially in the gaps under roofs. ■

FOOD AND FEEDING

Just about any food item available is consumed by one species of possum or another, although some are more specialist than others. The broadest diet is probably that of the common brush-tail: As well as fruits, flowers, buds, and insects, it eats the leaves of a huge range of plants. Cuscuses and the scaly-tailed possum also eat leaves, fruit, buds, and invertebrates; and the mountain brush-tail gets by on a mixture of leaves, fruits, pine cones, fungi, lichen, and bark. Breadth of diet aside, however, there are four main sources of food utilized by possums that are worth looking at in detail: leaves, plant exudates (gum, sap, and others), blossoms, and insects.

LEAF-EATERS

Ring-tailed possums are among the more specialist of possums in that leaves form the bulk of their diet; they live mainly in rain forests, where they find an endless variety of foliage. The lemuroid ring-tail leaps and clambers to the tips of branches, and, gaining extra grip with its tail, it pulls in the leaves of at least 37 different types of trees. The green ring-tail, on the other hand, likes fig trees and is one of the few possums able to eat their stiff, waxy foliage.

To eat leaves demands not only suitable molar teeth for chewing the fibrous material, but also a stomach that can digest it. Ring-tails have a large stomach chamber, rich in microbes that help break down cellulose in leaves. Digestion still takes time, however, and the ring-tail may even eat its feces to extract more nutrients. Probably because of this slow digestion, ring-tails tend to move slowly and thus conserve energy.

The leaves of eucalypts pose problems for leaf-eaters, because they contain substances toxic to most creatures. Some of those possums that can exploit this food source have been highly successful, among them the common brush-tail and the common ring-tail. Both these animals include other foods in their diet, but the greater glider eats only eucalypt leaves. The liver of this species can cancel out or detoxify the poisonous products of digestion from the bloodstream.

SAP-SUCKERS

Most other gliding possums of the eucalypt woodlands exploit not leaves of the trees but the fluids present in their woody parts: saps, gums, and manna—a sugary solution that exudes from sites where branches are physically damaged. They may also glean honeydew—droplets of sweet fluid secreted by sap-sucking insects.

C. & S. Pellitt/ANT/NHPA

Leadbeater's possum licks nectar and other plant fluids (above). *The light dusting of pollen that it inadvertently carries on its snout actually helps plants to cross-fertilize.*

SLOW FEEDER

With its leaf-eating habits, the slow-moving spotted cuscus (left) *has often been likened to the sloths of the South American rain forests. But since it also feeds on forest fruits and blossoms, its generalist feeding niche more closely mirrors that of monkeys.*

Exudates flow from places where bark has been damaged—often by the gliders themselves. Yellow-bellied gliders bite distinctive V-shaped notches through eucalyptus bark into the sapwood and then lick up the sap that seeps out. When the wounds plug up, the gliders open up new notches, and a favored tree may become heavily scarred. Fresh notches may also attract sugar gliders, but they too have strong enough teeth to bite holes in eucalypt bark to extract sap and manna. Also, the digestive systems of both the sugar glider and Leadbeater's possum can cope with the resinous gums exuded by acacias that grow in the woodland understory.

TOUGH STOMACH

The scaly-tailed possum (left) *is one of the few marsupials that can digest tough eucalyptus leaves; these contain substances that are toxic to most herbivores.*

Flower-Feeders

The feathertail glider licks up sap when it gets the chance, but what it really likes is nectar. It is one of many of the smaller possums, along with the eastern pygmy possum and the western pygmy possum, to visit flowers and feed on the sugary nectar and the protein-rich pollen they yield. Permitted by their light build and aided by their agility, their sensitive toe pads, and, in the case of the pygmy possums, their prehensile tails, they can clamber over flower heads, lapping up nectar and pollen with their brush-tipped tongues.

The eastern pygmy possum feeds from the blossoms of eucalypts, banksias, and bottlebrushes. When plentiful, pollen can provide virtually all the protein an eastern pygmy possum requires. But more often than not, the animal needs a secondary source. Both nectar-feeders and sap-feeders face potential imbalance in their diets, since these foods

Illustration Evi Antoniou

are rich in carbohydrates but poor in protein. This may especially be the case during the breeding season, when bodily demands are the highest. The readiest source for meeting this deficiency is insects.

In the breeding phase of spring and early summer, sugar gliders spend increasing amounts of time searching the foliage for moths, beetles, and larvae. Leadbeater's possum can find tree crickets beneath loose bark in its forest habitat all year round, a factor thought to be crucial in the animal's capacity to breed at any time of the year.

All pygmy possums feed to varying extents on invertebrates, including beetles, termites, grasshoppers, mantises, and spiders. They can catch flying moths too, but they bite the wings off before eating them. Even the smallest of possums, the little pygmy possum, is a voracious killer that tackles a wide range of insects and spiders not much smaller than itself.

But the most remarkable of the insect-eaters is probably the striped possum. Patterned like a skunk and nearly as smelly, it races over branches and fallen logs, investigating the crevices for wood-boring grubs and other insects. Using its long, jutting incisor teeth, the animal noisily jabs and gouges at bark to expose creatures beneath, sometimes producing a shower of wood fragments as it works. Larvae hidden deep within crevices or holes can be plucked out on the end of the possum's elongated tongue or dragged out using its elongated fourth finger with its sharp claw.

JUICE BAR

Though few possums have an exclusively specialist diet, most have a characteristic favored food source. Gliders (below) *feed heavily on the sap and gum of trees, and they often bite notches in bark to tap into these sugary exudates.*

FLOWER POWER

Some pygmy possums rely heavily on the nectar and pollen produced by certain flowers (below).

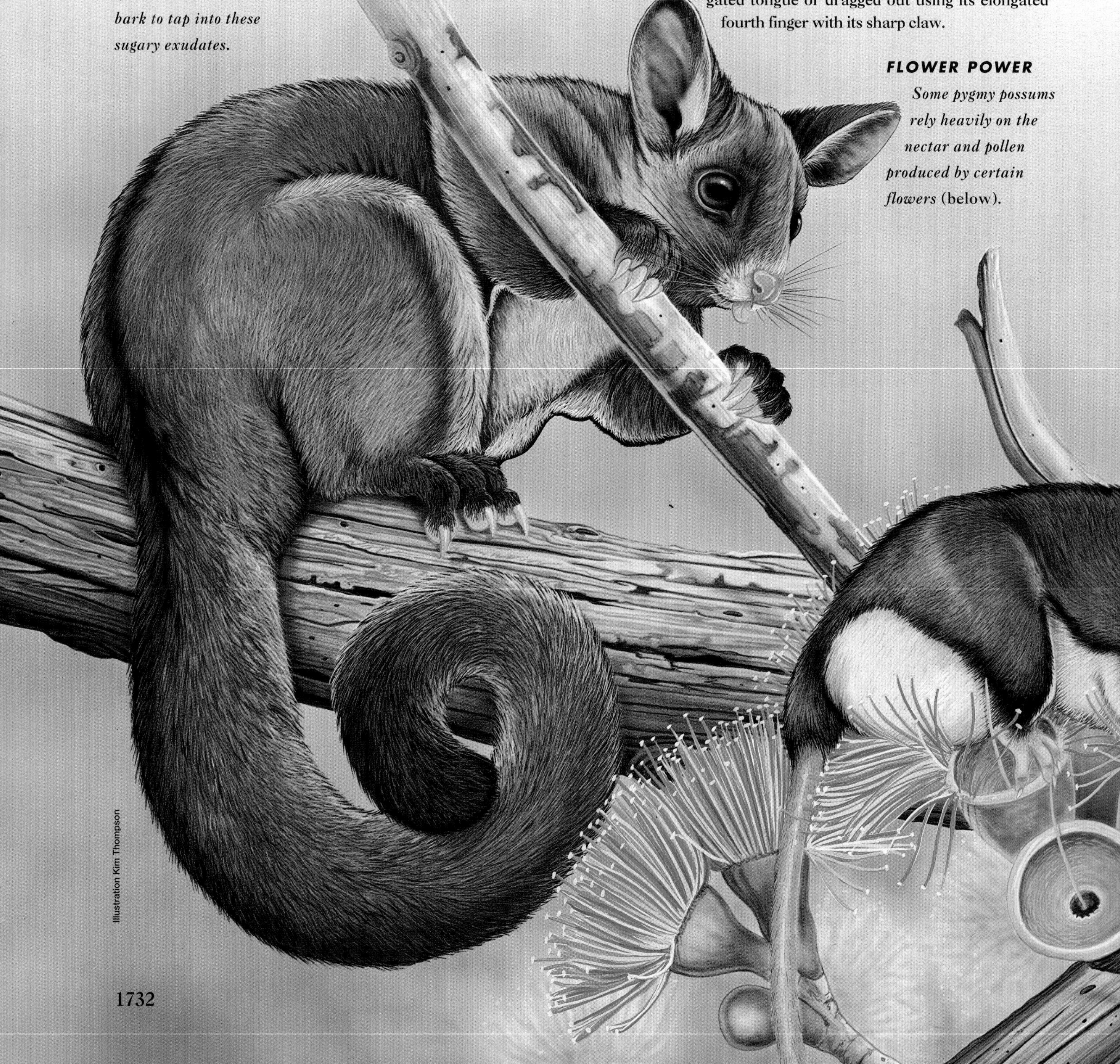

Illustration Kim Thompson

Alain Compost/Bruce Coleman Ltd.

Cuscuses are fond of fruits and flowers, although they also eat a few insects (above).

POSSUM POLLINATION

Blossom nectar is not an attractive food source simply by chance. It is provided by plants in order to lure nectar-feeders: insects, birds, bats, and marsupials. Banksia plants in the Australian heaths are closely associated with small, nocturnal marsupials, including the western pygmy possum. The pungent flower clusters are easily found in the dark by the possum and are robust enough to bear the animal's weight as it climbs around. Though some of the pollen is eaten, plenty more sticks to the possum's fur, ready to be brushed off against blooms the animal will visit later. The eastern pygmy possum performs a similar pollinating role in the understory of eucalypt woodland.

Some possums prey on animal food larger than insects and spiders. A little pygmy possum has been observed eating a lizard, holding the carcass down with its paws and tearing off chunks with its teeth. The spotted cuscus is believed to prey occasionally on small birds and small mammals, and the ground cuscus of New Guinea is also a carnivore.

The mountain pygmy possum's bladelike premolar side teeth are able to crack open hard seed coats and tough insect cuticles. This dexterous possum brings seeds up to the sides of its mouth in its forepaws. There is some evidence that it stores excess seeds for the winter in its nest or under loose bark. ■

DIGGING FOR DINNER

Striped possums feed mainly on insects, including wood-boring grubs, which they pry from bark (left).

SOCIAL STRUCTURE

Patterns of social organization vary among the possums, both between different species and, in some cases, within one species in different parts of its range. The yellow-bellied glider, for example, seems to form a stable bond with a single mate more readily in the southerly parts of its range than in the north. Nevertheless, most species fall into two camps: those that tend to be more solitary in their behavior and those that live more sociably.

SOLO POSSUMS

Cuscuses, brush-tails, and several ring-tails and pygmy possums lead rather lonely lives. Individuals keep to patches of forest called home ranges, which may overlap to some extent—particularly the larger male territories with those of nearby females—but neighbors seldom interact. Some, like the common brush-tail, jealously defend core areas within this patch, centered on good denning sites. The green ring-tail is probably the least sociable possum of all: Adults are seldom ever seen in the same tree unless they are mating. In others, such as the mountain brush-tail, the greater glider, and the mountain pygmy possum, mated pairs may share dens for the breeding period. At other times, when more than one animal is seen together, they are likely to be a mother with her dependent young.

in SIGHT

DEFENDING THE DEN

Common brush-tailed possums are jealous defenders of territory. Mature animals establish exclusive areas within their home ranges, marking them with scent. Though individuals of the opposite sex or of lower status may be allowed into the reserved zone, the resident will not tolerate rivals.

The exclusive areas are always centered on good den sites, suggesting that the territoriality is prompted by a shortage of dens. Many of the nesting sites that younger animals are forced to use after they have been driven from their mothers offer scant protection from predators, such as dingoes, pythons, and lace monitors. Older animals are set on holding on to secure sites such as tree hollows. So possessive are they that, in their native home, virtually all adult common brush-tails nest alone.

The common ring-tail and lemuroid ring-tail are more sociable. They often live in pairs or family groups and may sometimes feed in company with unrelated individuals. In the long-tailed pygmy possum, too, family groups of up to four may share a nest outside the breeding season.

But among the gliders the most complex forms of sociability have evolved. As a general rule of thumb, the smaller the species, the more sociable it is

FOR PROTECTION *against the winter cold, up to a dozen sugar gliders may spend the day huddled together in a nest* (below). *In summer the larger nesting bands break up into smaller groups.*

Illustration Darren Harvey/Wildlife Art Agency

inclined to be. Hence, in the north of their range, groups of up to six adult yellow-bellied gliders may be seen together, while twice as many sugar gliders may share a nest, especially in winter. The feather-tail glider, the smallest of all, forms extended family groups, and its feeding aggregations can at times number forty animals.

Groups of yellow-bellied gliders are basically harems. Each usually consists of a single male plus several females with their dependent young. The male, who mates with all the females, jealously defends a territory of up to 150 acres (60 hectares) against intruding rival males. In sugar gliders there may again be one dominant male in the group, but often there are other males, too, that may or may not have a breeding role but that help to defend the territory.

Natural Science Photos

Life will be hard for the young brush-tail (above) *when its mother drives it off to fend for itself.*

Leadbeater's possum displays a contrasting pattern. In this species, the most aggressively territorial individual is a dominant female, which excludes other females from her territory of 2.5 to 5 acres (1–2 hectares). She shares her territory with a mating partner and her dependent young, and she may also tolerate other adult nonbreeding males on the patch, making a group total of as many as eight animals.

Using scent

Possums mark their territories with scent from glands. Common brush-tails have nine scent glands, with those on the chest, chin, and anal area the most important. Secretions smeared on twigs serve not only to mark out an animal's presence, but probably also to indicate its status. In gliders, individuals, particularly those dominant in the group, smear scent on their companions during social contacts.

As well as using scent marks for communication, possums have a variety of calls, some of which, such as the guttural screeches of cuscuses, are uttered as part of territorial defense. Should intruders fail to be deterred from entering territories, the response from residents is often quite aggressive. Brush-tails rise up on their hind legs as a prelude to fighting, and combat between ground cuscuses involves biting and blows from any of the four limbs. ■

REPRODUCTION

Marsupial mammals have a fundamentally different reproductive system than that of placental mammals. Whereas the latter give birth to quite well-developed young after a prolonged gestation period, marsupials emerge from the womb at a stage barely more advanced than embryonic. Instead of prolonged development inside the mother's body, marsupials undergo the equivalent of fetal development outside her body, but attached to a teat inside the fold of belly skin that forms the mother's pouch.

A MATTER OF TIMING

The first stages in the possums' reproductive story are not, by and large, so unusual. As might be expected from a large group of mammals spread across widely different climatic zones, the timing and seasonality of breeding varies considerably. Some possums of humid areas, such as the New Guinea cuscuses and Leadbeater's possum, mate all year round, while those of drier zones tend to mate in wetter periods that last a few months. Courtship may be brief or ritualized, with mutual grooming and scent marking, as in the yellow-bellied glider. Mating in this species is gentle enough that it can take place while both animals are clinging under a branch. But in the striped possum it involves not only the intertwining and beating of tails but also much vigorous screaming.

BEAN-SIZED BABIES

It is after fertilization that the marsupial story becomes strange. The egg does not implant itself fully in the womb, and before three weeks have passed in some possums, the minute young is born. Weighing less than 0.035 oz (1 gram) and looking little more than like a featureless grub, the tiny creature instinctively wriggles its way laboriously from the birth canal, along the belly, and into the mother's pouch, clinging to her fur as it goes. Once in the security of the pouch, the newborn automatically attaches itself to a teat, which swells to fit its mouth, and stays there for at least seven weeks, drawing in through its mouth all the substances it needs to live and grow into a young possum.

Possums generally give birth to one or two young, but pygmy possums may produce three or four. The mountain pygmy possum sometimes produces more infants than its four available teats can accommodate,

A young spotted cuscus peers out from the safety of its mother's embrace (above). *She usually rears only one young, although she may give birth to three.*

EMBRYONIC

after only five days of life, a young brush-tailed possum (left) *is preoccupied with suckling. It is born with the ability to claw its way from the birth canal to this place of refuge and nourishment.*

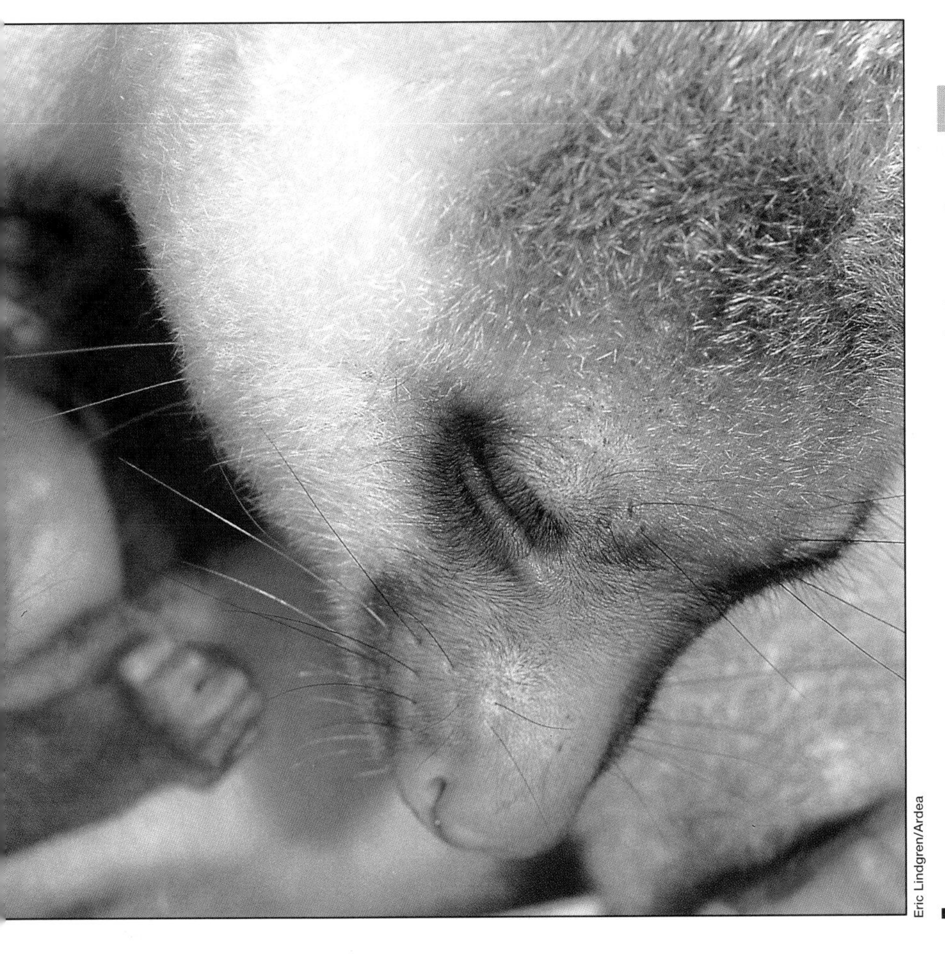

Eric Lindgren/Ardea

in SIGHT

MATERNAL DUTIES

One of the consequences of marsupial reproduction is that male possums play little part in the development of their offspring. During the extended period when the young are suckling in the pouch, the mother provides for all their primary needs—for food and safe refuge from predators.

After weaning, the bond built up between mother and offspring is such that the young still associate with this one parent and may ride on her back as she forages. She may alternatively leave them in the nest, although they utter distress calls when separated from her. Even in species such as Leadbeater's possum, in which partners form a strong pair bond and share territories, the male has little role or recognition as the father. In some species, such as the yellow-bellied glider, young males are harassed, and may even be killed, by their father.

in which case the last to reach the pouch dies. One or two litters per year is the norm, but the feather-tail glider may produce three litters in such quick succession that young are still being suckled while embryos are forming in the womb.

LETTING GO

The depth of the pouch is such that young are held safely inside even when their mother is moving quickly through the trees. Even so, there eventually comes a time when the young are too big to be accommodated. In the eastern pygmy possum this comes so quickly that the young have to cling to the mother's belly fur while still anchored to her teats. In other cases the young are sufficiently well developed to release their attachment before they outgrow the pouch. They may remain there for safety for a few more weeks, but eventually they have to vacate. At this stage their mother's milk still provides their sustenance, but they now either cling to her back while she forages, as in cuscuses, or are left behind in the nest, as in gliders, until they are weaned and can fend for themselves. ■

A young green ring-tail (below) *keeps a firm grip on its mother's fur: She rarely leaves her treetop home.*

Michael Morcambe/NHPA

FROM BIRTH TO DEATH

COMMON BRUSH-TAILED POSSUM

BREEDING: YEAR-ROUND IN THE NORTH; BIRTH PEAKS ELSEWHERE IN SPRING AND AUTUMN

GESTATION: 17–18 DAYS

LITTER SIZE: USUALLY 1

LITTER FREQUENCY: USUALLY 1 A YEAR, BUT IN SOME AREAS UP TO 2

WEIGHT AT BIRTH: 0.008 OZ (0.22 G)

LEAVE POUCH: 4–5 MONTHS

WEANING: 6–7 MONTHS

SEPARATED FROM MOTHER: 8–18 MONTHS

SEXUAL MATURITY: 1–2 YEARS

LONGEVITY: 8 YEARS OR MORE

Illustration Simon Turvey/Wildlife Art Agency

POSSUMS IN PERIL

SOME ARE HOLDING THEIR OWN, BUT MOST POSSUMS ARE IN DECLINE AS HUMAN INFLUENCE ON THEIR ENVIRONMENTS SPREADS; A FEW ARE ALREADY PRECARIOUSLY CLOSE TO THE BRINK OF EXTINCTION

In 1961 an eye-catching little animal brought excitement and a glimmer of hope into Australian wildlife circles. Zoologists surveying misty montane forests in the Cumberland Valley of southeast Victoria spotted with considerable surprise what turned out to be a Leadbeater's possum. Only the sixth specimen of the species ever recorded, it was also the first sighting of the animal in the wild since 1909. Since then Leadbeater's possum has been found to live in more than fifty localities spread across about 400 square miles (1,000 square kilometers) of mountain forest.

The symbolic importance of the discovery and later findings was that Leadbeater's possum had been assumed to have gone the way of at least ten other Australian marsupials since the arrival of Europeans on the continent in 1788: a plummet into extinction. The possum had been known to be rare and localized since its original discovery in 1867. This and the four subsequent recordings of specimens were all made in areas of the forest habitat that had been mostly destroyed by the 1920s.

In 1921 the sad assumption was made that Leadbeater's possum had joined the list of lost marsupials and increased the alarming record of extinctions among Australia's fauna. The irony is that, since the joy of its rediscovery, Leadbeater's possum has once again become a cause for serious concern. The species is in peril today because its restricted habitat is threatened by logging. This time the chances of discovering an unaffected population elsewhere are slender indeed.

POSSUMS UNDER PRESSURE

Leadbeater's possum is one of nearly a quarter of all possum species considered today to be in a precarious survival situation. Mostly they are threatened by habitat clearance and alteration, but other pressures, such as the introduction of nonnative animals and overhunting, play their part. To a degree, such threats have affected Australasian wildlife for several hundred years; but it has been the arrival and spread of European settlers in Australia over the last two centuries, and the more recent increase in settlement and forestry on the island of New Guinea, that have precipitated so many species into the predicament they now face.

John Dowrer/Planet Earth Pictures

Logging and deforestation continue unabated in New Guinea and Australia (above).

Jean-Paul Ferrero/Ardea

THEN & NOW

This map shows the former and current distribution of Leadbeater's possum.

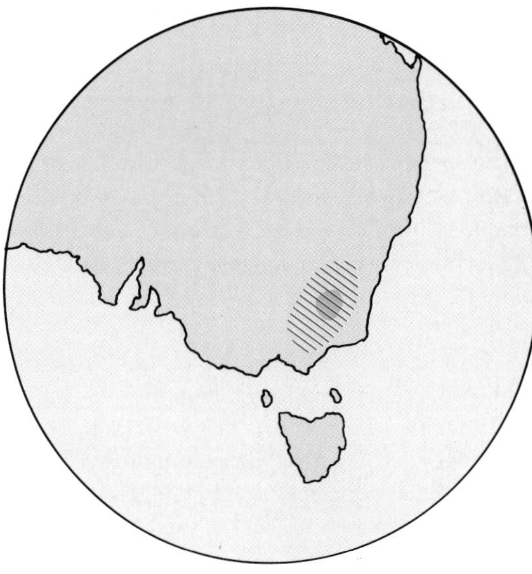

Leadbeater's possum lives up in the tree canopy of dense, humid primary forests at altitudes of up to 4,000 ft (1,200 m). Its distribution is thought to be restricted to some 200 sq miles (500 sq km) of mountain ash forest in the Cumberland Valley near Healesville, Victoria.

Its rediscovery in 1961 (see page 1738), a little less than a century after it was first discovered, gave hope to conservationists, who had believed the species to be extinct. The species now receives legal protection in Victoria, but its habitat continues to be threatened by commercial logging ventures and bushfires. Sympathetic forest management will be crucial to the survival of Leadbeater's possum, but there has been little evidence of this to date.

Across Australia, the landscapes both of the wooded coastal quarters and the dry interior have been modified by the needs of agriculture. Forests, scrub, and even semiarid plains have had vegetation cleared to make the land more suitable for grazing or cultivation. This process, taking place cumulatively decade after decade, may have opened up some habitats and made them more suitable for a

Lost, found, and lost again? Newly rediscovered, Leadbeater's possum is still in great danger.

few species, but for most possums it has resulted in a steady decline and contraction of range. Cutting down trees deprives possums not only of vital food supplies but also of resting sites and places of refuge from predators.

Clearance of bush for rural and urban development has driven the western ring-tail and the western pygmy possum from some of their former haunts, and the little pygmy possum has lost much of its dry forest habitat in mainland Australia. In the north, the removal and degradation of vegetation by roaming livestock as they browse may yet become a threat for the scaly-tailed possum and the rock ring-tail. This is one of the regions where farming is currently expanding fastest.

Part of the problem in such zones is not just deliberate clearance of vegetation. Bushfires after habitat alteration—such as that wrought by rough grazing—tend to be less frequent than in the past but more extensive and devastating. Fire-adapted vegetation can recover, but for small arboreal animals, such as pygmy possums, there is nowhere to escape from the flames.

OVERHUNTING THREATENS SOME POPULATIONS OF BLACK-SPOTTED CUSCUSES IN NEW GUINEA

The damper and more densely wooded regions have suffered greatly, too. One half of Australia's forests have already succumbed to land clearance. While its cousin the sugar glider has adapted quite well to the changes, the squirrel glider seems to have declined sharply as its forest homes in eastern Australia have been fragmented by land development.

LOGGING

Logging is the biggest threat today to the most luxuriant of all possum habitats, the rain forests. Temperate and subtropical rain forests in Tasmania and eastern Australia and tropical rain forests in Queensland, New Guinea, and its adjacent islands are all under grave pressure from industrial forestry businesses. Some of these logging companies are powerful multinationals; they can rapidly deplete forest habitats whether they are clear-cut (totally stripped of trees) or selectively logged (with only the most valuable trees removed). Selective logging removes big single trees that may offer important shelter and food supplies for possums, and at the same time alters the ecological balance of the forest, possibly disrupting the overall food web.

Leadbeater's possum is in such an uncertain position today because almost its entire remaining mountain ash habitat has been earmarked for

ENDANGERED ENVIRONMENT

NEW ZEALAND'S NEWCOMER

The first common brush-tailed possums were released in New Zealand in 1840. New Zealand had no native fur-bearing animals, and settlers hoped to establish a lucrative trapping business. In an empty land full of suitable food sources and shelter, the possums started breeding to their full and rapid potential. By the first detailed survey in 1946, common brush-tails were established across most of New Zealand, and today they exist wherever there is enough cover. The fur industry proved a great financial success, with peak exports in the 1960s and 1970s of around 1.5 million skins per year.

But the story does not end there. With an estimated 25 million common brush-tails in existence in New Zealand, this exotic species is probably now the country's most numerous mammal. It is highly adaptable, there are no natural predators on the island, and much of the plant life around it presents rich pickings. New Zealand's native trees have few defenses against leaf-eaters in the form of unpalatable oils, and their foliage is eaten with relish.

As possum numbers soared unchecked, the animals adapted their behavior. They relaxed their normal territoriality, occupying smaller and looser territories. The result is that population densities in many places are at least six times higher than the norm in the brush-tails' native Australia. The possums fed on favored trees with such intensity that foresters began to see native trees severely

Natural Science Photos

CONSERVATION MEASURES

- In 1993 the Australian government passed a new Endangered Species Protection Act and announced an extra $42 million for nature protection to supplement the $100 million already being spent per year. Though the new money will be spread thin and across all wildlife, additional resources to protect old-growth forests, expand the preserve network, control exotic animals, and increase rain forest

defoliated. By the 1950s fears spread that the marsupial invaders were destroying much of New Zealand's native vegetation, changing the composition of the forests and setting in motion further ecological imbalance. Through the use of a bounty plan and then culling campaigns involving shooting, trapping, and poison baits, attempts were made to control possum numbers. But even though millions were killed, the efforts had little effect on the overall population. Blanket extermination ideas were eventually dropped, and recent studies now raise doubts over the true destructiveness of possums. In many areas of established populations, the vegetation has changed negligibly in the long term. The jury is still out on New Zealand's bold newcomer.

Inset David Maitland/Planet Earth Pictures

THE COMMON BRUSH-TAIL WAS INTRODUCED TO NEW ZEALAND FROM AUSTRALIA AND TASMANIA.

replanting should benefit many species of possums. For the most critically endangered species, specialized funds may be allocated for intensive conservation efforts such as captive breeding and reintroduction into strictly controlled preserves. Hopes are high for a captive colony of Leadbeater's possums, which was established in the early 1970s and is so far proving successful.

POSSUMS IN DANGER

THE INTERNATIONAL UNION FOR THE CONSERVATION OF NATURE REGARDS THESE SPECIES AS PARTICULARLY THREATENED. A FURTHER FIVE ARE CONSIDERED RARE OR ARE SUSPECTED TO BE IN DANGER:

Species	Status
MAHOGANY GLIDER	ENDANGERED
LEADBEATER'S POSSUM	ENDANGERED
MOUNTAIN PYGMY POSSUM	ENDANGERED
TATE'S TRIOK	ENDANGERED
BLACK-SPOTTED CUSCUS	VULNERABLE
OBI CUSCUS	VULNERABLE
TELEFOMIN CUSCUS	VULNERABLE
WOODLARK ISLAND CUSCUS	VULNERABLE
WESTERN RING-TAIL	VULNERABLE
NORTHERN GLIDER	VULNERABLE
RAT-TAILED TRIOK	VULNERABLE

ENDANGERED MEANS THAT THE ANIMAL IS IN DANGER OF EXTINCTION AND ITS SURVIVAL IS UNLIKELY UNLESS STEPS ARE TAKEN TO SAVE IT. *VULNERABLE* MEANS THAT THE SPECIES IS LIKELY TO ENTER THE ENDANGERED CATEGORY IN THE NEAR FUTURE IF THE CAUSES FOR ITS DECLINE CONTINUE TO EXIST.

clear-cutting. The logging would take place on a 40- to 80-year rotation, but this would not be a long enough span to ensure sufficient remaining old trees to meet the animal's needs. Leadbeater's possum nests inside hollows, and only trees about 150 years old develop cavities of a suitable size. Even after wildfires, at least some such mature trees naturally remain to provide the possums with shelter. But clear-cutting, even in phases, will not permit such trees to remain, because any regrowth is felled before the trees achieve maturity. Continued logging also puts a long-term question mark over the future of the little pygmy possum in its refuge of Tasmania. The yellow-tailed glider has suffered in some areas because the tall, mature eucalyptus forests it prefers are also sought after by loggers.

TROUBLE IN QUEENSLAND

In the pockets of tropical rain forest in Cape York, Queensland, logging poses serious dangers for the long-tailed pygmy possum, the lemuroid ring-tailed possum, and the mahogany glider, whose principal feeding tree, the red mahogany, is selectively felled. Outside Australia, logging and spreading settlement pose potential threats for several of the cuscuses, including the black-spotted cuscus of northern New Guinea and the Woodlark Island cuscus from the island of that name to the east.

One exception to the rule is provided by the green ring-tail, which lives in the rain forests of northeast Queensland. Although it is under threat from logging and is now sparse, it is more resilient to the effects of selective logging. The fig trees that provide it with its favorite food do not yield commercial timber, so they are often left undamaged after a clearance operation. Studies suggest that it may survive even in small remnants of rain forest that have been logged two or three times.

UNWELCOME VISITORS

As well as habitat loss, another grave pressure that besets the wildlife of Australia is the harm caused by nonnative animals that have been introduced to the continent. Many of the native species, having evolved for millions of years in isolation from the rest of the world's wildlife, have been hard hit by the sudden

FROM 1923 TO 1955, SOME 7.5 MILLION COMMON RING-TAIL PELTS WERE COLLECTED FOR THE FUR TRADE

release of prolific or rapacious competitors and predators. Marsupial mammals have been particularly harmed by some placental counterparts—rabbits, dingoes, foxes, and cats. It is the latter two—stealthy versatile hunters able to pursue their prey in dense vegetation—that have proved the curse of possums. Recent estimates suggest that some 5 million red foxes and 12 million feral cats presently run wild in Australia, killing an estimated 6.4 billion native animals every year. Predation by cats is thought to be one of the major reasons for the western ring-tailed possum's current rarity, and both domestic and feral cats certainly find the diminutive western pygmy possum easy prey. Attempts to restock a national park north of Sydney with common ring-tailed possums in the early 1990s were ruined by predation by foxes and cats. Of 84 common ring-tails released, no fewer than three-quarters were killed.

ALONGSIDE MAN

CATTLE KILLERS?

Given their adaptability, it is perhaps not surprising that brush-tails have been the possums that have had the most important encounters with humanity. Not only are common brush-tails the most likely marsupials to colonize artificial habitats, but they have also proven to be among the most economically costly to human interests. In both Australia and New Zealand, common brush-tails raid gardens, orchards, plantations, and crops, while the mountain brush-tail damages pine plantations in Australia by stripping bark from trees.

But one of the most feared discoveries about the common brush-tail is that it can be a carrier of bovine tuberculosis (TB). Cattle are grazed throughout New Zealand, and the dairy industry is crucial to the country's economy. Localized infections of possum populations in New Zealand were found in areas where there was a high incidence of TB among cattle on nearby pastures. The implication was that possums formed a reservoir for the disease and could readily pass on the infection. Possums dwelling at the edges of woodland or pasture may forage as far as half a mile (800 m) across the open ground; they may also den in pastures, feed in hay barns, and drink from water troughs. Since infected possums have skin lesions that contain masses of TB bacteria, there is a high chance of contamination. Expensive poisoning efforts have recently been targeted at the twenty-three sites in New Zealand's North and South Islands where local possums are known to harbor the disease, but so far the infection has not been stamped out.

Jean-Paul Ferrero/Ardea

HUMAN HUNTERS

Hunting by people presents a threat to possums, especially to the larger species in New Guinea, whose meat has long been a traditional source of food. Spreading human populations now mean that such pressures on species can become severe.

Hunting on a commercial scale has in the past been responsible for a far greater slaughter of possums in Australia. The mountain brush-tail used to be hunted widely for its pelt, as were the thickly furred Tasmanian forms of the common brush-tail and the common ring-tail. Large-scale hunting is now at an end, and the deliberate taking of possums no longer poses a major threat on the continent. ■

The limited habitat of the mountain pygmy possum is threatened by development and global warming.

INTO THE FUTURE

Many of the possums that are widespread in distribution are unlikely to be put in danger, although their total numbers are likely to decline further with habitat alteration. This applies equally to larger and more adaptable species, such as the common brush-tail and common ring-tail, as well as to smaller but elusive creatures like the eastern pygmy possum and the feathertail glider. But for those possums with a more restricted distribution or that are dependent on the maintenance of extensive tracts of mature forest, the outlook is far less secure.

The mountain pygmy possum still survives at quite healthy densities in its subalpine refuges, but these patches of suitable habitat are small and separated by large tracts of unsuitable habitat. Adverse changes to their surroundings could rapidly put these animals in jeopardy. Leadbeater's possum is one of several Australian forest possums whose survival depends on the future practices of the logging industry. Unless forest management takes the animal's needs for food and shelter into consideration, it cannot survive. Deforestation and logging are a dire threat for many island cuscuses, such as the Obi cuscus, and are even putting some New Guinea species such as the black-spotted cuscus under pressure.

In the face of such problems, conservation has made some gains. Possums are protected in some national parks and sanctuaries in Australia. There is hope, too, that careful felling patterns in state forests could preserve enough older trees in pockets, so that those species dependent on old growth, such as Leadbeater's possum, the greater glider, and the yellow-bellied glider, can still inhabit logged areas. Public pressure on logging companies just might persuade them to change their ways—for although the future of logging remains a volatile issue in Australia, there is a good deal of political support for conservation in general. ■

PREDICTION

PRESSURE ON ISLAND SPECIES

Deforestation and overhunting are likely to place an increasing number of island species under threat, and the combined threats of logging, habitat conversion, and introduced predators are unlikely to abate in the near future for some vulnerable mainland species, especially those restricted to pockets of suitable habitat.

Illustration Sean Milne

ROOM WITH A VIEW

One conservation strategy for possums that has yet to be tried out extensively is the provision of artificial nest boxes in areas where logging or fire has deprived local populations of vital shelter. A key species that could benefit is Leadbeater's possum, which may be better able to survive if nest boxes allow it to inhabit areas of forest where the trees are regenerating but are too young to develop the natural hollows required for shelter.

Studies have identified at least seven species that are prepared to use boxes: the common brush-tail, the mountain brush-tail, the common ring-tail, the greater glider, the sugar glider, the feathertail glider, and the eastern pygmy possum. Nest boxes might be tailored to meet the size and shape preferences of different species.

SCANT KNOWLEDGE

One of the fears of conservationists is that too little is presently known about the ecological needs and population status of many possum species outside Australia. The impact of rapidly spreading human settlement could put some of them in danger of dying out before anyone realizes they are even declining. Logging practices present a further threat, and the circumstances of many New Guinea species with limited distributions and that live in remote terrain are little known. They include the Weyland ring-tail and the Arfak ring-tail of western New Guinea. The same applies to some other island species, among them the small Sulawesi cuscus, the Waigeo spotted cuscus, and the Biak glider.

PRONGHORNS

RELATIONS

The pronghorn and chevrotains are members of the order Artiodactyla. Other members of the order include:

PIGS & PECCARIES

HIPPOPOTAMUSES

WILD CATTLE

DEER

CAMELS

GAZELLES

Jeff Foott/Survival Anglia

The pronghorn is a two-toed ungulate (hoofed mammal). It is classified in its family Antilocapridae. Chevrotains are four-toed ungulates, in their own family of Tragulidae.

ORDER
Artiodactyla
(even-toed ungulates)

FAMILY
Antilocapridae

SUBFAMILY
Antilocaprinae

GENUS AND SPECIES
Antilocapra americana

FAMILY
Tragulidae

GENUS AND SPECIES
Hyemoschus aquaticus
(water chevrotain)
Tragulus meminna
(Indian spotted chevrotain)
Tragulus javanicus
(lesser Malay chevrotain)
Tragulus napu
(greater Malay chevrotain)

SURVIVORS OF THE PAST

THE PRONGHORN (*ABOVE*) AND THE CHEVROTAIN ARE NO MORE CLOSELY RELATED TO EACH OTHER THAN THEY ARE TO PIGS OR CAMELS: ONE OF THEIR FEW COMMON FEATURES IS A HIGHLY PRIMITIVE ANCESTRY

As the morning mist rises over the plains of western North America, a deerlike animal with strange, curved horns stands alert, ready to flee at the first sign of danger. This graceful creature is a pronghorn, often referred to as the American antelope, and the swiftest-running animal in America.

Far away in equatorial Africa a creature the size of a lapdog is foraging among the undergrowth of a rain forest. It is a chevrotain, or mouse deer, and its deerlike appearance is about all it has in common with its distant cousin the pronghorn. Both animals, however, are relics of the past. The pronghorn is the sole survivor of the family Antilocapridae, which arose in North America and which, about 1.5 million years ago, included at least thirteen genera.

Chevrotains are the world's most primitive artiodactyls (even-toed mammals), and have changed little since the Oligocene and Miocene epochs. In those times they were found all over the world, but

A pronghorn cleans the afterbirth from her newborn calf.

Stan Osolinski/Oxford Scientific Films

today they are restricted to the rain forests of western Africa and Southeast Asia. They form the family Tragulidae, just four species in two genera.

The pronghorn is not considered to be a true antelope. This is because, unlike deer, which shed their bony antlers, or most bovids, which keep their horns, the pronghorn sheds the horny sheaths of its horns each year. There are, however, a few bovids that also do this, and during the 1970s a decision was made to classify the pronghorn in the family Bovidae, but in a separate subfamily, Antilocaprinae. This is still debated today; many zoologists maintain that the pronghorn's horn structure evolved separately from bovids and that this, together with the lack of antelopes in the Americas, places the animal in its own family Antilocapridae.

PRONGED HORNS

Pronghorns seem to have existed only in North America. The fossil record begins in the middle Miocene epoch with *Merycodus*, which had more elaborately branched horns than the modern pronghorn. Horns are carried by all male pronghorns and most females. A large, bony knob forms the permanent core of the horn; this is surrounded, as in all antelopes, by a horny sheath, which in the pronghorn's case is shed after the breeding season. The sheath is formed by a specialized growth of skin. At the tip this is initially soft and fleshy, but it

P. Morris/Ardea

Chevrotains are truly tiny inhabitants of Asian rain forests (above).

rapidly hardens into true horn. The rest of the skin bears bristly hairs and this gradually changes from the top downward into horn. The pronghorn's horns stand upright from the head and curve back at the tips. In the male, each horn has a short, forward-pointing branch, or prong, in the sheath—hence the common name. The male's horns are about 10 in (25 cm) long, while the female's are much smaller and usually have little or no prong.

A male pronghorn may stand more than 3.3 ft (1 m) at the shoulder; the female is smaller. The upper parts of the coat are reddish brown to tan, with a black mane. The underbelly is white, and the rump bears a white patch. The buck has a black face and a patch of black hair on the side of the neck; these features are less obvious or missing in the doe. The feet have two toes and, unlike all other artiodactyls, there is no trace of other toes; in other words, there are no dewclaws.

Cat-sized mouse deer

Chevrotains, as their other name of mouse deer implies, are tiny. The largest is the water chevrotain of western Africa, which is roughly the size of a small terrier. The three Asian species are even

Stan Osolinski/Oxford Scientific Films

The pronghorn is named after the sharp projections near the tips of its horns (above).

THE PRONGHORN'S FAMILY TREE

Both the pronghorn and the chevrotains belong to the order Artiodactyla, or even-toed ungulates. Forming one of the most diverse of all mammal orders, the 187 artiodactyl species include pigs and peccaries, camels, giraffes, wild cattle, and antelopes. Many of these are ruminants, animals that possess a specialized digestive system.

more diminutive: The lesser Malay chevrotain (or lesser mouse deer) is no bigger than a domestic cat. Chevrotains have a fairly robust body, but their legs are only the thickness of a pencil.

The coats of the four chevrotain species vary a little. The water chevrotain is a blackish red-brown, with rows of pale spots. The flanks are striped, and the throat and chest sport a herringbone pattern. The Indian spotted chevrotain (or spotted mouse deer) has similar markings but is paler. The coat of the lesser Malay chevrotain is more or less uniformly red, but the characteristic throat markings are present. The greater Malay chevrotain, too, is generally red all over.

Pig parallels

Chevrotains have no horns or antlers, but they do have upper canine teeth that grow continuously, like those of pigs, and the premolars have sharp, rather than flattened, crowns. Their sexual behavior is also somewhat like that of pigs, in that it is relatively simple and copulation usually takes longer than in other ruminants. Their genitalia, too, are not unlike those of a pig. Chevrotains do not indulge in visual displays, so their means of communication is limited to sounds and scents.

That said, they also lack the specialized scent glands below the eyes or between the toes that are found in most ruminants. Like pigs, they also lie down rump-first and their feet have four toes, rather than just the two normally found in ruminants, although the central two are more fully developed than the others. Of them all, the water chevrotain is the most piglike. All these characteristics indicate that chevrotains are, in evolutionary terms, somewhere between the pigs (Suidae) and the ruminants with horns and antlers (Pecora). ■

CHEVROTAIN

Tragulus, Hyemoschus

(TRAG-yoo-luss, hie-eh-MOSS-kus)

Chevrotains, or mouse deer, are primitive, even-toed ungulates of the African and Asian rain forests. They lack horns but possess distinctive upper canines. There are three species in the genus* Tragulus*, plus a single species in the genus* Hyemoschus*.

DEER

GIRAFFE

PIG

PECCARY

HIPPOPOTAMUS

ARTIODACTYLA

B/W illustrations Ruth Grewcock

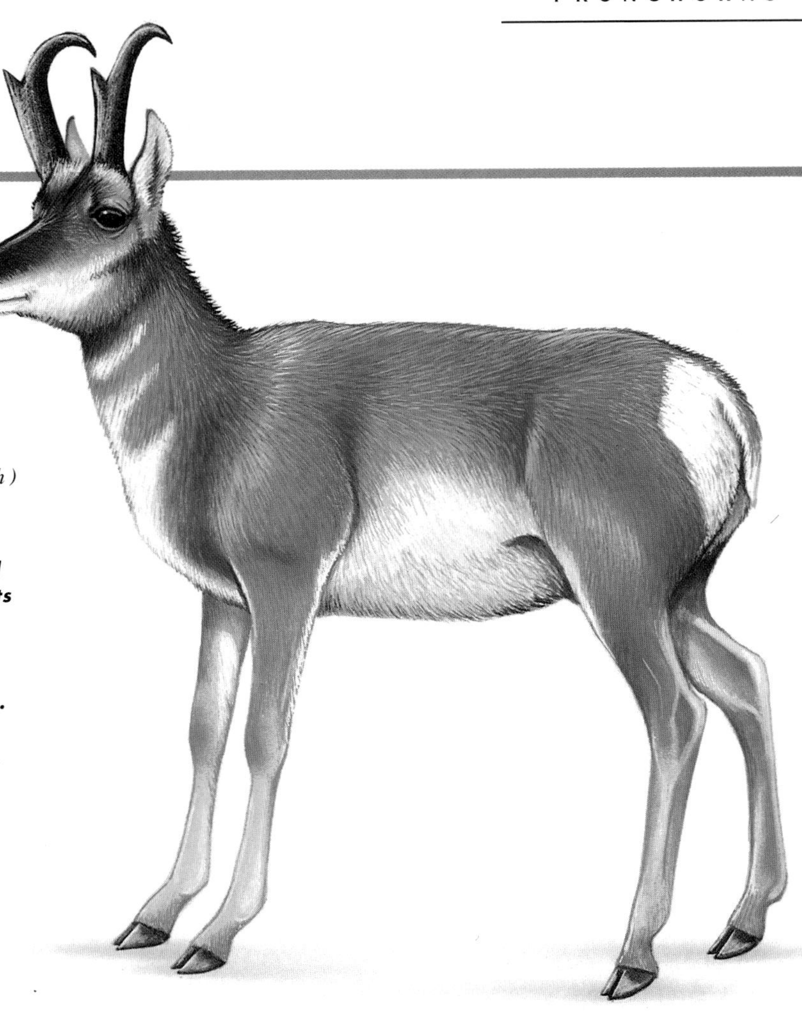

PRONGHORN

Antilocapra americana

(ann-til-o-CAP-rah ah-mer-ee-CAH-nah)

Pronghorns live in western North America, from Canada south to Mexico. They are herbivores and may be found in a range of different environments from open prairie to desert, where they can survive for long periods without drinking. They are constantly on the move during both day and night, but they are most active at dawn and dusk. They once numbered in the millions, roaming the plains and prairies alongside the American bison.

Color illustrations Kim Thompson

ANCESTORS

The most primitive living ruminants, chevrotains may represent a link with the nonruminants. Similar animals lived 50 million years ago, but by the early Miocene epoch tragulids had diverged from most ruminant animals. *Dorcatherium* (*dor-cah-THEER-ee-um*), found in Eurasia and Africa, was very like modern Asian chevrotains, but could not have been the ancestor of later horned and antlered animals. A late Miocene ancestor of the pronghorn was *Ilingoceros* (ih-ling-o-KARE-oss), shown below.

BOVIDS

WILD CATTLE

CAMEL

ANATOMY: THE PRONGHORN

THE RUMP

bears a patch of pure-white hairs. When disturbed, the pronghorn raises these hairs to flash an alarm signal and also releases a scent from rump glands.

Male pronghorns measure 3.3–5 ft (1–1.5 m) from head to rump, with a tail of 3–4 in (7.5–10 cm). The shoulder height is 31.5–41 in (80–104 cm). Females are smaller.

The water chevrotain is the largest of its family. It has a head-and-body length of 23.6–33.5 in (60–85 cm), with a shoulder height of 12–16 in (30–40 cm). The lesser Malay chevrotain has a head-and-body length of only 17.3–19 in (44–48 cm), and stands just 8 in (20 cm) high at the shoulder.

THE LIMBS

are slender, but they give the pronghorn astonishing agility: It can cover 27 ft (8 m) of ground in a single leap.

THE HOOVES

are long and pointed. Springy pads of gristle act as shock absorbers when the animal is leaping and running at full tilt.

THE COAT

comprises an outer layer of long, protective guard hairs over an undercoat of dense, woolly fur that retains warmth. The pronghorn flexes special muscles to erect or relax the guard hairs in order to regulate its body temperature.

Anatomy illustrations Wayne Ford/Wildlife Art Agency

X-RAY

The pronghorn's bone structure is fine and lightweight, offering a profile not unlike the true antelopes. The limbs, however, are highly resilient, easily capable of sustaining the shocks induced by the animal's rapid pace. The forefeet take the brunt of the pressure when the pronghorn runs fast.

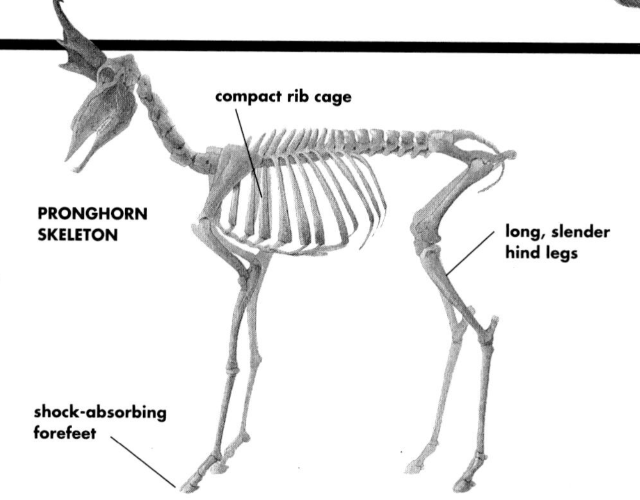

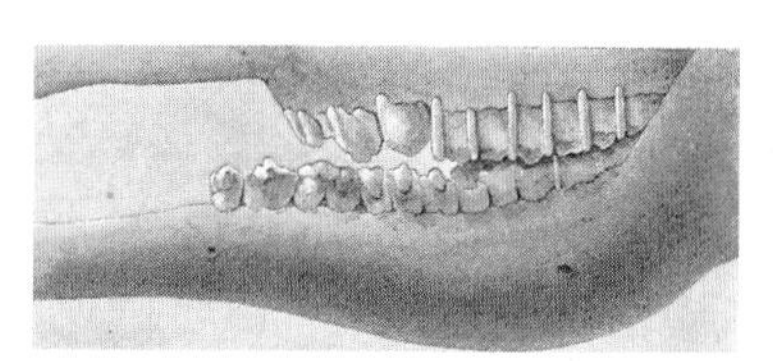

TEETH

The pronghorn has a row of sharp incisors and canines in the lower jaw; these bite onto a hard pad in the upper jaw. Behind these teeth is a space, behind which lie the flat, high-crowned premolars and molars for grinding up vegetation.

X-ray illustrations Elisabeth Smith

FACT FILE:

THE PRONGHORN

CLASSIFICATION

GENUS: *ANTILOCAPRA*

SPECIES: *AMERICANA*

SIZE

HEAD-BODY LENGTH: 3.3–5 FT (1–1.5 M)

TAIL LENGTH: 3–4 IN (7.5–10 CM)

SHOULDER HEIGHT: 31.5–41 IN (80–104 CM)

COLORATION

LIGHT BROWN TO TAN

THE UNDERSIDE HAS A RECTANGULAR WHITE PATCH BETWEEN THE SHOULDERS AND THE HIND LEGS

THERE ARE TWO WHITE PATCHES ON THE FRONT OF THE NECK AND WHITE PATCHES ON THE RUMP

THE MALE HAS A BLACK MANE

FEATURES

SLENDER LEGS, LONG BACK, AND SHORT TAIL

MUZZLE IS HAIRLESS ONLY AROUND THE NOSTRILS

A PAIR OF FORKED HORNS THAT GROW ON LARGE, BONY KNOBS. THE LATTER ARE PERMANENT BUT THE HORNS ARE SHED EACH YEAR

THE EYES

are protected from the sun by long, black lashes. Surprisingly large and prominent, they are set well back in the skull to give 360° vision. The pronghorn can reputedly detect objects up to 4 miles (6.5 km) away.

THE NOSE

is sensitive, particularly to the sexual, territorial, and alarm scents given off by other pronghorns.

THE FOREFEET

are used by the pronghorn to dig latrine holes in the soil, and to scrape away snow to expose food.

HORN

The pronghorn sheds only the sheath of its horns each year. The sheath is formed from skin covered in bristlelike hairs, which gradually turns into true horn. Central to the horn is a laterally flattened, bony core: This is not shed.

sheath

horn core

The chevrotain has a similar dentition to that of the pronghorn, except that it possesses a pair of canines in the upper jaw. In the male these are elongated into the form of saberlike tusks, while in the female they are mere studs.

Clearly visible on the pronghorn's skull (far right) is the placement of the eye orbits far back in the cranium.

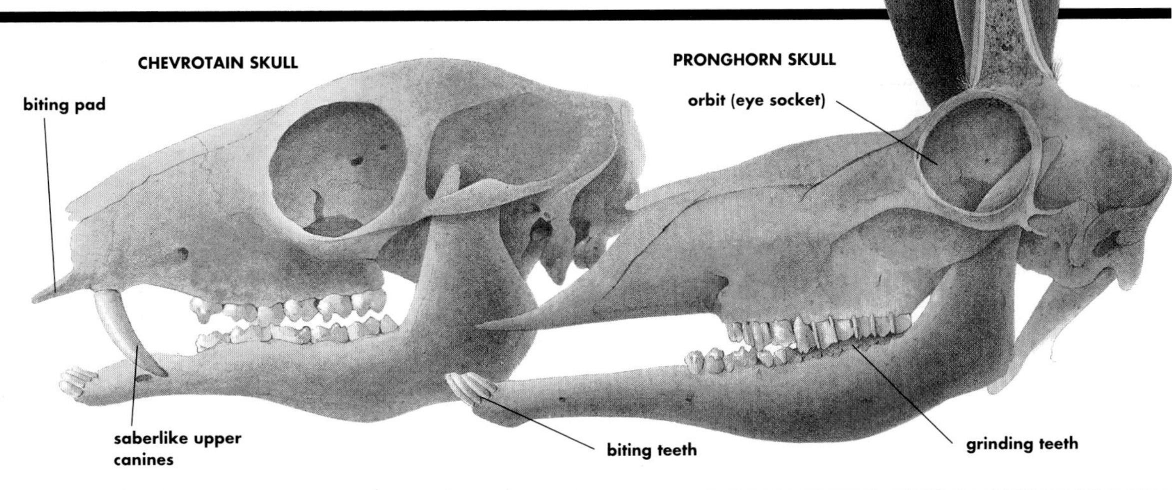

GROUP ASSETS

THE PRONGHORN HAS A LOT TO GAIN BY LIVING IN A GROUP: WITH A FEW ANIMALS WATCHING OUT FOR PREDATORS, ALL MAY GRAZE IN RELATIVE SAFETY

Pronghorns live in small groups in summer, but for a few solitary, older bucks. In winter, these groups join up to form much larger herds. This socializing is mainly for reasons of self-preservation. Today the pronghorn's main natural enemy is the coyote, but throughout its history it has been preyed on by swift predators: this may be why it is now America's fastest mammal. Speeds of over 43 mph (70 km/h) have been recorded; pronghorns cruise at about 30 mph (48 km/h) and can keep this up for some 3.7 miles (6 km) before tiring.

The pronghorn's coat has two layers: A woolly undercoat retains warmth, while long, coarse guard hairs keep out the elements. The pronghorn can control its body temperature by altering the position of the guard hairs. In cold weather the hairs lie flat and cold air cannot reach the underlayer. In hot conditions, special skin muscles are used to raise the guard hairs and allow air to cool the skin. For this reason, the animal can exploit both temperate and desert climates.

A pronghorn raises its rump hairs to deliver a clear warning to others in the herd (right).

Fawns remain close to their mother even in full flight (below). *She guards them with utter determination.*

Judd Cooney/Oxford Scientific Films

Jeff Foott/Bruce Coleman Ltd.

An Indian spotted mouse deer calf hides in forest undergrowth in Sri Lanka (below).

Joanna van Gruisen/Ardea

The pronghorn uses the same technique to give a warning signal. When it stands sideways, it blends into the landscape, but when danger threatens, it rapidly raises and lowers the long hairs on the white rump patch, so that the patch "flashes." At the same time, a pungent scent is released from glands in the rump. The rump flashes can be seen from up to 2–3 miles (4 km) away, long after the rest of the animal has become invisible.

Secretive chevrotains

Water chevrotains live deep in the forests of Africa and are rarely seen. They are solitary animals, hiding during the day in caves. If surprised, they tend to slip into water and dive to escape pursuit.

It is claimed that water chevrotains sometimes climb trees to flee enemies or simply to sun themselves

The Asiatic chevrotains, too, are shy and rarely seen, although they are fairly numerous. They, too, are solitary, except when breeding. Females are more active than males and follow tiny, tunnel-like trails through the jungle. If startled, a chevrotain will usually "play dead." But if approached closely, it leaps up and dashes away.

A chevrotain treats any unfamiliar object with great caution, inspecting it slowly with the head stretched forward and one forefoot raised. In the end, fear usually overcomes curiosity and the animal takes off in a series of long, arching jumps. If caught, chevrotains have been known to bite as they attempt to escape. ■

HABITATS

Pronghorns and chevrotains have contrasting lifestyles. Pronghorns prefer open spaces, where potential predators can be seen from some distance away and where they can rely on their speed to escape. Chevrotains, on the other hand, like to live in dense jungle, where they can hide from their enemies.

Hot and Cold Climates

Pronghorns are most at home in the tall- and short-grass prairies of central and western North America. When the first settlers arrived in the west in the early 1800s, they found huge herds of pronghorn, and bison on the plains between the Missouri River and the Rocky Mountains. Both species were slaughtered in large numbers, sometimes for their meat and hides, but often just for sport. During the next 100 years the bison were all but wiped out and the pronghorn population was reduced from an estimated 35 million to some 19,000 animals.

Since then, the pronghorn population has recovered somewhat, due to strict conservation measures

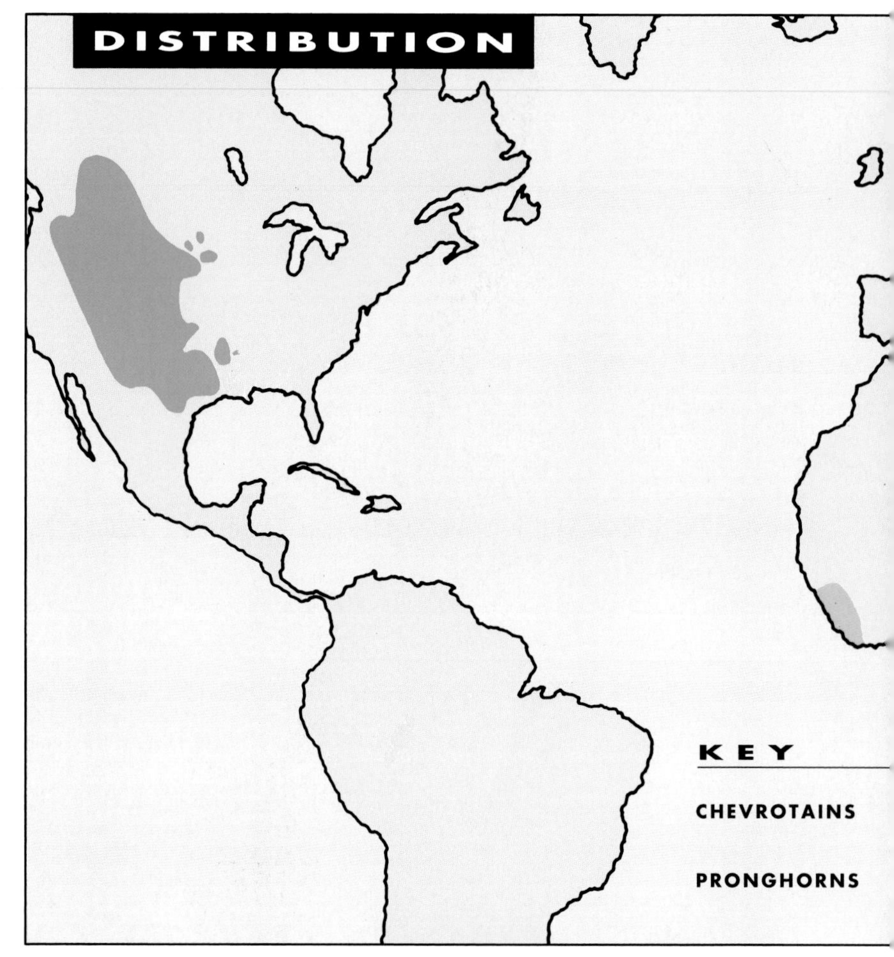

Pronghorns rake the snow to expose grasses in a Montana winter.

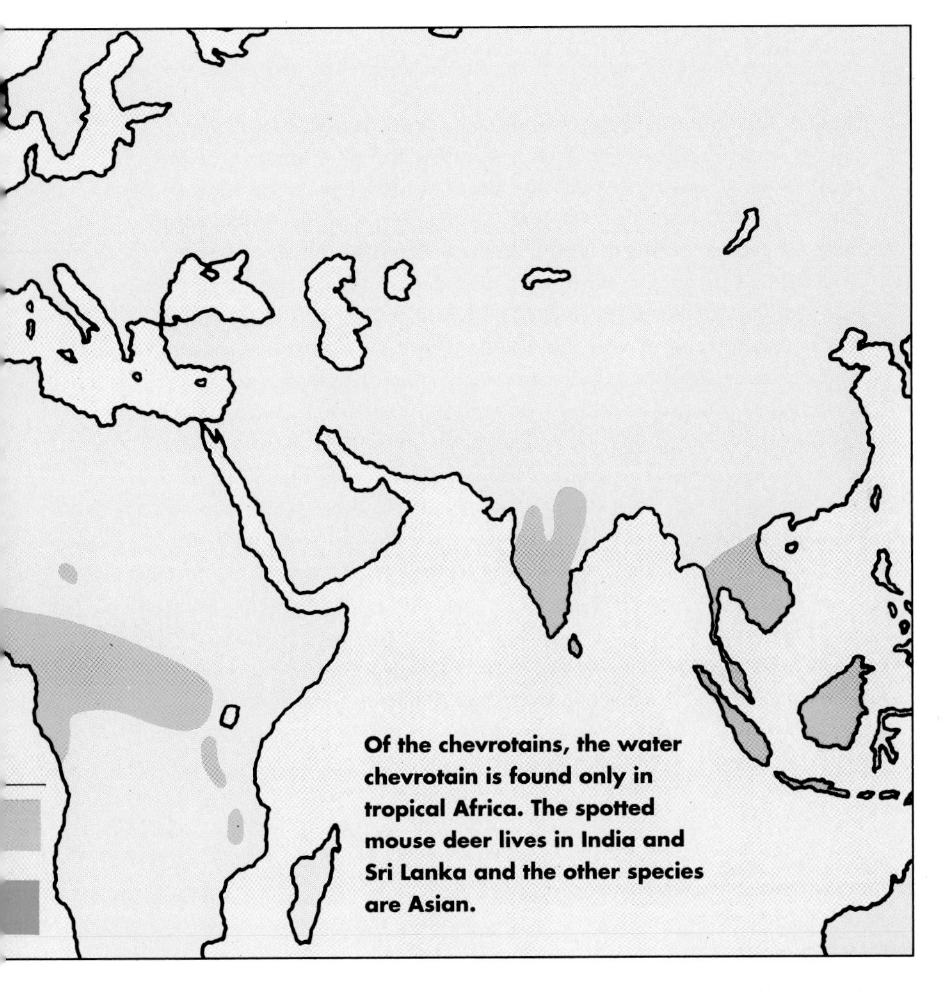
Of the chevrotains, the water chevrotain is found only in tropical Africa. The spotted mouse deer lives in India and Sri Lanka and the other species are Asian.

being enforced. But much of their former range is now farmland, and so today's pronghorns are largely confined to the short-grass prairies of western North America. Fortunately, this highly adaptable species can tolerate a wide range of different conditions. It is found as far north as Canada, where it survives the icy winters by growing a dense undercoat that is then molted in the spring. The pronghorn can also be found as much as 11,000 ft (3,350 m) above sea level. By contrast there are pronghorns in the hot, rocky deserts of western America, as far south as northern Mexico.

Another major influence on the pronghorn's evolution has been the fact that prairies, especially tall-grass areas, are often swept by fire. Such fires are destructive, but by temporarily razing the grass they make way for a range of high-protein herbs and grasses. These plants make up a large part of the pronghorn's diet and, whenever possible, pronghorns prefer to graze on burned prairies.

Home on the Range

Pronghorns are active day and night, but there is a slight increase in activity just after sunrise and just before sunset. In summer, female pronghorns form groups of about twenty animals and range over a fairly small area, perhaps about 2 sq mi (5 sq km); the group may travel up to 0.8 mi (1.3 km) in a day. In winter, however, when there is less food available and the groups are larger, this may increase to about 6 mi (10 km). The range of a group may shift several times during the year as it seeks new sources of food, and the distance between the summer and winter ranges may be as much as 100 mi (160 km).

Other Creatures

With the bison now greatly depleted, pronghorns are the only large herbivores on the prairies today. However, they share their habitat with many other animals. Now that the wolf has largely been eliminated from these regions, their main enemy is the coyote. Neither of these predators has any hope of catching a fleeing adult pronghorn, but the young are vulnerable. Mothers are fiercely protective of their calves, and have been seen using their front hooves to drive off coyotes, foxes, eagles, and even humans. Other more peaceable neighbors include the prairie dog, the jackrabbit, the prairie fowl, and the American badger.

River Deer of the Jungle

The habitats preferred by chevrotains, or mouse deer, could hardly be more different. The water chevrotain is found only in the dense rain forests of

KEY FACTS

- **The pronghorn's sight is excellent; it can see a moving object several miles away. However, its visual acuity is poor, and a human standing motionless only 330 ft (100 m) away may remain unobserved.**

- **Pronghorns are reported to have been observed racing alongside vehicles, apparently for the fun of it.**

- **The pronghorn has a habit of setting its lower jaw out of line as it stands resting or chewing the cud, so that the mouth sags noticeably on one side. One observer likened it to a man with a chew of tobacco in his mouth.**

- **Compared to sheep, the pronghorn has a huge heart in relation to its weight; it also has a surprisingly wide windpipe. When in full flight, the animal opens its mouth to take in air, since its oxygen demands are so great.**

- **The pronghorn has specialized joints in its lower legs with highly developed tendons, enabling it to place immense pressure on its limbs without suffering damage.**

western Africa. It has earned its name from its habit of diving into water when disturbed, and it is seldom found more than 820 ft (250 m) from a river or standing body of water. Curiously, however, it only enters the water when threatened.

At ground level the water chevrotain's domain is relatively open, as no grasses and very few herbs or shrubs grow on the forest floor. This makes the water chevrotain more vulnerable to predators, and so, perhaps, this is the reason why it has developed the defensive technique of hiding in water, and why it may, if indeed it does, climb trees.

The water chevrotain is not the only hoofed mammal of the jungle. Others include the reclusive okapi (a relative of the giraffe), the bongo, buffalo, and bushbuck, a number of duikers, and the tiny royal antelope, which is only a little larger than the chevrotain. Predators in the rain forests include the leopard, golden cat, forest genet, and various civets (catlike species related to mongooses).

The three Asian species of chevrotain live in more dense surroundings and, although they are more frequently seen than the water chevrotain, very little is known about how they make use of their habitat. They are found in primary and secondary rain forests and in the dense bush zones more characteristic of cultivated areas. It seems likely that the impenetrable vegetation gives them plenty of cover for their activities, and presumably stealth and secrecy are their main defense. Such tiny creatures must otherwise be extremely vulnerable to the forest predators, which include a number of forest cats, snakes, crocodiles, and birds of prey, not to mention humans.

Mouse deer share their environment with an enormous variety of other creatures: The Malay peninsula alone is said to contain five times the number of animal species found in Great Britain. ■

FOCUS ON

INDIAN COUNTRY

Native American tribes were once spread across the entire North American landmass, but it is the North American Plains Indians who were perhaps the most significant in the history of the early United States settlers. Occupying a huge north-south strip of prairie, the various tribes survived by hunting bison and other big game. With bow and arrow, knife, and trap, they hunted the native wildlife for food, but never exhausted their natural resources. From the 1840s a steady stream of miners and ranchers arrived. They overexploited the land and eventually evicted or killed the majority of the Indians.

In earlier, happier times, the North American prairie formed a seemingly endless sea of waving grass, from the edge of the deciduous forests of Pennsylvania and Ohio, westward to the Rocky Mountains, and southward from the Mackenzie River in Canada to the Gulf of Mexico. The eastern region was dominated by tall grasses, which once grew high enough to hide a man on horseback. Farther west, short grasses prevailed.

All these grasslands were home to the pronghorn, which were probably among the first inhabitants of the prairies, arriving long before even the American Indians and before most of the other animals now present.

TEMPERATURE AND RAINFALL

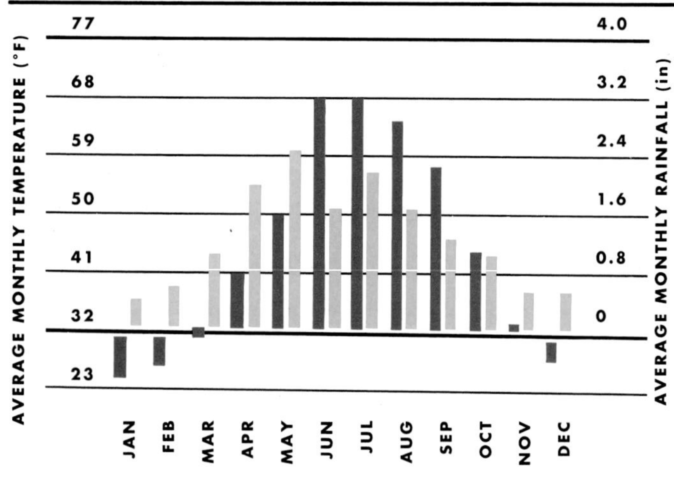

The eastern plains receive about 40 in (100 cm) of rain annually. In the west the land rises to about 3,000 ft (920 m) at the Rockies, where the rainfall is much lower. The figures given here are for Cheyenne in Wyoming.

NEIGHBORS

Since large mammals are now scarce on the prairies, some of the more familiar native species are numerous rodents and reptiles, as well as birds and insects.

RATTLESNAKE

The prairie rattlesnake preys on rodents, and even seeks winter refuge in the burrows of prairie dogs.

JACKRABBIT

Jackrabbits are highly alert grazers and browsers, and can run almost as fast as the pronghorn.

All illustrations Evi Antoniou

David Hosking/FPLA

INDIAN COUNTRY

CANADA
ROCKY MTS
USA

The grasslands once occupied by the North American Plains Indians ranged from Saskatchewan and Alberta in the north, right through to New Mexico, Texas, Oklahoma, and Arkansas in the south. From Montana in the west they stretched east to the Mississippi River.

ENEMIES

EXTREMELY DANGEROUS

GRAY WOLF

The wolf is now rare on the prairies, and presents an occasional—but very real—threat to young pronghorns.

EXTREMELY DANGEROUS

COYOTE

One of North America's most adaptable mammals, the coyote is the supreme opportunist hunter.

BLACK-FOOTED FERRET

Perhaps the rarest mammal in the United States, this ferret preys on prairie dogs, pursuing them into their burrows.

RED-TAILED HAWK

This hawk ranges over most of North America. In the prairies, it preys mainly on mice and other rodents.

PRAIRIE DOG

One of the most sociable of all rodents, this squirrel forms "towns" in extensive burrow systems.

DUNG BEETLE

Dung beetles break up the excrement of other animals and feed it to their own larvae underground.

AMERICAN BADGER

A relative of the European badger, this expert digger eats almost anything, from rodents and insects to roots.

TERRITORY

In the spring the social hierarchy changes from the loose, unstructured arrangement of the winter. Some of the pronghorn bucks, usually those over three years old, become territorial and start to compete with one another for females. Each of these territorial bucks tries to defend a particular area of land and the older ones often return to the same territory each year, occupying it as soon as the large herds break up at the end of the winter.

MATURE PRONGHORNS SNORT TO CONVEY ANGER OR ANXIETY, AND MALES ROAR DURING THE MATING SEASON

Illustrations Guy Troughton/Wildlife Art Agency

The bucks try to form their territories where females are most likely to come to browse, but in very dry conditions this is less easy to accomplish. So, in desert areas, instead of defending fixed territories, territorial bucks tend to join up with and defend itinerant herds of females.

A territory may measure anything from 50 acres (20 ha) to over 990 acres (400 ha). It usually includes a permanent source of water and the borders are often marked by prominent physical features, such as rocky outcrops or trees. The pronghorn marks the borders with urine, feces, and scent produced by the cheek glands.

When a territorial pronghorn buck confronts a rival, the encounter begins with a staring match: The message is clear and highly aggressive. One of the males may submit at this point by simply avoiding eye contact; if both males hold their ground, they start to roar, each trying to produce terrifying sounds. If this does not achieve a result, one male will approach the other and a chase, or sometimes even a fight, may ensue. The sharp horns of a pronghorn can cause serious injury, so fighting is usually a last resort.

Territories are not always clearly delineated and defended. On occasions a large buck that has defeated neighboring males may later allow some or all of them onto his territory. As a result, some bucks roam several territories, others have access to just a few, while others patrol just one area and can only drive very old or very young bucks out of it.

FIGHTS

between feuding males usually occur only as a last resort; pronghorns seem reluctant to inflict injury with their sharp horns (above).

Rod Planck/NHPA

in SIGHT

SCENT MARKING

Pronghorns rely a great deal on scent to convey information. They have scent glands on the cheeks, at the base of the tail, on their hindquarters, between their toes, and on each leg. Gland-produced scent is used as a warning signal together with tail fur flashes. Males daub scent from their cheek glands to mark territories, and reinforce these boundaries with urine and feces.

Both male and female chevrotains also use scent to mark out territories or to indicate their presence. The male Malayan mouse deer will smear a female with scent to signify that he has claimed her.

***TERRITORIAL** disputes between pronghorn males are usually settled with nothing more aggressive than a staring match* (above). *The loser averts his gaze in submission.*

During the summer each buck tries to keep "harems" of females, which number up to about twenty-three in each group, within his territory. Despite his endeavors, however, the groups of females wander freely from one territory to another; only rarely does a group remain in just one territory. Outside the territories, the females are pursued by herds of bachelor bucks, but they try to avoid them.

TERRITORIAL CHEVROTAINS

Of the chevrotains, the most extensively studied is the water chevrotain of Africa. Like all the chevrotains it is solitary, so its social behavior is unlike that of the pronghorn. When two water chevrotains meet, for example, the event is sufficiently unusual that they must call to each other before approaching, and the individual that makes the first call must await an answer.

Female water chevrotains establish themselves in a home territory and remain there all their lives. Males never remain longer than a year in the same place. A water chevrotain leaves its "calling card" by rubbing scent from glands on its lower jaw onto leaves, tree roots, or the ends of branches.

Studies in captivity show that Asian chevrotains also do this. Males seem to maintain territories or at least aggressively protect the females around them. A captive lesser Malay mouse deer uses scent from its cheek glands to mark places in its enclosure; it anoints the sites several times each hour, marking even more frequently when moved into an unfamiliar enclosure. It also smears the same scent over the backs of females.

THE LESSER MALAY MOUSE DEER IS THE ONLY RUMINANT TO SIT ON ITS RUMP AND DEPOSIT SCENT FROM ANAL GLANDS

Mouse deer also drum on the ground with their feet when agitated. When male strangers meet, they usually fight, although when males are forced to live with one another in the same enclosure, they rarely antagonize one another. When fighting, water chevrotains thrust with their muzzles and bite with the intention of inflicting wounds with the long canines of the upper jaw, as well as the incisors and canines of the lower jaw. ■

Slim Sreedharan/Biophotos

The lesser mouse deer may seem tiny and fragile, but can be bullish in defending a territory or mate.

FOOD AND FEEDING

Like most grazers, pronghorns must spend a large part of their lives eating in order to obtain sufficient nutrition from their relatively low-protein food. The plant material they eat is coarse and tough, and is often dusty. This acts like sand-paper on the teeth, wearing them away constantly. To compensate for this, the grinding teeth of prong-horns have open roots and grow continuously. In the pronghorn, sharp teeth in the lower jaw bite onto a hard pad in the upper jaw. Toward the back of the jaw lie the flat premolar and molar teeth that grind up the plant material.

Pronghorns feed on a wide range of herbs, shrubs, grasses, and, in desert areas, they even find ways of tackling prickly cacti. The species of plants eaten depend on the locality and the time of year; pronghorns are adaptable animals and will basically eat what is available. They commonly eat sage-brush, a type of wormwood, and seem to have a preference for the tough, wiry grasses of the plains; they do not thrive if fed the type of lush, green grass preferred by cattle.

The set of the pronghorn's eyes far back in its skull are a great advantage when grazing. Its wide-angle vision helps it to spot predators stalk-ing up from behind, and the extra distance of the eyes from the jaws helps to keep it clear of the prickly vegetation on which it feeds.

HARD TIMES

In winter on the prairies, food is often in short sup-ply, but pronghorns adapt as usual, foraging more widely and eating more shrubby leaves than at other times of the year. When snow lies on the ground they use their forefeet to dig down to the grasses and herbs underneath. They also do this to dig scrapes in the ground for their droppings.

A pronghorn drinks freely when water is avail-able, but in times of drought it can survive on the moisture in its food. In desert areas, cacti and other succulent plants are a valuable source of moisture. Normally the pronghorn travels only a few miles each day in search of food and water, but if these are scarce it will range far and wide.

CHEWING THE CUD

Despite their many primitive characteristics, chevrotains, like pronghorns, deer, antelope, and cattle, are ruminants (see page 1761). As in all ruminants their four-chambered stomachs contain bacteria that help break down the cellulose in their plant food. At intervals, while they are digesting

Tom McHugh/Oxford Scientific Films

The tusks of a mouse deer are used for fighting, rather than gathering food (above).

PRONGHORNS *graze in groups or, as below, in family units.*

Main illustrations Barry Croucher/Wildlife Art Agency

Illustrations Ruth Grewcock

A WATER CHEVROTAIN
feeds on fruit in the hazy light of an African-rain forest dawn (above).

their food, they regurgitate lumps of partly digested material so that it can be chewed a second time.

Like other ruminants, chevrotains possess lower canines that resemble incisors and form the two outer members of the row of cutting teeth used for biting off pieces of food. The tusklike upper canines are not used in feeding. All the premolars are used for cutting rather than grinding, and the molars bear crescent-shaped ridges on their crowns.

The water chevrotain eats a variety of foods. Fallen fruit forms a large part of the diet, but it also feeds on grass, water weeds, and lily roots. Captive animals readily feed on fish, small crustaceans, and insects, so it seems likely that these forms of food may also form part of their diet in the wild. Asiatic chevrotains have a similarly varied diet in which grass plays a large part, together with the leaves and buds of low bushes and seedlings, and fallen fruit. Again, the lesser Malay chevrotain is known to eat insects when in captivity, and so invertebrates probably feature in the diets of all three Asiatic species. ■

in SIGHT

PRIMITIVE RUMINANTS

The chevrotain is a somewhat primitive ruminant, as the third of the four chambers in its stomach is poorly developed; these four species are considered to be at least illustrative of the change from the nonruminant nature of the pig to the fully developed ruminant digestive system of deer, antelope, and cattle.

However, this underdevelopment is not much of a hindrance to chevrotains, as they live in an environment where food is plentiful and where they need not survive on plant leaves alone. The rain forests contain an abundance of highly nutritious fruits and nuts, many of which fall to the ground where chevrotains can easily find them. Because the rain forests lack the extreme seasonal variations of other areas, this means that such food is available more or less all year-round.

LIFE CYCLE

At the start of the rut (mating season) in September, the territorial bucks move off, each with a chosen female. Young bachelor bucks pursue females but are usually rejected. The older, territorial bucks lead their mates into secluded sites such as ravines. Here they mate, hidden from all rivals. The most dominant bucks have the most mating hideouts. Courtship is ceremonious; the buck circles the doe with exaggerated steps and shows her the black patches on his cheeks. Only after this do they mate.

A FEMALE WITH TWIN CALVES HIDES THEM IN SEPARATE SITES, TO REDUCE THE RISK OF A PREDATOR FINDING THEM BOTH

After the rut the bucks shed their horns. They are, at this stage, so exhausted that they would be easy prey for predators, but without their horns they are virtually indistinguishable from females, whose tiny, but lethal, horns are worth avoiding.

Calves are born in May after a gestation period of 230–240 days. A doe usually has one calf in her first season and thereafter twins or, rarely, triplets. At birth a pronghorn calf weighs 4–6.6 lb (1.8–3 kg). It suckles its mother's rich milk, and at four days it can outrun a human. At three weeks it is already grazing, and its coat bears adult coloration. It is weaned at about four to five months. Does become sexually mature at fifteen to sixteen months, while bucks probably do not mate until over two years old. Both sexes seem to breed throughout life.

The water chevrotain mates at any time of year. The only form of courtship is a cry; this brings the

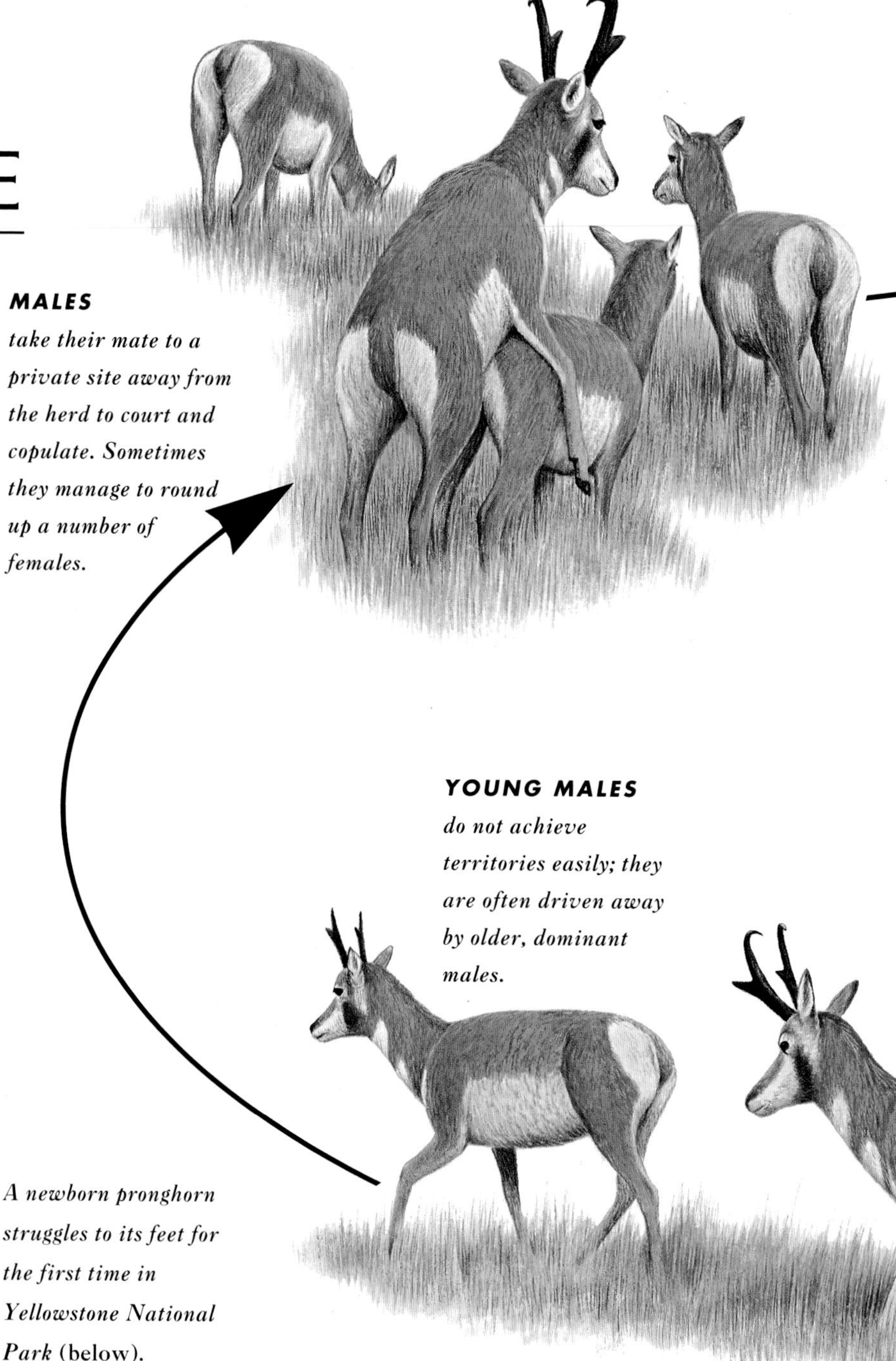

MALES
take their mate to a private site away from the herd to court and copulate. Sometimes they manage to round up a number of females.

YOUNG MALES
do not achieve territories easily; they are often driven away by older, dominant males.

A newborn pronghorn struggles to its feet for the first time in Yellowstone National Park (below).

Stan Osolinski/Oxford Scientific Films

AMAZING FACTS

EMBRYONIC COMPETITION

Unborn pronghorn calves fight to the death inside their mother's womb. Although usually only two fetuses reach full term, four to six are actually implanted in the wall of the uterus at the start of pregnancy. Research has shown that long projections grow out of the embryonic membranes: Some of these projections puncture the membranes of other embryos, killing them. In the end all but two, occasionally three, of the embryos are reabsorbed into the mother's body.

GROWING UP

The life of a young pronghorn

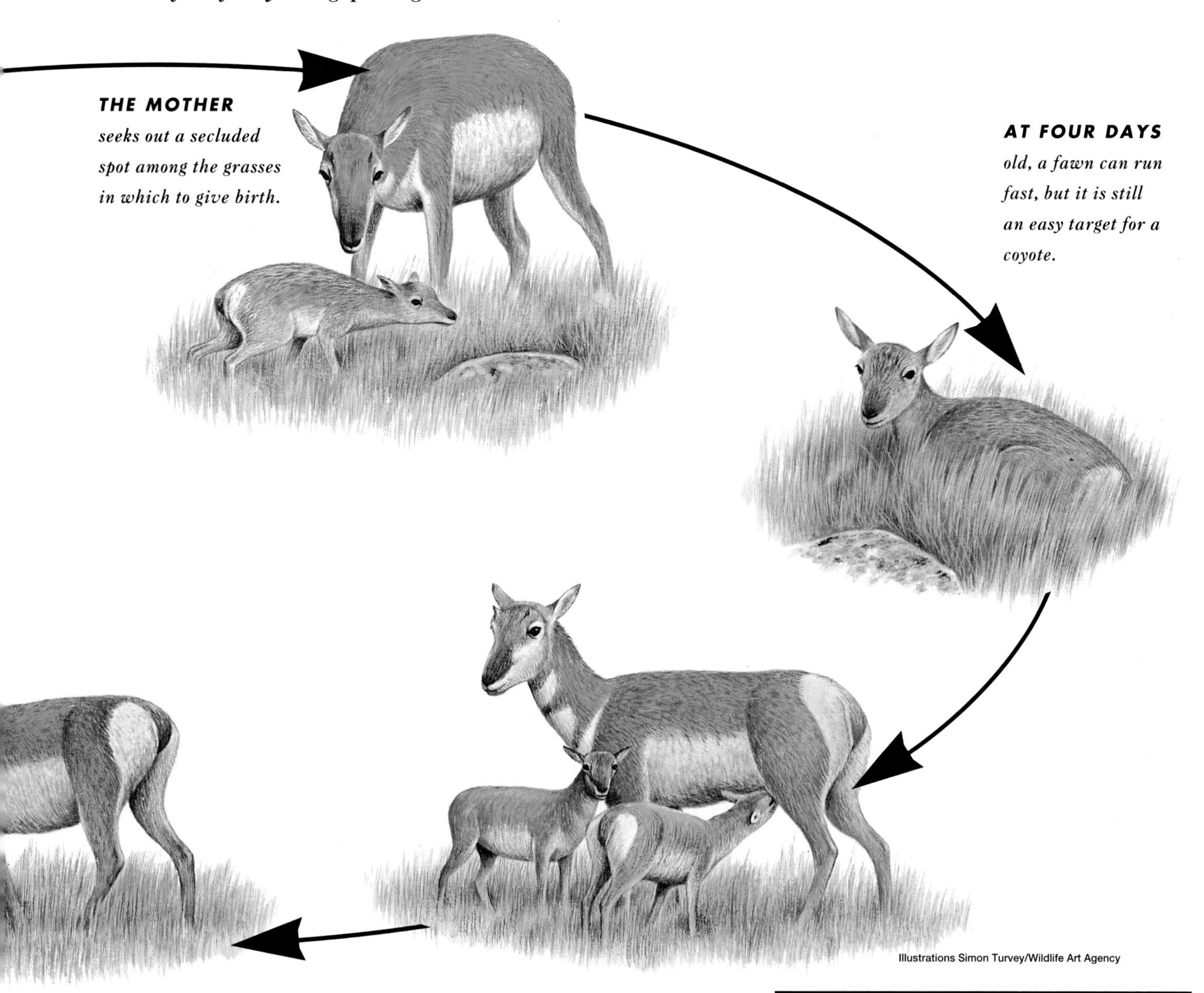

Illustrations Simon Turvey/Wildlife Art Agency

female to a halt, ready for copulation, which may last only a couple of minutes. Gestation takes six to nine months, and only one offspring is born. Most calves are born at the end of the rainy season, when there is plenty of lush vegetation available. Weaning takes place at about three months and the young reach sexual maturity at ten months.

The greater Malay chevrotain mates at any time of year, while the other two Asian species mate in June and July. Gestation in all three species lasts about five months. The lesser Malay chevrotain produces a single calf that is weaned at three months and reaches sexual maturity at four to five months. The greater Malay chevrotain and the Indian spotted chevrotain may produce two offspring, and the adults mate again just two days after the birth of their young. ■

FAWNS
spend twenty to twenty-five minutes each day with their mother. She nurses them for four to five months.

FROM BIRTH TO DEATH

PRONGHORN

GESTATION: 230–240 DAYS
LITTER SIZE: 1–3
WEIGHT AT BIRTH: 4–6.6 LB (1.8–3 KG)
EYES OPEN: AT BIRTH
FIRST WALKING: WITHIN HOURS OF BIRTH
WEANING: 4–5 MONTHS, SOMETIMES SHORTER FOR MALES
SEXUAL MATURITY: DOE AT 15–16 MONTHS, BUCK AT 2 YEARS
LONGEVITY IN WILD: USUALLY 7–10 YEARS

WATER CHEVROTAIN

GESTATION: 180–270 DAYS
LITTER SIZE: 1
WEIGHT AT BIRTH: NOT KNOWN
EYES OPEN: AT BIRTH
FIRST WALKING: WITHIN HOURS OF BIRTH
WEANING: 3 MONTHS
SEXUAL MATURITY: 10 MONTHS
LONGEVITY IN WILD: NOT KNOWN

DEATH ON THE PLAINS

SWIFT AND ADAPTABLE, PRONGHORNS ONCE ROAMED THE PRAIRIES IN THEIR MILLIONS. YET LESS THAN 100 YEARS AGO THEY WERE ALMOST WIPED OUT—VICTIMS OF SPEEDING BULLETS AND THEIR OWN CURIOSITY

In the early 1800s a herd of pronghorns in winter must have been an awe-inspiring sight. Thousands of animals spread out as far as the eye could see made the plains seem like a hunter's paradise, and it was probably this, together with the obvious crop-growing potential of the rich land, that attracted the settlers that moved westward from the early American colonies.

The very success of the pronghorn in adapting to a diverse range of habitats desired by settlers—particularly rich grasslands—contributed greatly to its own decline. Today, it is no longer possible to see the herds that the early settlers saw; only a fraction of them survives today, and most of their prairie home no longer exists in its natural state.

Where formerly there were seas of waving grain, now there are oceans of waving corn. The pronghorns' domain has quite literally become the "bread basket" of America, and the land that once fed them and the herds of bison with which they coexisted is now needed to feed the ever-growing

Judd Cooney/Oxford Scientific Films

David E. Rowley/Planet Earth Pictures

Pronghorns being rounded up for tagging (above). *Once hunted almost out of existence, the pronghorn is now a symbol of conservation in the United States.*

In some areas the plains can be inhospitable and even deadly. This fawn (right) *died after becoming stuck in the mud of a drying water hole.*

THEN & NOW

This map shows the former and present range of the pronghorn.

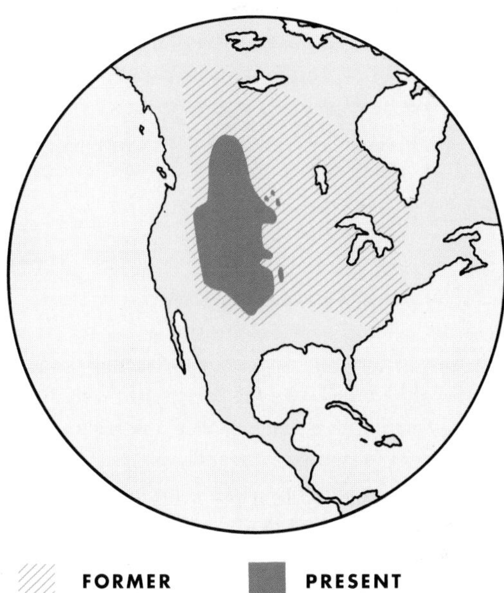

FORMER RANGE   PRESENT RANGE

Pronghorns once ranged from the foothills of the Rocky Mountains in the west, across to the Hudson Bay and the North Carolina coast in the east, and from Canada's Yukon Territory in the north, to the shores of the Gulf of Mexico in the south. Today they occupy a strip of western North America from British Columbia in the north, south to Texas, but their eastern distribution in particular has been severely limited, and few are found east of the Mississippi River.

human population. Pronghorns are no longer really welcome and their numbers will almost certainly never return to what they were before people usurped their habitat.

THE PRONGHORNS' LIGHTNING-SWIFT PACE DID NOT COMPENSATE FOR THE NATURAL CURIOSITY THAT HELPED TO KILL THEM

It is, perhaps, ironic that today people are realizing that, by wiping out the natural inhabitants of the prairie—the pronghorn and the bison—the people of North America removed what could have been a most valuable resource that, in some areas, made better use of the land than the crops and domestic animals introduced by farmers. Being ideally suited to the natural grasses that exist on these prairies, pronghorns are very much more productive, in terms of meat, than cattle, which feed on lush, green grasses that require the injection of copious amounts of fertilizer. On the open range they do much less damage than cattle or sheep, and in many places grazing pronghorns make much better use of the soil than farmers who plant crops. In the past, constant cultivation of the soil has led to erosion and the creation of useless, desertlike dust bowls. Today, some of the old dust bowls still remain and others are even now being created.

Easy targets

In 1880 there were probably thirty-five to forty million pronghorns roaming the American prairies. Animals in such enormous numbers present a sitting target, and the early settlers set about killing them with great vigor. Pronghorns were killed for their meat, for their hides, for their tongues, or simply for sport—a pronghorn's head made a handsome trophy to hang on the wall.

Between Denver and Cheyenne there were perhaps three or four million pronghorns living near the relatively new railway line, and during the winter of 1868–1869 dead animals were transported along the tracks to the cities by the wagonload. Each carcass could be bought for around six to eight cents.

THE MALE PRONGHORN, WITH ITS UNIQUE HOOKED HORNS, WAS GREATLY PRIZED AS A HUNTING TROPHY

The pronghorn's speed, normally an excellent defense against predators, was no help to it against the new invaders of the prairie; even a pronghorn cannot outrun a speeding bullet. And its innate inquisitiveness did nothing to improve the situation. In most antelope and deer, instinctive caution and fear form part of their natural defense mechanism, but in pronghorns this is often overcome by a curiosity that leads them, quite against their own basic interests, to investigate anything out of the ordinary.

This curiosity soon became apparent to the settlers. As the wagon trains rumbled across the prairies, pronghorns could often be seen following at distances as close as 330 ft (100 m). At night pronghorns would sometimes race through the travelers' campsites. It was not long therefore before hunters saw that they could turn the pronghorn's inquisitiveness to their advantage, and the practice of "flagging"—planting a stick in the ground with a fluttering flag on the end in order to

ENDANGERED ENVIRONMENT

SURVIVAL OF THE FOREST

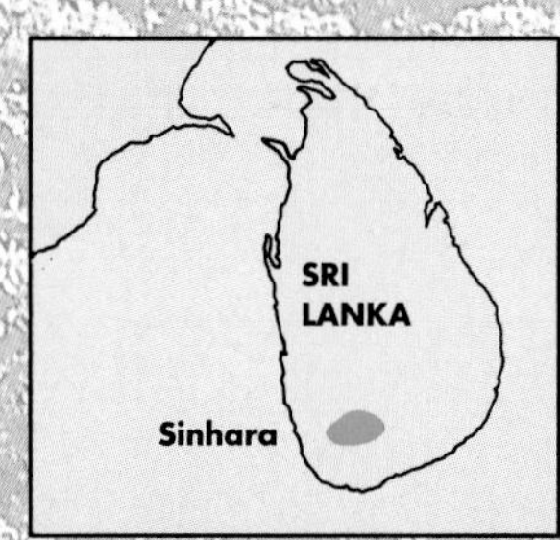

Because so little is known about chevrotains, their status is uncertain. In Asia they are frequently observed by the native people and so they do not appear to be rare. The water chevrotain of western Africa, on the other hand, appears to be under threat. This can be seen by looking at what is happening to its environment. Every year huge tracts of its native forest are removed to provide timber and cleared land for farming. But this process is hardly unique to western Africa; the forests of Southeast Asia are also being stripped at an alarming rate. And if the forests are threatened, so too must be the animals that live there, including the three species of chevrotain.

Fortunately, steps are being taken to save some of the rain forest. As an example, there is the project designed to ensure the long-term survival of the Sinhara Forest of Sri Lanka, the last extensive lowland forest on this island and home to the Indian chevrotain, or spotted mouse deer.

This forest covers nearly 24,700 acres (10,000 ha) of land and contains about half of the plant species

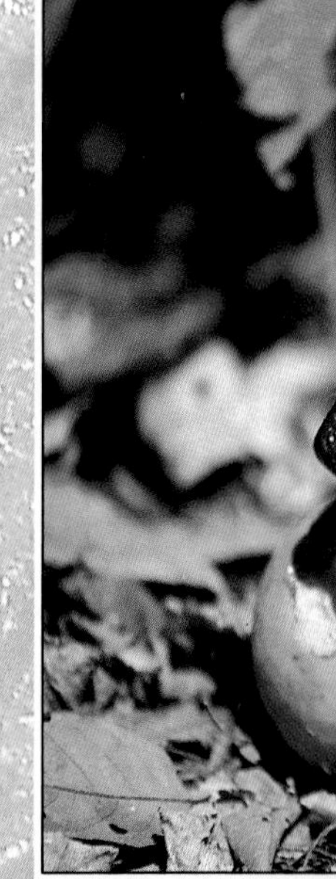

A WATER CHEVROTAIN EATING FRUIT DROPPED BY A MONKEY. BOTH ANIMALS DEPEND ON THE SURVIVAL OF THE RAIN FOREST.

John & Gillian Lythgoe/Planet Earth Pictures

Conservation Measures

As with so many animals, the only effective way of conserving chevrotains is to conserve their habitat and prevent overexploitation.

- The North American subspecies of pronghorn has been successfully conserved by controlling hunting and by offering financial incentives to farmers to compensate for loss of revenue or damage to crops.

endemic to the island, including 60 percent of the island's tree species. Sinhara has been a wet-zone forest preserve since the 1970s, but despite this it has remained under threat from encroachment by shifting cultivation, and from a combination of both controlled and illegal exploitation of the forest's natural products, both animal and plant.

A multidisciplinary management plan has now been set up to try to preserve the forest. The aim of the plan is to ensure that the forest products are used on a sustainable basis. Illegal exploitation is to be brought under control and, toward this end, local people are to be encouraged to become aware of the forest and the long-term benefits, such as tourism, local sustainable use, and the potential of carefully conserved genetic resources.

Inset picture Nick Gordon/Survival Anglia

- The sale of pronghorn meat was banned early this century. At around the same time, nature preserves were established and animals were reintroduced into parts of their former habitat.

- The Sinhara Forest in Sri Lanka, habitat of the Indian chevrotain and other rare wildlife species, was established as a wetland preserve in the 1970s.

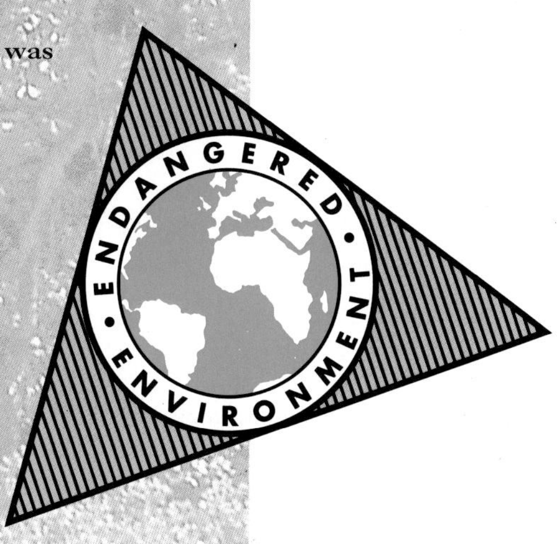

PRONGHORNS IN DANGER

NOT ALL PRONGHORNS ARE OUT OF DANGER. ALTHOUGH THE NORTH AMERICAN SUBSPECIES *ANTILOCAPRA AMERICANA AMERICANA* APPEARS TO BE SAFE FOR THE MOMENT, THE THREE OTHER SUBSPECIES ARE ALL CLASSIFIED AS ENDANGERED BY THE INTERNATIONAL UNION FOR THE CONSERVATION OF NATURE (IUCN).

SONORAN PRONGHORN	ENDANGERED
MEXICAN PRONGHORN	ENDANGERED
CALIFORNIAN PRONGHORN	ENDANGERED

ENDANGERED MEANS THAT THE ANIMAL IS IN DANGER OF EXTINCTION AND ITS SURVIVAL IS UNLIKELY UNLESS STEPS ARE TAKEN TO SAVE IT.

Hans Christian Heaps/Planet Earth Pictures

attract pronghorns within rifle range—became common. Even if no flag was available, a man lying on his back waving his feet in the air could achieve the same effect.

CONSERVATION MEASURES

By 1910, the pronghorn population had fallen to just 19,000 animals and it was beginning to look as though the species would be completely wiped out. Just in time, however, the people of America began to take an interest in conserving this uniquely American animal and the situation began to improve.

OIL EXPLORATION AND STRIP MINING FOR COAL COULD POSE THREATS TO THE PRONGHORN'S HABITAT

Between 1913 and 1915 the sale of pronghorn meat became illegal. Nature preserves were set up and animals were reintroduced into areas where they had been eradicated. Flagging was made illegal and hunting became strictly regulated, with a hunting season that had to be rigidly adhered to, and very strict limits on the numbers that could be killed.

Today, in some states, farmers are offered financial incentives not to kill pronghorns as pests, so that even if the animals do damage crops the farmers do not lose money as a result. Hunters face financial disincentives, too. In Wyoming a hunter who wishes to kill pronghorns is obliged to pay the

ALONGSIDE MAN

INTO THE SUBURBS

Pronghorns are not always confined to the prairies. They are intelligent animals and are quick to learn from experience. Many have now learned that where there are people there is food and, in harsh winters, many move close to towns to feed on hedges. Pronghorns can even be found grazing and browsing in suburban backyards. Their adaptability is such that they quickly learn to ignore harmless sounds, such as traffic noise, the roar of aircraft taking off, and even gunfire on military ranges and exercise areas.

Stan Osolinski/Oxford Scientific Films

A pronghorn mother and calf (above) *cross a road in Yellowstone National Park . The sound of traffic does not seem to bother this inquisitive creature.*

Jeff Foott/Survival Anglia

A pronghorn standing by a fence at Custer State Park, South Dakota (left). *Whenever possible, fences are adapted so that the pronghorn can roam from one grazing area to another.*

farmers on whose land he is hunting $5 for each pronghorn. In Texas he may have to pay up to $30. These may seem only token payments, but the legislation represents a step in the right direction. Today the annual harvest of pronghorns is about 40,000 animals.

The story of the conservation of the American pronghorn is by and large a successful one. By

ILLEGAL HUNTING AND HABITAT DESTRUCTION ARE THREATENING THE FUTURE OF THE MEXICAN PRONGHORN

1924, numbers had risen to 30,000 and today there are about 750,000–1,000,000 animals roaming the North American plains. Farmers have been persuaded to allow them to wander freely and, fortunately, barbed-wire fences do not pose much of a problem to pronghorns. They do not jump fences, but crawl under them, even relatively low ones. Farmers are advised to place the lowest strand at a height that does not hinder pronghorns as they migrate from one area to another. ■

INTO THE FUTURE

Americans today are proud, and rightly so, of the pronghorn. It is, after all, a unique animal, being the only American antelope in existence, and its conservation history has, in the main, been a resounding success. Numbers are rising in most areas, and much of the remaining wild prairie land receives official protection. This animal has become a symbol of American conservation and its image has been used on the cover of the *Journal of Mammalogy*, the organ of the American Society of Mammalogists, since it was first published in 1919.

However, although the North American subspecies *Antilocapra americana americana* appears to be safe for the moment, the three other subspecies are endangered. The Mexican subspecies, *A. a. mexicana*, numbers fewer than 1,200 animals, and its populations are declining due to illegal hunting and changes in the habitat. This subspecies is listed on Appendix 2 of CITES, the Convention on International Trade in Endangered Species of Wild Flora and Fauna.

The CITES agreement, drawn up in 1975 and now undersigned by more than 100 countries, aims to protect wildlife under any current or perceived future threat. Appendix-listed animals are graded according to the threats facing them: There is, for example, a total trade ban on animals in Appendix 1, with more relaxed restrictions in lower appendices. In Appendix 1 are the Sonoran pronghorn, *A. a. sonoriensis*, which is found in southern Arizona and northwestern Mexico, and the Californian pronghorn, *A. a. peninsularis*, of Baja, California. ■

PREDICTION

SURVIVAL IN THE MAIN

With the continuing careful husbandry of both existing herds and prairie habitat, the North American pronghorn's future seems assured. However, attention must now be given to the endangered subspecies if they are to survive.

CAPTIVE BREEDING

Pronghorns rarely thrive in zoos east of the Mississippi River, and in many cases they do not survive more than a year. No one knows why this should be so, as when they are kept in captivity in their natural habitat, they thrive. In New Mexico Zoo near Albuquerque, there used to be a very successful breeding group. In the east coast zoos, however, pronghorns reproduce only rarely and only a few live longer than seven years.

Similarly, pronghorns seldom survive for very long in European zoos. Even the Hanover Zoo, renowned for its experience and ability in keeping rare ungulates, has had considerable difficulties. In 1961, this zoo began working on the captive breeding of pronghorns, but for a long time their animals were so ill that they were constantly close to death and most eventually succumbed. By 1966 only two remained, but these two became the first pronghorns to reproduce in Germany.

The female delivered twins after a difficult labor and at first remained in poor health. After the birth she was given a linseed preparation to drink, and later began to eat large amounts of food. Her condition gradually improved, and, although she had some difficulty in suckling two healthy growing calves, the outcome was successful. But this was just one success after five years of keeping pronghorns.

Chevrotains are nearly as difficult to keep in zoos. No zoos at present keep African water chevrotains, and the greater Malay chevrotain is found only in some North American zoos. In this species' case the entire zoo population can be traced back to a single breeding that took place in the Bronx Zoo in New York. The lesser Malay chevrotain is kept in zoos, but the Indian spotted chevrotain is not.

Illustration Steve Kingston

PUMAS

RELATIONS

Pumas are members of the order Carnivora. They belong to the family Felidae along with all the other New World small cats. Some other New World members of the family are as follows:

OCELOT

JAGUARUNDI

LYNX

BOBCAT

MARGAY

KODKOD

PAMPAS CAT

GEOFFREY'S CAT

D. Robert Franz/Planet Earth Pictures

All cats are carnivores and belong to the same order. There are thirty species of small cats in one genus. Of these, ten are found only in the New World, eighteen are found only in the Old World, the lynx is found in both, and the domestic cat is worldwide.

ORDER

Carnivora
(carnivores)

FAMILY

Felidae
(felids)

GENUS

Felis

SPECIES

concolor
(puma)

SPECIES

yagouaroundi
(jaguarundi)

SPECIES

rufus
(bobcat)

SPECIES

lynx
(lynx)

SMALL BUT DEADLY

LESS WELL KNOWN THAN THEIR LARGER RELATIVES, THESE NEW WORLD CARNIVORES POSSESS THE KEEN SENSES, NIMBLE MOVEMENT, AND DAGGERLIKE FANGS THAT MAKE CATS HIGHLY EFFICIENT PREDATORS

With the exception of the jaguar, the cats of North and South America are grouped together in the category known as small cats. This can be misleading; the puma, also called the mountain lion and the cougar, can be every bit as large as the jaguar, the only so-called big cat of the Americas. However, the puma comes within the small cats group for other reasons.

Anatomical differences in the hyoid bone—the bone at the root of the tongue—mean the puma and other small cats purr instead of roar, like big cats. Also, the big cats have hair that extends all the way to the front edge of the nose, while the puma and other small cats have a naked strip along the top of the nose. Except for the ocelot, small cats bend their forelimbs as they rest, wrapping them in front of, or just underneath, the body, then curl their tails around themselves, like a domestic cat; big cats, on the other hand, usually rest with their forelegs

Michael Leach/Oxford Scientific Films

The ocelot (above) *is one of the few small cats that readily takes to water.*

stretched out in front of them and extend the tail behind them. Finally, small cats tend to feed crouching over their prey, while big cats more frequently eat in the resting position.

Small cats are found in every continent of the world except Australia. The puma, above all, is proof of the adaptability of cats to varying environments for it has been found in almost every type of habitat—from bleak, snow-covered mountains to steamy tropical forests, from sea level to elevations of 14,765 ft (4,500 m) or more. The bobcat also ranges over a large area in North America, and it, too, has adapted to a wide variety of habitats.

The first ancestors of today's cats evolved in the Eocene period some 50 million years ago, although the best-known prehistoric cat precursors, the saber-toothed tigers, appeared sometime between 38 to 26 million years ago. Recent research seems to indicate that modern cats evolved through three major lineages, now divided into three modern subfamilies. The subfamily Felinae includes all thirty species of cat in the genus *Felis.* The puma, jaguarundi, bobcat, and lynx are in this subfamily. The Pantherinae include all the large cats in the genus *Panthera* as well as the clouded leopard, which is the only representative of the genus *Neofelis.* The Acinonychinae is represented only by the cheetah, whose unusual characteristics, such as partly retractile claws, are probably very similar to the earlier felids that gave rise to all cats.

Jeff Foote/Survival Anglia

COAT COLORS

Rod Williams/Bruce Coleman Ltd.

Geoffroy's cat *(above)* is one of the smaller cats in this group. It is beautifully marked with small black spots on a yellowish background—which has made it a prize target for the fur trade. A near neighbor, the kodkod, is also spotted, while the even smaller little spotted cat has dark stripes and blotches. The pampas cat has a long, soft coat that is spotted, and the mountain cat has irregular spots and stripes. All these cats are found in the forests and scrublands of South America.

The puma (left) *is the most widely distributed mammal—besides humans—in the Western Hemisphere.*

With its long, slender body, the jaguarundi (below) *is the most unusual looking of all the small cats.*

G. I. Bernard/NHPA

PUMA

Felis concolor (FEE-lis CON-co-lor)

The puma is the best-known and most widely distributed of all the small cats. Although it is a native only of the New World, it is now found in other countries—notably the United Kingdom—proof of its adaptability to a wide range of differing habitats.

SUBSPECIES:
FLORIDA PUMA
EASTERN PUMA
CENTRAL PUMA
PATAGONIA PUMA

Most cats lead solitary lives, and the New World small cats are no exception. The puma undoubtedly evolved as a lone killer and, as such, is the most adept large carnivore in the United States, frequently killing animals up to eight times its size.

Although all the New World cats share the characteristics common to most cats—lithe, muscular bodies; sinewy legs; round, soft feet with retractile claws; and long, sharp, and slightly curved canines—they vary considerably in size and outward appearance. The largest, the puma, is yet quite light in build and has a small head. Its coat is a yellowish tawny shade with no spots or stripes. The slightly smaller lynx also has a uniform coat color, generally a pale tawny brown mixed with blackish hairs, but its flatter face is characterized by large pointed ears that have long ear tufts. These tufts act as sensitive antennae and help improve the lynx's hearing. The bobcat also possesses pointed ears, but the ear tufts are not as long, and its coat is barred and spotted with black on a paler background.

The jaguarundi is an extremely unusual-looking cat: Its long, low-slung body, short legs, and very long tail give it an appearance reminiscent of a marten. Its uniform-colored coat is a reddish brown, gray, or almost black. The elegant ocelot has distinct markings of dark spots, bars, and rosettes on its tawny yellow to reddish gray coat. The margay is similarly colored and marked, but is smaller with a relatively longer tail.

ALL CATS ARE DIGITIGRADE—THAT IS, THEY WALK ON THEIR TOES. THEIR BODY WEIGHT IS DISTRIBUTED EQUALLY OVER THE LARGE SOLE PADS

Most cats stalk their prey silently and stealthily, siezing it after a short dash or a swift pounce and killing it by piercing between its neck vertebrae with sharp canines. The victim, meanwhile, is held firm by the cat's sharp claws. These claws are retracted for much of the time, so that they are protected from the wear and tear that would quickly reduce their sharpness. Besides being essential for the firm holding of prey, the claws also assist in climbing; most cats are agile climbers and some even take their prey up into the high branches to consume it.

A well-developed physiological sense in cats is that of equilibrium—extremely useful to animals that habitually climb in their daily lives. If a cat loses its footing on a high branch, it is able to regain an upright position before hitting the ground. The head turns upright first, followed by the fore body and then the hind end.

THE PUMA'S FAMILY TREE

The family tree shows the relationship between the so-called big cats and the New World small cats. There are also a number of small cats—some eighteen or so species all included in the genus Felis*—distributed throughout the Old World, in Africa and Asia in particular. The lynx is one of the few species found in Europe as well as Canada and the United States.*

OTHER SPECIES:

- BOBCAT (*FELIS RUFUS*)
- LYNX (*FELIS LYNX*)
- OCELOT (*FELIS PARDALIS*)
- GEOFFROY'S CAT (*FELIS GEOFFROYI*)
- KODKOD (*FELIS GUIGNA*)
- MARGAY (*FELIS WIEDII*)
- MOUNTAIN CAT (*FELIS JACOBITA*)
- PAMPAS CAT (*FELIS COLOCOLO*)
- LITTLE SPOTTED CAT (*FELIS TIGRINUS*)
- WILDCAT (*FELIS SILVESTRIS*)

Illustrations William Oliver

JAGUARUNDI

Felis yagouaroundi

(*FEE-lis YAG-oo-ar-un-dee*)

In spite of its markedly different appearance from most small cats, the jaguarundi is, nevertheless, a member of the same genus. it has a small, somewhat flattened head, a relatively long neck, and a long slender body. It is at home in a variety of habitats, extending from Southern Texas down into South America.

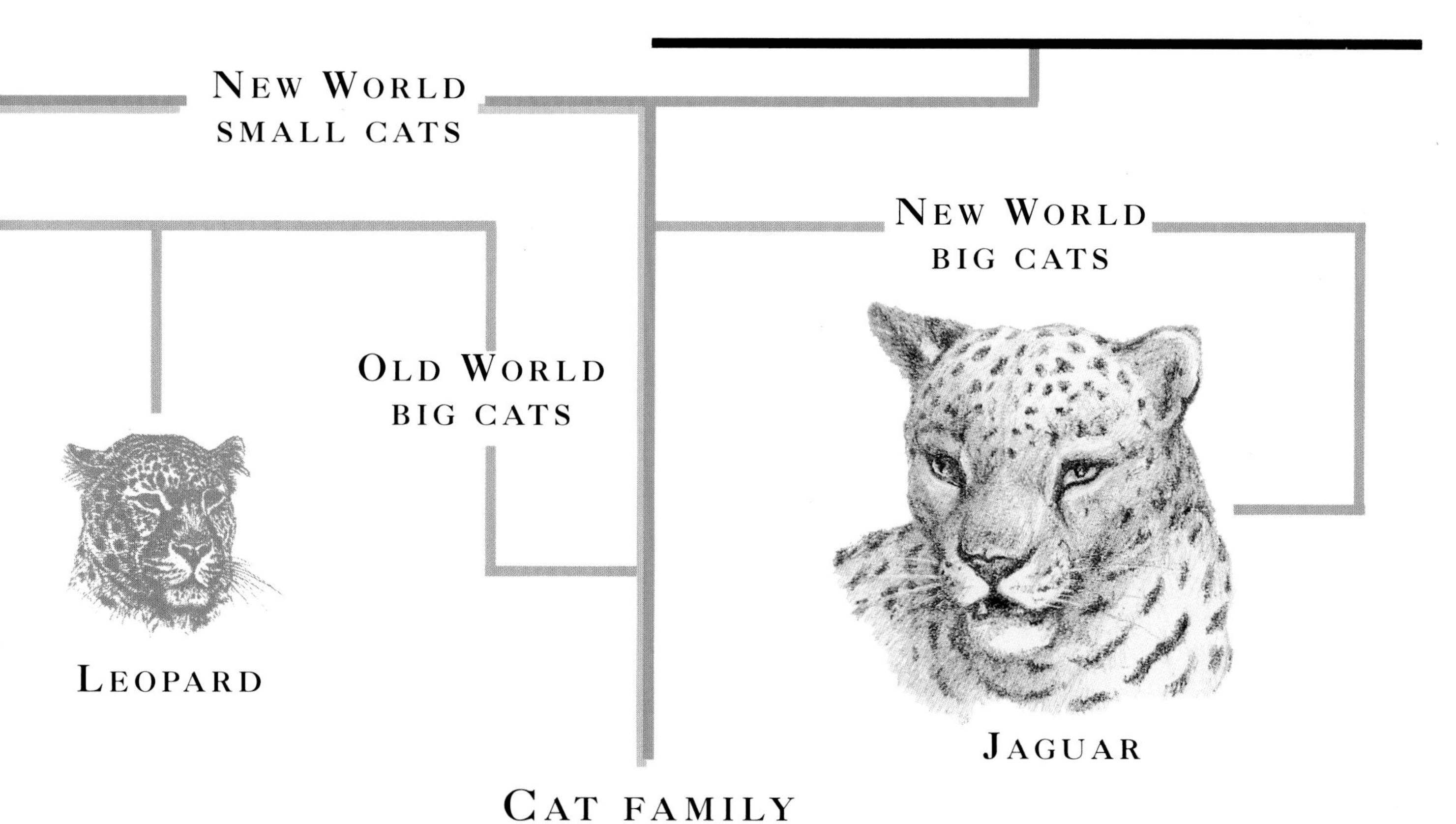

ANATOMY: THE PUMA

RED-BROWN FUR

The male puma (above left) is the largest of the New World cats and, in spite of being classed as a small cat, is as large as the jaguar (see Fact File). Females (above center) are slightly smaller. The lynx (above right) has a head-and-body length of 26–43 in (67–110 cm). The little spotted cat and kodkod are the smallest at about 20 in (52 cm).

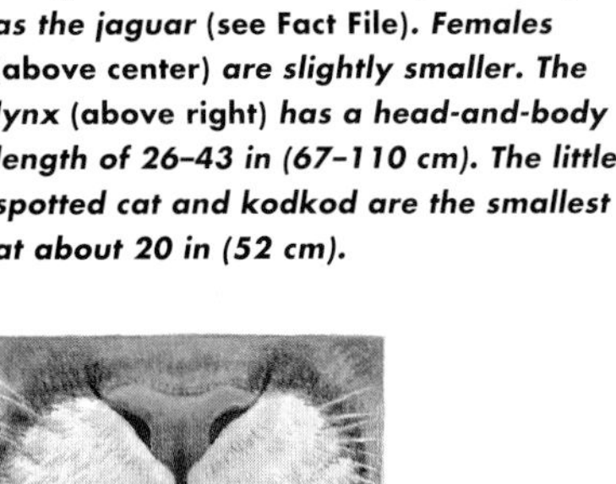

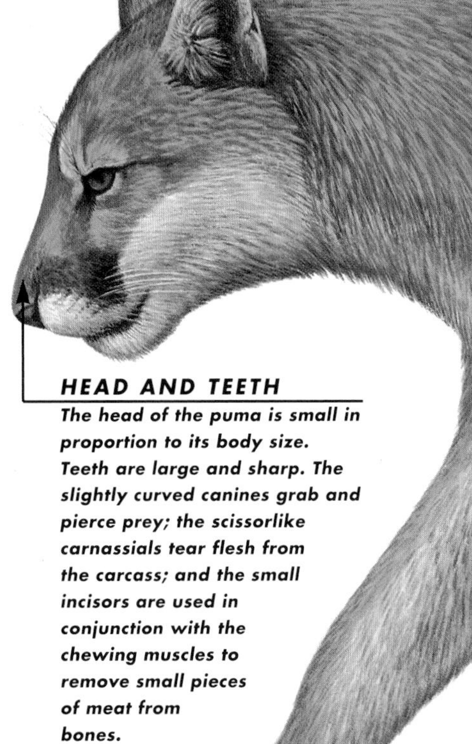

EARS

These are relatively small. However, the refined muscular control of the ears, possessed by all cats, increases both the sensitivity of hearing and ear mobility.

HEAD AND TEETH

The head of the puma is small in proportion to its body size. Teeth are large and sharp. The slightly curved canines grab and pierce prey; the scissorlike carnassials tear flesh from the carcass; and the small incisors are used in conjunction with the chewing muscles to remove small pieces of meat from bones.

LEGS

The legs seem longer than they are because cats are digitigrade—that is, they walk on their toes. In the puma, a cat with remarkable leaping ability, the hind legs are considerably longer than the front ones.

NOSE AND MOUTH

Besides the nasal olfactory sensors possessed by most animals, cats have a vomeronasal organ (above right)—two auxiliary olfactory membranes located in canals that lead from the roof of the mouth on each side. Their function is not known.

Illustrations Simon Turvey/Wildlife Art Agency

X-RAY

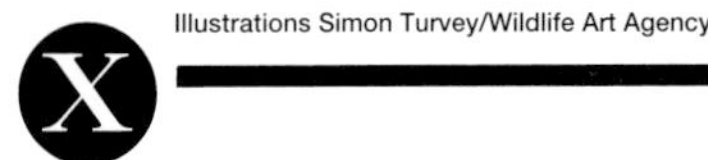

The puma's skeleton shows a vertebral column that is curved like a taut bow. This shape supports the body but allows great flexibility of movement.

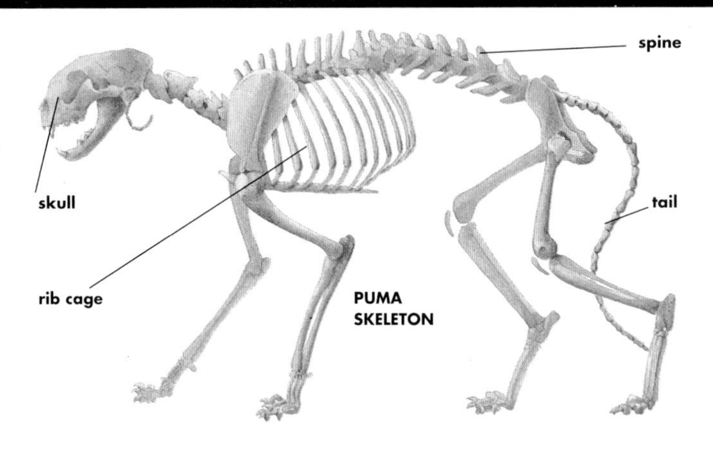

Pumas have retractile claws, which are contained in sheaths in the feet when not in use. This means they are elevated above the ground and are not subject to constant wear that would quickly make them dull. The claws are controlled by ligaments and extensor and flexor muscles.

X-ray illustrations Elisabeth Smith

FACT FILE:

PUMA

CLASSIFICATION

GENUS: *FELIS*

SPECIES: *CONCOLOR*

SIZE

HEAD–BODY LENGTH: 41–79 IN (105–200 CM)

TAIL LENGTH: 26–31 IN (67–78 CM)

WEIGHT: 79–231 LB (36–105 KG)

SIZE VARIES GREATLY ACROSS THE RANGE; MALES ARE A LITTLE LARGER THAN FEMALES

WEIGHT AT BIRTH: 8–16 OZ (226–453 G)

COLORATION

SOLID COAT COLOR, USUALLY A TAWNY YELLOW ABOVE AND PALER UNDERNEATH

CUBS ARE BORN SPOTTED WITH RINGED TAILS; THESE MARKINGS FADE AFTER A FEW MONTHS

FEATURES

EYE COLOR IS AMBER

EARS ARE SMALL, SHORT, AND ROUNDED; BACKS ARE DARKER

TAIL IS LONG WITH A BLACK TIP

HIND LEGS ARE CONSIDERABLY LONGER THAN FRONT

FEET ARE LARGE

BLUE-GRAY FUR

BLACK FUR

COAT COLORS

The puma's varying coat colors are associated with different locations. Reds are more common in the tropics, and blue-gray is found in northern areas. Black is very rare anywhere.

BODY SHAPE

Fairly long and streamlined with powerful limbs, the body is designed for bursts of speed.

FEET AND TRACKS

The puma's large feet leave rounded tracks, usually with all four lower toes imprinted, although there are generally no claw marks. The fore prints are slightly larger than the hind prints.

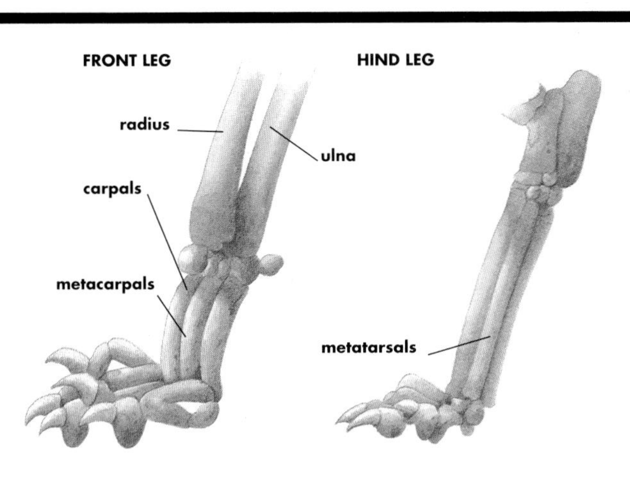

Like other cats, the puma has a relatively small skull. However, its eyes are unusually large for the skull size. Large eyes have better light-gathering abilities for vision in poor light.

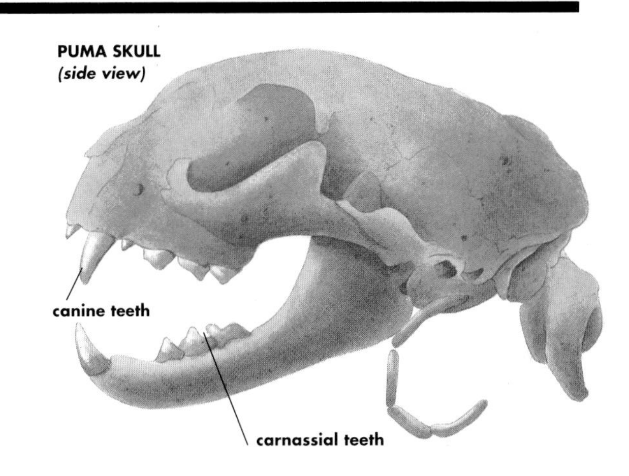

EVERYWHERE AND NOWHERE

THE MOST WIDELY DISTRIBUTED CAT IN THE AMERICAS, THE PUMA IS EXTREMELY ELUSIVE AND HARD TO SEE IN THE WILD—EVEN THOUGH EVIDENCE OF ITS PRESENCE MAY BE APPARENT

The New World's small cats, like most wild animals, are perfectly adapted to life in their chosen habitats. All are mainly solitary, occupying territories that vary in size, principally according to food availability, and all are well equipped for their life as nature's top predators.

Many of these cats are nighttime hunters, although some, including the puma, are often active by day. This may reflect the habits of a particular cat's principal prey: In certain areas, for example, the puma's main source of food is the Columbia ground squirrel, which is a diurnal species. Or it may be related to the time of year and weather conditions: Pumas will often hunt and roam through the daylight of long summer days, or when snow is falling. Heavy daytime rain, however, seems to be a deterrent, and in such wet conditions pumas tend to lie up in caves or sheltered spots among rocks. Whatever the weather or food availability, pumas are more likely to be active during daylight hours in areas that are uninhabited by humans.

GENERALLY NOCTURNAL, MANY CATS WILL HUNT BY DAY IN AREAS REMOTE FROM CIVILIZATION AND HUMAN INTERFERENCE

The superiority of cats' vision is also an indication of their hunting habits. Usually a cat's eyes appear to be large for the size of its head; their positioning in all species gives stereoscopic, or binocular, vision, which allows the cat to judge distances with great accuracy. This is important; a cat usually creeps up on its prey and must be able to gauge just the right moment to make its last-minute dash and pounce in order to make a successful kill.

In daylight, cats and humans have a similar degree of vision, but in darkness that of cats is vastly superior. Cats can open their pupils to a maximum area that is about three times greater than that of humans, thereby allowing the layer of cells behind the retina to absorb even the dimmest light. In order to protect the eyes in bright light, they can also reduce the pupil to the merest slit, so that the light-sensing cells are not overwhelmed.

Another feature that helps cats move with confidence and accuracy in the dark is their whiskers. Extremely sensitive to the touch, whiskers help cats determine whether they can pass through narrow spaces. Cats' hearing is thought to be good, too, and in some species—such as the lynx, for which hearing is important to their way of life—it is heightened by the presence of ear tufts. All cats have strong

Leonard Lee Rue/Bruce Coleman Ltd.

Born blind and helpless, all kittens, like these week-old bobcats, are dependent on their mothers.

Hans Reinhard/Bruce Coleman Ltd.

A family of lynx (left), *the most northerly ranging of the New World's small cats*

The bobcat (below) *has a range extending from southern Canada to southern Mexico.*

Stephen J. Krasemann/Bruce Coleman Ltd.

muscles that move the outside ear. This probably helps the cat hear better by locating the direction of the sound more accurately. The most poorly developed sense is thought to be smell.

Although cats are aggressive hunters, they are not particularly hostile toward members of their own species. When fights do occur, they are most likely to be over food; if food is plentiful within an area, then aggression is not necessary. Territories are marked with a system of claw scratches and scent marks of urine and feces, often very discreetly placed so that they are only detectable by cats of the same species rather than by others. As such they are information markers as much as warnings to stay away.

All cats use a variety of sounds for communication. These tend to be unique to each species, and similar in males and females. Some sort of meow is common to most cats, although the sound will vary in different species. All cats hiss and growl as warning and confrontation signals.

The puma, although most usually silent, nevertheless has an impressive range of vocalizations. Its most bloodcurdling sound is said to be the scream of its mating call. It can also produce a high-pitched, whistlelike call, which tends to sound as if it should be coming from a much smaller animal. ■

HABITATS

As a species, cats are found in almost every habitat, from steamy, low-level rain forests to arid sandy deserts or rugged high mountains. The only places they tend not to inhabit are the treeless tundra regions or polar ice.

Generally cats will seek habitats that offer some sort of shelter, such as trees, rocky outcrops, or fairly dense scrub growth, because they need such cover to hide in as they silently creep up on their prey. The pampas cat of the Andes' high steppes is one of the few cats anywhere to be chiefly an animal of open country. Grasslands are its main habitat, although it will venture into thin forest and scrubland. Primarily a ground-dwelling animal, this cat is rarely found in trees.

North America's principal small cat, the puma, has proved adaptable to most types of habitats from tropical forests and swamps to hilly forests and snow-covered mountains. In fact, increasingly across its range it appears to be withdrawing into inhospitable mountainous areas, where it is likely to be left alone by humans. Being a particularly good climber, this cat likes to live around trees. It is a good swimmer, too, but it will take to water only when absolutely necessary.

Studies of pumas in different habitats have shown there to be a variation in size according to locations. Those found in equatorial rain forests are apparently much smaller than those living in the northern and southern extremes of the range.

THE PUMA'S LONG BACK LEGS ENABLE IT TO COVER A CONSIDERABLE DISTANCE IN A SINGLE BOUND OR LEAP

The bobcat ranges from southern Canada to southern Mexico. Within this vast area, it has also adapted to a variety of habitats. Scrubby brush country with rocks and areas of dense vegetation are its preferred environments, but it will also be found in swampy areas, farmland, and even more arid country—although it does still need some shelter and cover.

The lynx, which occupies territory farther north than the bobcat, is found in dense coniferous forests. The ocelot, an inhabitant of the middle and southeast United States down to northern Argentina, is another forest-dweller, although it is also found in areas of arid scrubland and low evergreen oaks. The ocelot is a good swimmer and takes readily to water,

Stephen Krasemann/NHPA

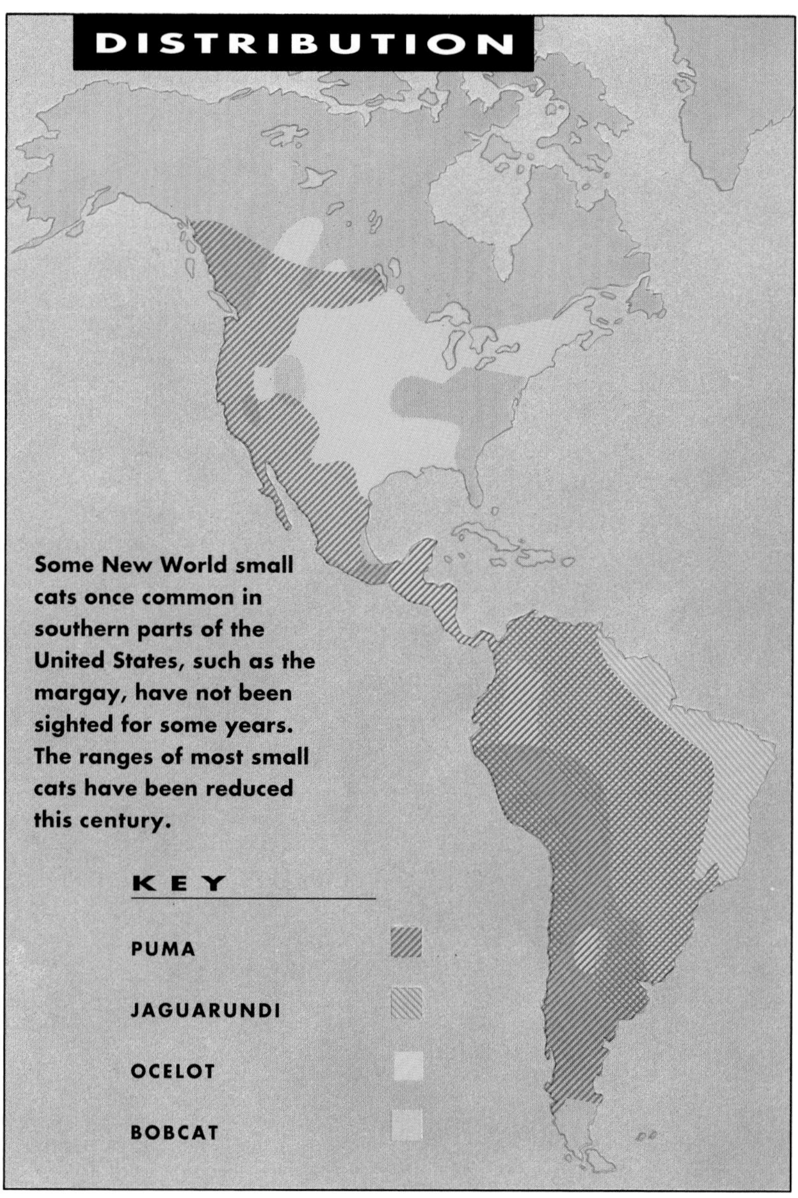

Andy and Sandy Carey/Oxford Scientific Films

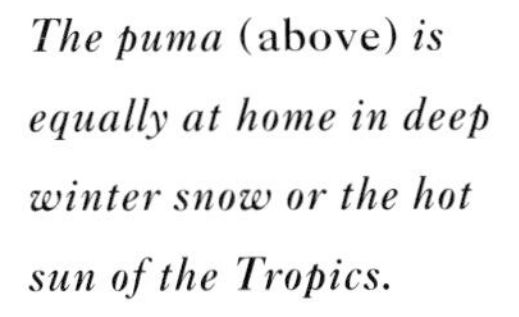

The puma (above) *is equally at home in deep winter snow or the hot sun of the Tropics.*

The margay (right) *has disappeared from the northernmost parts of its range.*

KEY FACTS

• The puma is one of the most agile of all cats. Its long back legs give it an extraordinary leaping ability: It has been seen to clear obstacles of over 6 ft (2 m) high while on the run. It is also an excellent climber and escape artist; it will leap over steep cliffs in order to escape.

• According to Native Americans, jaguarundis were tamed by natives before the Spanish invaded South America. They were used as domestic cats are used today—to control rodent populations.

• The deadly canine teeth of cats are longer and stronger in relation to the size of the skull than those of the canids.

• The margay's hind feet are more flexible than those of other felids. They can rotate 180 degrees.

• The greatest age ever recorded in a member of Felidae, excluding the domestic cat, was that of a bobcat. It lived to be over thirty-four years old.

• The margay has not been seen in Texas since the mid-19th century.

often hunting along streams.

The margay ranges from northern Mexico to northern Argentina (although recently it has been sighted only rarely in the United States) and is almost exclusively an animal of the forest. Mainly a tree-dweller—it is thought to forage almost exclusively among the branches—it is the only North American cat known to climb down trees headfirst. It has been observed hanging from high branches, holding on with the claws of one hind foot. Because its markings are similar to the ocelot's—although it is smaller and slimmer—and because of its arboreal habits, the margay is also known as the tree ocelot.

SMALL CATS ARE FOUND IN EVERY CONTINENT OF THE WORLD EXCEPT AUSTRALIA

The weasel-like jaguarundi has a range that extends from southern Texas through Mexico, Central America, and into South America, east of the Andes to northern Argentina. Again, though, it is rare over much of this range, particularly in the United States. It was once a creature of varied habitats, seemingly at home in fairly open spaces, but it is now found mainly in brushy thickets, particularly of cacti or other spiny plants. Often active by day, this is another cat that takes readily to water and is sometimes found near rivers.

Found only in South America, from Bolivia through southern Brazil to Patagonia, Geoffroy's cat inhabits scrubby upland woods up to altitudes of 11,000 ft (3,300 m) as well as more open country. Found at even higher levels—up to 16,500 ft (5,000 m)—the mountain cat lives in the arid and semiarid zones of the Andes from southern Peru to northern Chile. On the other hand, the kodkod, an inhabitant of Chile and Argentina, appears to be a forest-dweller. Some experts, however, claim that the kodkod actually lives on the ground and rarely takes to the trees, although it is undoubtedly an adept climber. The little spotted cat ranges from Costa Rica down through most of South America; it is another forest-dweller, although it, too, lives on the ground as well as in trees. ■

CATS DISPLAY A GREAT FLEXIBILITY OF BEHAVIOR, ACCORDING TO THE DEMANDS OF THE HABITATS IN WHICH THEY LIVE

FOCUS ON

THE EVERGLADES

Situated in southern Florida, the Everglades were once a wetland wilderness, providing a unique American habitat or, more accurately, habitats. The whole area slopes very gradually south toward the sea. It is essentially a low region of saw-grass prairies and swamps in a shallow basin. Saw grass is a sedge, the edges of which are covered with minute sharp teeth, that grows to a height of 10–15 ft (3–5 m). There are areas of open water and there are myriad small islands, called hammocks, which may be of saw grass, or of various vegetation—palms, pines, oaks, cypresses, and numerous tropical shrubs all tangled together. Mangrove swamps are a feature of the borders of the Everglades, as are the adjacent pine forests.

The Everglades were once the stronghold of the puma—known in this area as the Florida panther. It shared its habitat with a rich array of animal life, for wetlands of this sort provide habitats for literally thousands of species of plants and animals. Mangrove forests alone drop some 13 tons of organic detritus per acre (12 tonnes per 0.4 hectare) annually, and this provides the basis of numerous food chains. More than 300 species of birds have been observed in the Everglades.

Nevertheless, the Florida panther has not been sighted in the Everglades since 1991, even though it has been protected since 1958 and was named Florida's official state animal in 1982.

TEMPERATURE AND RAINFALL

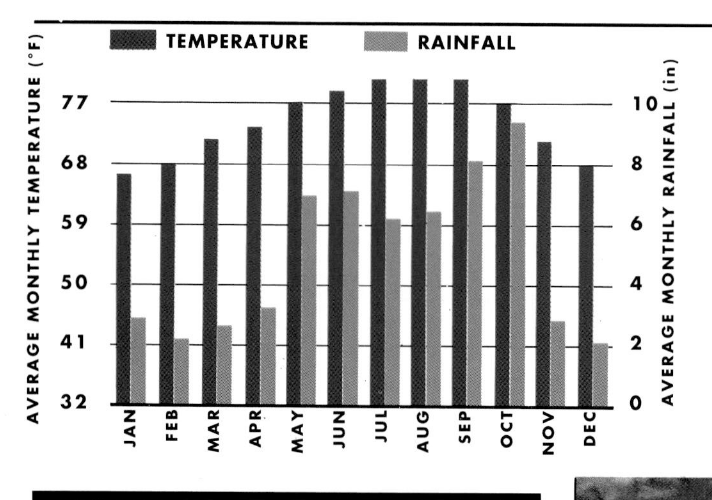

The climate in the Everglades is subtropical with two distinctive seasons. From about May to October, the wet season brings heavy rainfall and permanent warm humidity. During the winter, however, the rain stops and the water levels all over the area tend to drop dramatically. The effect of this has been exacerbated by vast drainage projects throughout this century.

WETLAND OR FARM?

When drained, wetlands yield rich soil for agriculture. To this end and to satisfy the demands of tourism, the Everglades have been systematically drained for many years. Much of the area has been lost and the ecological balance of the remainder has been seriously affected, resulting in changes in vegetation and loss of animal life.

NEIGHBORS

The Everglades are home to one of the richest diversities of animal life found anywhere in the world, including rare species found nowhere else.

FLORIDA SANDHILL CRANE

This sandhill crane is found only in Florida. Habitat loss is making it increasingly rare.

MANATEE

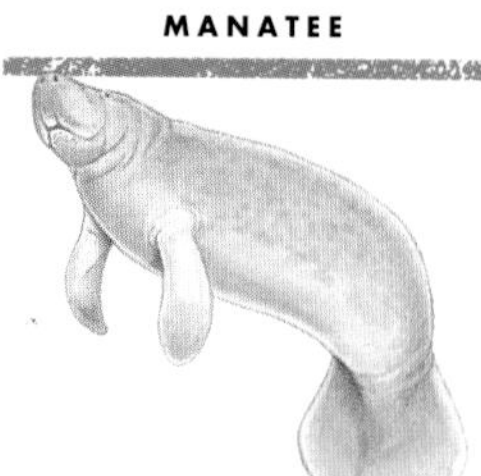

Florida is one of the last strongholds of this shy, aquatic mammal. It feeds on aquatic vegetation.

Illustrations Tracey A. Stitch/Wildlife Art Agency

FLORIDA'S IMPORTANT WETLAND

The 4,000 sq miles (10,000 sq km) of wetland that make up the Everglades are located on the edge of the Tropics in the southernmost tip of Florida. Concerted efforts are being made to restore this important environment to the condition it was at the beginning of the 20th century.

Pat Morris/Ardea

GREEN TREE FROG

The toes of tree frogs help them cling to bark and twigs, but these frogs prefer low shrubs to high trees.

LONGNOSE GAR

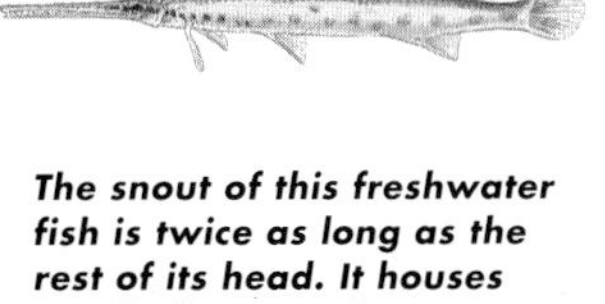

The snout of this freshwater fish is twice as long as the rest of its head. It houses small, sharp teeth.

CORN SNAKE

This is just one of the many snakes that make their home in the wooded areas of the Everglades.

ALLIGATOR

The alligator is one of the Everglades' most threatening—and best-known—inhabitants.

GREEN HERON

Unlike most herons, the green heron tends to be solitary. It favors marshy areas for breeding.

HUNTING

Wherever they are found, cats are generally at the top of the food chain. Most adult cats have few predators in the wild; only cubs and weak or old cats are likely to fall victim to any carnivores, such as coyotes, with which they share their environment. However, some of the small cats can be at risk from other species. The lynx, for example, has been known to fall prey to the larger puma where their ranges overlap; and the lynx will also sometimes fall victim to gray wolves.

All cats are almost entirely carnivorous—that is, they eat almost nothing but flesh, mainly of other warm-blooded mammals. For this reason, they have a relatively simple digestive system. Animal tissue—flesh—is rich food and needs less extensive digestion than vegetable matter, for example, which has to be broken down more thoroughly to release its nutrients.

The other feature perfectly adapted to a cat's carnivorous nature is its teeth. The most noticeable and awe-inspiring of these are the fierce canines—upper and lower ones on either side of the jaw. These killing weapons are the first to pierce live prey, usually delivering the fatal stab behind the neck. Together with the three pairs of upper and lower incisors, they also rip into the flesh. There is little emphasis on grinding and chewing in the dentition of a cat. Whatever chewing a cat does occurs at the corners of its mouth, where the masticating muscles are located. The rough-surfaced tongue scrapes flesh off bones. Because they prefer their

Marty Stouffer/Oxford Scientific Films

Like the lynx, the bobcat preys on the snowshoe hare. Here a bobcat makes its final assault on the hapless victim. Small prey is consumed immediately. Larger prey is cached.

THE PUMA'S KILL

To the puma, the most consistently important prey victim across its range is deer, the species varying according to location. Up to eight times its own size, a kill of an adult male mule deer or an elk will last a puma at least a week. After the kill, the puma remains nearby until it has consumed all the flesh. The puma knows it must guard its kill closely, for it shares its habitat with a number of scavengers. The fact that deer are the principal prey of the puma is often viewed as a natural way of culling these animals, preventing the herds from overpopulating.

AFTER THE KILL

The puma is strong enough to drag its heavy prey to a protected site, where it covers it with whatever vegetation is available.

PREY

The diets of all small cats are extremely varied, for cats are opportunist hunters. Birds, lizards, and frogs, as well as small animals, are welcome fare.

LIZARD

meat to be fresh, cats are opportunistic hunters across their ranges, taking whatever animals or birds are the most abundant and easily caught. Seldom do cats feed off carrion, although the lynx is an exception.

Small cats, particularly, are not active pursuers of their victims in the way that most wild dogs are. They are the silent stalkers; the patient waiters who crouch in hiding, then slink along the ground in a creeping run, freezing for seconds at a time, waiting to pounce. ■

MARGAY'S KILL
One of the most arboreal of the small cats, the margay drops on unsuspecting ground prey from its perch in the trees above. It also eats birds.

Barry Croucher/Wildlife Art Agency

B/W illustrations Craig Robson/Wildlife Art Agency

TERRITORY

Far less territorial than many wild animals, most of the New World small cats do, nevertheless, operate within a home range that they mark out with urine and feces, by scratching key trees, and by making scrapes in the ground. Usually the sizes of such ranges tend to be linked to the availability of food, rather than to a deep territorial instinct.

Pumas are generally widely spaced out across their habitats. This is not, as it might seem, entirely because of an antisocial nature, but also because of a need for a large area in which to find sufficient food. Even when pumas were plentiful, there was never a danger that they would overrun the land; their territorial habits act as a natural limit to their own numbers.

A puma's home range may vary from an area of 16–113 sq miles (41–292 sq km) for a male and 12–80 sq miles (31–207 sq km) for a female. The higher figures indicate the extent of the summer range, which tends to be larger than the winter range. A range will also alter to coincide with seasonal migration patterns of the puma's principal prey, such as mule deer and elk.

The size of a female's territory also relates to whether she has young or not. When she is nursing small cubs, she will not wander far from her den, so the size of her home range is generally

LONE BOBCAT

Bobcats mark out and occupy home ranges; those of males often overlap. Females occupy smaller areas; these do not overlap with other females' but may overlap with males'. The cats travel well-worn paths within their territories and mark these by squirting urine or scraping with their paws. The information given by these signs help males to gauge whether females are ready to mate.

Illustrations Steve Kingston

OTTER CAT

is another name for the jaguarundi because it looks sleek and likes water.

BOBCAT'S RANGE

As with those of most cats, the size of a bobcat's territory will generally depend on the availability of food within an area.

contracted. When the cubs are a little older and she is teaching them to hunt, a female puma is likely to wander over a much larger range. Puma cubs often stay with their mother for up to two years, and the size of her home range will vary throughout this time.

The home ranges of male pumas tend to be quite distinct from one another, while those of females may overlap, possibly with those of a few females and a male. A male's territory may overlap with several females', and a female's territory may overlap with more than one male's. Where such overlaps occur, the animals tend to use different areas at different times, thus respecting each other's solitary status. They come together only to mate.

Young and transient animals may pass through another's range, but they will not be tolerated for long. It seems that territorial rights are relinquished mainly by death. Young males seldom challenge older males to gain access to a prime territory.

MOST SMALL CATS ARE NOT AGGRESSIVELY TERRITORIAL. NEVERTHELESS, MOST OF THEM OCCUPY DEFINED HOME RANGES

Within its home range, a puma travels extensively. It is not unusual for one animal to roam up to 25 miles (40 kilometers) in a night. Generally there is no one fixed den where the puma sleeps, although breeding females rearing young are an exception to this. Instead, pumas rest where the mood takes them, seeking shelter in caves, among rocky outcrops, or beneath dense vegetation. ■

Jeff Lepore/Oxford Scientific Films

A bobcat (right) *rubs itself against a branch to mark its presence.*

SOUTH AMERICA

Little is known about the territorial habits of South America's small cats. Habitats tend to be more tropical than in North America, which usually means the availability of prey is steady throughout the year and territories are likely to be stable from month to month. In ocelot studies in Peru, females occupied small, exclusive home ranges of about three quarters of a square mile (2 sq km).

LIFE CYCLE

The mating season is the only time of the year that most New World cats stay in each other's company for any length of time. Although males of most species will be able to tell by their urine markings if the females in their territory are sexually receptive, it is quite often the females that seek out males, making loud mating calls to attract them.

Across much of its range, the puma has no set mating season, and it is the act of mating itself that stimulates the female to ovulate. In the northern part of its range, females generally give birth in late winter and early spring, when the weather is better and more prey is available. Having come together, a male and female will stay in each other's company for a couple of weeks, hunting and sleeping side by side.

As the gestation period of 90 to 95 days comes to an end, the female will find a cozy, protected den for herself, usually in a cave or between rocks. She lines the ground with foliage to make it warm and comfortable, and here she gives birth to up to six cubs—three or four being the common number.

All cats are born blind and helpless, but they are generally fully furred. Initially, the female puma does not stray too far from the den; she spends a lot of time suckling the young. If the cubs survive, the female will not come back into estrus for about two

AT BIRTH *the coat of the 12-in- (30-cm-) long puma cubs is spotted and the tail is ringed. These markings fade when the cubs are six months old or so. The eyes open at ten days old and gradually change from blue to amber.*

YOUNG ADULTS *establish their independence at two years old, but males will not mate for another year. Females are sexually mature at two-and-a-half years old.*

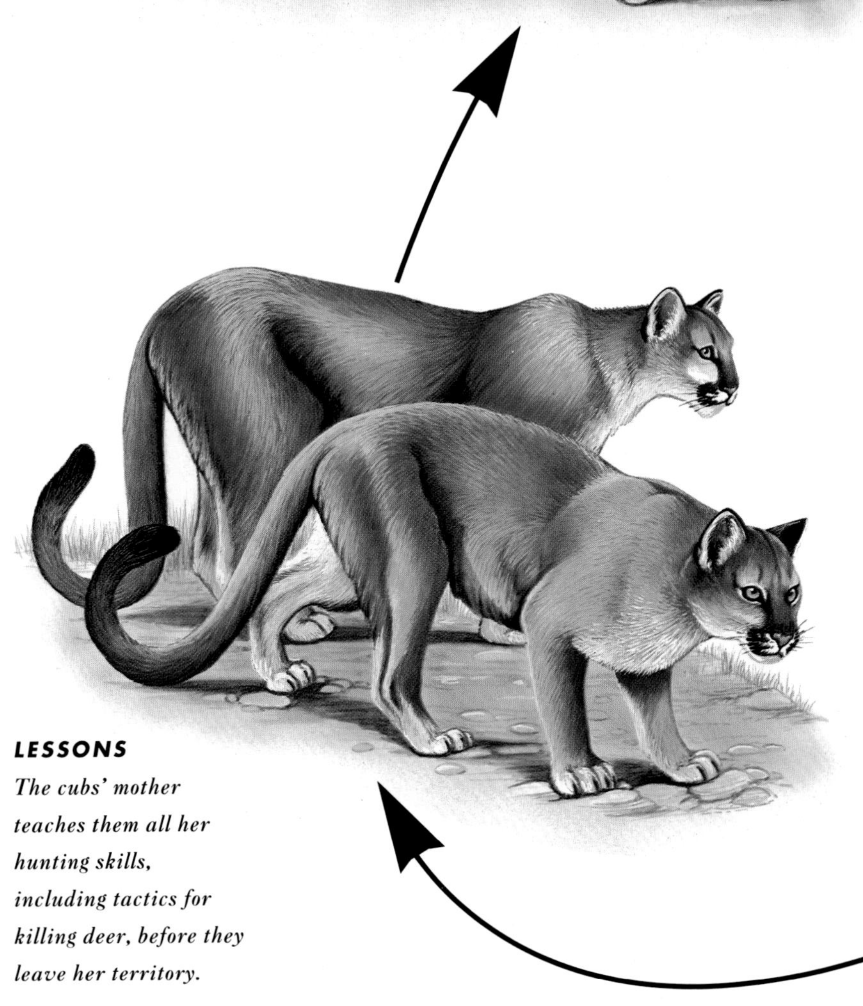

LESSONS *The cubs' mother teaches them all her hunting skills, including tactics for killing deer, before they leave her territory.*

FROM BIRTH TO DEATH

PUMA
GESTATION: 90–95 DAYS
LITTER SIZE: 1–6
WEIGHT AT BIRTH: 8–16 OZ (227–454 G)
EYES OPEN: 6–10 DAYS
WEANED: ABOUT 3 MONTHS
INDEPENDENCE: 1–2 YEARS
SEXUAL MATURITY: MALES, 3 YEARS; FEMALES, 2.5 YEARS
LONGEVITY: UNKNOWN IN THE WILD; OVER 20 YEARS IN CAPTIVITY

LYNX
GESTATION: 63–70 DAYS
LITTER SIZE: 1–5, USUALLY 2–3
WEIGHT AT BIRTH: 7–7.5 OZ (198–213 G)
WEANED: 5 MONTHS, BUT TAKE SOLID FOOD AT 1 MONTH
INDEPENDENCE: 9–10 MONTHS
SEXUAL MATURITY: MALES, 33 MONTHS; FEMALES, 21 MONTHS
LONGEVITY: UNKNOWN IN THE WILD; OVER 26 YEARS IN CAPTIVITY.

JAGUARUNDI
GESTATION: 72–75 DAYS
LITTER SIZE: USUALLY 2, OCCASIONALLY 3.
TAKE SOLID FOOD: 6 WEEKS

BOBCAT
GESTATION: 60–63 DAYS
LITTER SIZE: 1–6, USUALLY 3
WEIGHT AT BIRTH: 10–13 OZ (283–369 G)

GROWING UP

The life of a young puma

***HIDDEN IN** the undergrowth, a cub waits for its mother to return from hunting. It will eat meat at six weeks old, but suckles for about six weeks more.*

***WITHIN WEEKS** baby pumas have developed into strong, playful kittens, ready to try most things. When they learn to climb trees, they are merely following an inborn instinct.*

All illustrations Kim Thompson

in SIGHT

THE BOBCAT'S YOUNG

The bobcat mother commonly gives birth to two or three young in a cozy, sheltered nest during the spring. They open their eyes when they are nine days old and suckle for about two months. At three to five months old, they will go on hunting forays with the mother. By their first winter, they become totally independent and leave the mother, and she is ready to mate again.

ZEFA

years. Females begin breeding soon after they are two years old; males usually do not mate until they are at least three years old.

North America's bobcat generally mates in the late winter. Birth occurs after a 60- to 70-day gestation period in late April to early May. It seems, however, that some females—probably younger ones or those that have lost a litter for some reason —may sometimes give birth later on in the year, toward the end of the summer or in early autumn. A male bobcat may mate with several females, chasing off any intruding males at this time. It is also at this time that the bobcat is at its most vocal—loudly yowling to attract mates.

The lynx's breeding habits are similar to the bobcat's, although these cats tend to mate and give birth a little later in the year.

Although there seems to be no fixed breeding season, the majority of jaguarundi births occur in the spring and summer. The common litter size is two, born in a sheltered den after a gestation of 72–75 days. Like the puma, the cubs are born spotted, although these marks quickly fade. Cubs are often found with different colors within one litter.

Little is known about the breeding habits of South America's small cats, but in the Tropics there is probably no particular breeding season. ■

ENDANGERED OR A DANGER?

THE FUTURE OF MOST SMALL CATS HAS A QUESTION MARK HANGING OVER IT, BUT IN PLACES, CONSERVATION MEASURES HAVE SO INCREASED NUMBERS OF PUMAS THAT SOME PEOPLE CONSIDER THEM A DANGER

Most of the small cats—those with spotted or striped coats in particular—have been massively exploited during the 20th century for their fur. To satisfy human vanity, these cats have been slaughtered in the thousands. The ocelot is one such; during the 1960s more than 130,000 skins were imported to the United States from South America. The United States was quicker than most European countries to enforce a ban on such imports, though, doing so in 1972. In the mid-1970s Great Britain was importing more than 75,000 skins yearly. In the early 1980s people in some European countries were paying $40,000 or more for a coat made of ocelot skins.

The ocelot is reported to be easy to catch, either by trapping or shooting, which has made it particularly vulnerable. In past years, it was also much in demand as a pet, and females were often killed when they tried to protect their cubs from being captured. These cats had a reputation for being affectionate and easily tamed when young—and at one time people would pay as much as $800 to acquire one as a pet. However, as they get older, they become less predictable and are often aggressive. The selling of live ocelots as pets has been banned in many countries, including the United States. In spite of this and its protected status across most of its range, however, the ocelot is still listed as vulnerable by the International Union for Conservation of Nature (IUCN), or the World Conservation Union.

The margay has also been persecuted for its fur, with more than 30,000 skins being exported annually in the late 1970s. Once the margay was given protection, the number of skins dropped to about 20,000 in 1980, and by 1985 it was apparently only just over 100. In spite of this, the margay is another cat listed as vulnerable by the IUCN, as, too, is the little spotted, or the tiger cat (although its status has improved to some extent—it was previously listed as endangered). The mountain cat is classified as rare by the IUCN, while the Convention on International Trade in Endangered Species (CITES) has placed it in its Appendix 1, which includes "all species threatened with extinction which are or may be threatened by trade." Geoffroy's cat is also known to have been heavily exploited by the fur trade, with thousands of skins being exported in previous years.

Where the fur trade is concerned, what has led to such decimation in so many species is that it takes an enormous number of skins to make one coat. Each animal is an individual, and the markings on

A puma skin (right) *is held up. Puma skins have little commercial value, except as trophies.*

Martin Wendler/NHPA

The spoils of game hunting: Jaguar, ocelot, and margay skins all stretched out for display.

Martin Wendler/NHPA

THEN & NOW

This map shows the comparative distribution of the puma in 1900 and in 1990.

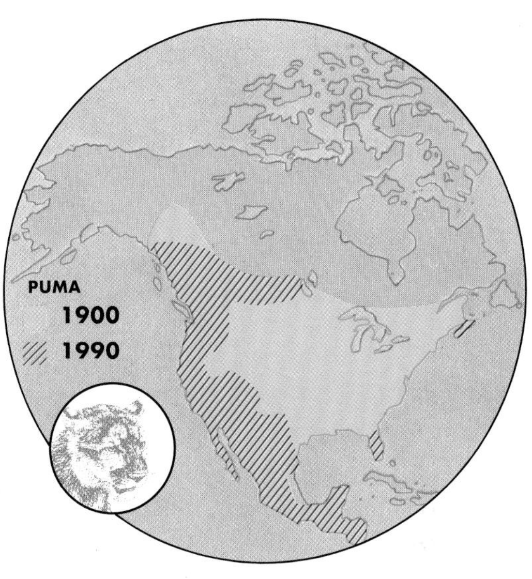

The march of human civilization is the principal reason for the considerable contraction of the ranges of the puma.

Pumas came into conflict with man when man wanted to cultivate "puma country," and the cats—seen as predators of domestic livestock—were killed in the thousands. Soon they withdrew into the more rugged, inhospitable parts of their terrain, where man had not yet penetrated. They have disappeared from huge areas across the central and eastern United States. In other places, populations became more and more isolated from one another as their ranges were split up by great cultivated tracts of land. This can have a detrimental effect on a species, reducing the number of animals available for breeding and eventually forcing them out of their natural cover in search of mates.

The lynx—another solid-colored cat whose coat, therefore, is not considered particularly valuable to the fur trade—has also been affected mainly by the spread of agriculture and human civilization. It has disappeared from much of its most southerly ranges and is thought to be extinct in many former areas where human population is now widespread. Again, its range has become considerably fragmented, leading to small, isolated populations.

its fur will not always match that of another animal, even of the same species. Because the international fur trade was prepared to pay so much, cats have been killed indiscriminately and in huge numbers, so populations have become smaller and smaller and more widely dispersed. It is feared that some species may never recover from this.

THE FATE OF THE PUMA

The fate of the puma has followed a somewhat different course across its range. It has been persecuted by humans not for its valuable fur, but because it has been seen as a threat to domestic animals, apparently finding them easy prey. It was

THE PUMA WAS REGARDED AS A THREAT TO DOMESTIC LIVESTOCK BY EARLY SETTLERS IN THE UNITED STATES

also seen as a competitor for deer and other game. Wherever humans settled in "puma country" the two came into conflict, and humans invariably won.

The principal way of hunting the puma was with dogs, chasing the cat until it took refuge in a tree, where it became an easy target for the gunman. At least until the 1960s, farmers and ranchers considered pumas little better than vermin and shot or poisoned them mercilessly in the thousands. The bobcat, with which the puma shares a lot of its range, suffered a similar fate. At one time both animals carried a price on their heads and so attracted bounty hunters.

It seems that the result of this kind of killing was to almost eliminate the puma from everywhere north of Mexico except in the mountainous parts of the west, as well as in southern Texas and Florida. The puma was pushed into ever

MOST STATES NOW GIVE THE PUMA PROTECTED STATUS, BUT IN A FEW HUNTING THEM IS STILL PERMITTED

more remote regions, isolating small populations.

Eventually different states began to initiate protective action. Not everyone agreed with this, and killing continued. In California, for example, bounty hunting of the puma continued until the early 1960s. Then, in 1963, as people began to show concern for its fate, even fearing it may become extinct in this state, it was designated a nongame animal. Since that time, however, this status has been subject to constant change, with two official bodies taking opposing views.

The California Department of Fish and Game

David Middleton/NHPA

HIGHWAYS AND HABITATS

Much of the puma's—and other small cats'—demise over former ranges has been through loss of habitat, mainly cleared for agriculture. The ocelot, too, suffered through habitat loss in the United States—in Texas, in particular, where much of the brush country that it favored was cleared.

It is loss of habitat, rather than hunting, that mainly accounted for the serious plight of the puma in Florida, where it is called the Florida panther. However, this is one of the states that has gone out of its way to try and preserve the species. Besides giving protection and making people aware of it, Florida has also set up wildlife crossings beneath stretches of the interstate route between Fort Lauderdale and Naples. This enormous highway cuts right through what was thought to be one of the last remaining habitats of the Florida panther. Very few have been killed on the highway since it was built in the 1960s. The wildlife crossings have cost millions of dollars.

In South America, habitat loss for the small cats is equally if not more devastating. Many of them are inhabitants of the rain forest, and it is this habitat that is among the most threatened of all. The Amazon and Orinoco Basins of South America constitute some of the main concentrations of tropical rain forest left in the world, yet they have already been massively exploited. In 1987 alone, Brazil burned an area of forest almost equal to the size of Austria. Since then protective measures have caused a significant drop

CONSERVATION MEASURES

Small cats that live in rain-forest areas are particularly vulnerable. Described as the lungs of the world, these forests are being felled at an alarming rate.

- A study undertaken in 1987 concluded that over one million species of animals and plants found exclusively in tropical rain forests are likely to become extinct over the next 15 years.

in forest clearing, and it is currently estimated that Brazil will lose only about 8 percent of its rain forests over the final two decades of this century. Eight percent, however, actually means 243,240 sq miles (630,000 sq km)—an area equivalent to three medium-sized European countries.

To many of South America's small cats, forest trees are a vital component of their habitat. If the forests disappear, the cats will disappear with them, for they will not survive in a different environment—even presuming there is somewhere else for them to go.

David Middleton/NHPA

WHOLESALE CLEARING OF FORESTS HAS LED TO CONSIDERABLE LOSS OF PRECIOUS HABITAT.

• It has been estimated that a typical 4-sq-mile (10-sq-km) patch of rain forest is home to 1,500 species of flowering plants, 750 species of trees, 125 species of mammals, 400 species of birds, 100 species of reptiles, and 60 species of amphibians.

ENDANGERED • ENVIRONMENT •

SMALL CATS IN DANGER

THE CHART BELOW SHOWS HOW THE INTERNATIONAL UNION FOR THE CONSERVATION OF NATURE (IUCN), OR THE WORLD CONSERVATION UNION, CLASSIFIES THE STATUS OF THE PUMA, THE OCELOT, THE MARGAY, AND THE JAGUARUNDI:

PUMA	ENDANGERED THESE SUBSPECIES ARE ENDANGERED: FLORIDA PANTHER EASTERN PANTHER
OCELOT	VULNERABLE
MARGAY	VULNERABLE
JAGUARUNDI	INDETERMINATE

ENDANGERED MEANS THAT THE ANIMAL'S SURVIVAL IS UNLIKELY UNLESS STEPS ARE TAKEN TO SAVE IT. *VULNERABLE* INDICATES THAT THE ANIMAL IS LIKELY TO MOVE INTO THE ENDANGERED CATEGORY IF THINGS CONTINUE AS THEY ARE. *INDETERMINATE* MEANS THAT IT IS KNOWN THAT THE ANIMAL IS ENDANGERED, VULNERABLE, OR RARE BUT THERE IS INSUFFICIENT INFORMATION TO SAY WHICH CATEGORY IS APPROPRIATE.

Topham Picture Source

recommends that there should be regulated hunting of pumas, claiming that the population has more than doubled since the early 1970s and that some control is necessary in order to protect human property and lives. The Mountain Lion Preservation Foundation, on the other hand, opposes all hunting of the puma in California. In 1990 the people of California voted to ban puma hunting for sport. In 1992 there were an estimated 5,000 pumas in the wild, roaming up and down the coastal mountains, as well as in Sierra Nevada and southeast deserts. The state has pledged to spend $30 million annually for the next 30 years to protect the habitats of pumas, deer, and other endangered species.

Today, the killing of pumas is regulated in just about every state where it is still found, except for Texas, which still allows it to be killed at any time. In the many national parks and preserves where it is found, it is protected, although this was not always so (see page 1795). The result of this, some people say, is that pumas are beginning to make a comeback, repopulating former habitats, particularly in the west. Other people, however, remain pessimistic about the fate of this cat in much of the United States—especially in the east, where there are apparently few pumas in spite of the fact that there is still a considerable amount of suitable habitat.

The most southerly home of the puma is at the tip of South America in the Torres del Paine National Park, described as a United Nations biosphere preserve in southern Chile's portion of Patagonia. Covering an area of 935 sq miles (2,420 sq km), this is also home to Geoffroy's cat. The park is not actually part of the puma's natural habitat, but in recent years it has gained an impressive stronghold in the preserve.

The puma that roams the Torres del Paine National Park is sometimes given subspecies status, (see also Into the Future, page 1795). Known as the Patagonia puma (*F. c. patagonica*), it is also reckoned to be one of the largest pumas to be found anywhere across the range.

As in many places, pumas in Chile have not always been welcomed by humans. Earlier this century, the country was covered by huge ranches, each one of which would employ one or two *leoneros*—hunters paid to keep the puma population in check to protect the domestic livestock.

Now, not only have many of these large ranches been broken up, but in 1980 the killing of pumas was prohibited by law in Chile. The ranchers say they still suffer losses from the pumas in the area. Conservationists, however, view the recovery of the puma in this area as a triumph for South American wildlife conservation in a continent that has been slow in its conservation approaches.

Martin Wendler/NHPA

The keeping of pumas as pets is now discouraged by local, state, and federal laws.

Rod Williams/Bruce Coleman Ltd.

The shy pampas cat now numbers fewer than 10,000 animals.

Topham Picture Source

ALONGSIDE MAN

A MAN-KILLER?

Although a powerful predator, a puma, like most wild animals, would normally retreat from people rather than attack them. However, they sometimes encroach on densely populated towns. When this happens, wildlife protection officers are called in and often end up having to shoot the animal *(left)*.

In the last hundred years, there have been less than sixty recorded attacks on humans in the United States and Canada, of which nine were fatal. Californian biologist, Paul Beier, who has made a study of attacks by pumas on people, points out that about forty people in the United States die each year from bee stings and double that number from lightning strikes, which perhaps puts some perspective on the small number of attacks by pumas.

INTO THE FUTURE

Despite intense controversy, at the beginning of the 1990s the Florida Panther Interagency Committee approved a breeding program to attempt to raise animals that could be released into the wild. While some people saw this as a way to preserve the animals, others felt it was too risky to remove from the wild the animals that would take part in the program.

In 1991 six kittens of known parentage were captured in the wild. The intention was to mate them with kittens that possess different genetic traits. The offspring from these matings have already been released in selected areas across their range.

The puma in Florida, known, too, as the Florida panther, is given subspecies status by some experts who classify it as *Felis concolor corvi*. Other subspecies are the eastern cougar, *F. c. cougar*, which ranges from eastern Texas to Florida, and *F. c. costaricensis* of Central America. All of these are listed as endangered. Geneticists still disagree about whether the subspecies are really one and the same with the puma, *F. concolor*.

PREDICTION

FASHION FURS

Unless countries forbid the trapping or killing of cats for their fur, or for sport, the small cat populations will continue to drop. Particularly badly affected are the cats with patterned coats, such as the ocelot.

THE JAGUARUNDI

The jaguarundi has fur of poor quality, making it of little value to the fur trade, and yet this weasel-like cat has still suffered enormous losses from its population. In fact, in an area from southern Texas and Arizona to Panama, it has become almost extinct. Within this range, some people recognize four subspecies of jaguarundi, all of which are listed as endangered.

Its demise has been brought about by several factors: It has been hunted by humans for sport; killed by farmers because they fear it may prey on their livestock; and its natural habitat has been destroyed, either to cultivate the land or to erect dwellings for fast-growing human populations.

YELLOWSTONE PARK

Established in 1872, Yellowstone National Park is America's oldest national park. It is also the largest—at 3,636 sq mi (9,417 sq km), it is about three times the size of Rhode Island. It has some 400 miles (650 km) of roads and 1,000 miles (1,600 km) of trails and is blessed with a diversity of carnivores. Certainly when it was first established, grizzly bears were one of its main attractions. It is now also home to a wide diversity of deer. It had a number of pumas at the beginning, but federal policy decreed in the early 1900s that large predators were to be killed in order to protect the other species.

Soon after the puma was given protection, it returned to an area just north of the park. By 1972 there were thought to be eighteen or so resident adult pumas actually in the park. Despite its vast size, only about 200 sq miles (518 sq km) of territory is considered to be suitable winter habitat for pumas.

PETS IN THE WILD

Besides sightings of the native species of wildcat,* Felis silvestris*, there have been numbers of reported sightings over the last decade of other larger wildcats, such as pumas, in Great Britain. At first the sightings were thought to be rumored, but many of these have now been substantiated: Wildcats of various species are undoubtedly roaming in parts of the countryside.

This situation is thought to have come about as a result of the 1976 Dangerous Animals Act, which introduced stringent regulations about the keeping of large wild animals in domestic situations. Unable to meet the demands of the act, and unwilling to put the animals down, it is thought that people simply released their one-time pets into the wild. Sightings have been reported in County Durham and on Exmoor and Dartmoor. It has been confirmed that the cats are surviving well—and breeding.

Illustrations Joanne Cowne

RABBITS

RELATIONS

Rabbits belong to the order Lagomorpha. There are two families in this order with eleven genera and fifty-eight species. Other members of the order include:

JACK RABBITS
HARES
PIKAS
SNOWSHOE HARE

Rabbits and hares are so closely related that it is difficult to classify them. The four species of rockhare, for instance, are usually described with rabbits.

Jane Burton/Bruce Coleman Ltd.

SHORT BUT SWEET

FEW RABBITS SURVIVE FOR MORE THAN A YEAR IN THE WILD, BUT DESPITE THIS THEY ARE AMONG THE MOST SUCCESSFUL ANIMALS ON EARTH

As the shadows lengthen at the field's edge, the rabbits emerge to feed. Creeping forward in the fading light, they work their way into a crop of newly sprouted wheat, nibbling off the succulent shoots and chewing them to a pulp. Their long ears twitch, listening. Occasionally one sits up on its hind legs to check the terrain with its big, high-set eyes, then settles down again. The rabbits creep on, nibbling, nibbling. Then they freeze. There is a fast, muffled drumming and the nibblers sprint for cover, their white tails flashing in the gloom. They vanish into their bolt-holes and wait for the danger to pass. It may be a false alarm, but the rabbits will not take the risk. Life is short enough.

Almost defenseless, highly edible, and fast breeding, rabbits might have been designed as ideal prey. Capable of living on vegetation that is inedible to most animals, they convert it into fast food for a host of carnivores ranging from weasels to wolves.

Rabbits belong to the order Lagomorpha, along with hares and pikas. Pikas belong to the family Ochotonidae and rabbits and hares belong to the family Leporidae, of which there are a total of forty-seven species in eleven genera. Rabbits are classified as follows:

ORDER

Lagomorpha

(pikas, rabbits, and hares)

FAMILY

Leporidae

(rabbits and hares)

GENERA

ten

SPECIES

twenty-four

Species include:

European rabbit
Amami rabbit
Bunyoro rabbit
Volcano rabbit
thirteen species of cottontails

Yet although each individual rabbit is lucky to survive for more than a year before it becomes part of the food chain, most rabbit species are thriving. The European rabbit is so numerous that it is regarded as a major pest—despite having been almost wiped out in the 1950s by a killer disease. Clearly rabbits have hit upon a formula for success. The origins of this formula are a mystery.

THE SOLES OF THE RABBIT'S FEET ARE COVERED WITH HAIR TO ABSORB THE IMPACT OF RUNNING ON HARD GROUND

Together with hares and pikas, rabbits form an order of 58 species known as the lagomorphs—which means "harelike." Superficially they resemble the rodents, a vast group of over 1,700 species that includes the rats, mice, squirrels, and cavies, and at one time they were classified in the same order. Like rodents they are small to medium-sized gnawing mammals with chisellike front teeth that grow constantly to compensate for wear and, like rodents, they have lost the sharp canine teeth that are so important to many carnivores, such as cats and dogs. But they seem to have acquired these

Gerrad Lacz/NHPA

European rabbits being reared for the table. All domesticated rabbits descend from this species.

PANORAMIC VIEW

Ian Beames/Ardea

The rabbit's side-mounted eyes give it a virtually all-around view. This is achieved at the expense of the binocular vision that allows animals with forward-pointing eyes to see in depth. Because of this a rabbit lives in a largely two-dimensional world, but this is not necessarily a disadvantage. An enemy may be more conspicuous if it is moving through a landscape that appears flat and two-dimensional, giving the rabbit more time to bolt.

adaptations coincidentally. Blood analysis indicates that the lagomorphs are no more closely related to rodents than to any other mammals, and there are distinct physical differences.

Lagomorphs have an extra pair of "peg teeth" in the top jaw, behind the main incisors, something that does not occur in any rodent. All the teeth have a full coating of enamel, whereas rodent incisors are only enamel coated on the front. These differences may seem minor, but they appear in fossil skulls dating from over 45 million years ago, showing that the lagomorph line was flourishing at least 40 million years before primitive humans began walking on two feet. These early remains

Before leaving the burrow, a rabbit will stop and sniff the air for the scent of enemies.

Ian Beames/Ardea

are almost as specialized as those of modern lagomorphs, so we can only guess at their ancestry. They might have evolved from insect-eaters like shrews, or from primitive grazing animals like tapirs. Until someone finds some even older remains, we will probably never know.

By 30 million years ago there were recognizable rabbits nibbling the grasses of North America, and the leporid line has since developed into two branches: the rabbits and the hares. Essentially hares are bigger, faster animals adapted to life in the open; they depend on their ability to outrun their enemies and rarely take refuge underground. Rabbits are more compact, less athletic creatures adapted for burrowing; they rely on their bolt-holes for security, and rarely stray far from them. So although hares may feed in the middle of a large open space, rabbits will nearly always feed at the edge, close to their refuges.

Both rabbits and hares have acute senses for detecting predators. The ears of a rabbit are its most conspicuous feature; long and mobile, they are capable of picking up the slightest sound and detecting its precise direction—so the rabbit always knows which way to run.

Its eyes are equally efficient. Large and sensitive, they are adapted to work well in dim light, and being mounted high up on the sides of its head, they provide virtually all-around vision, all the time.

A rabbit's sense of smell is also an important aid to survival. Its slitlike nostrils are shielded by folds of skin, and as it feeds, a rabbit will often test the air for the scent of danger by "winking" these folds to expose the highly sensitive nasal membranes beneath. The slightest hint of an alien scent will put the rabbit on full alert, ready to run for cover.

Although not the fastest of animals, the rabbit is quick enough to gain the safety of a bolt-hole before a predator can cut off its retreat. It propels itself with its long hind legs, and in a more relaxed mood will often use both feet together to hop from place to place. ■

ANCESTORS

Ancestral rabbits were feeding on the grasslands of western North America during the Oligocene period, from 24 to 37 million years ago. Virtually complete fossil skeletons of an animal known as *Palaeolagus* (pale-ee-o-LAEG-us) have been found in rocks laid down during this period, and they are so like the bones of modern rabbits that we can assume the living animals looked much the same. The hind limbs are shorter, however, indicating that the rabbit's ability to leap and run fast has evolved more recently.

THE RABBITS' FAMILY TREE

This family tree shows how the rabbits, hares, and pikas are related to each other. The rabbit and hare family, Leporidae, can be divided into two groups. One group (genus Lepus*) includes jackrabbits and hares. The other group consists of the ten genera of rabbits, six of which at various times were thought to be hares. These are the bushman, hispid, Sumatran, and three species of red "rockhare."*

COTTONTAILS

(Genus *Sylvilagus*)

There are thirteen species in this genus. Most species are common.

European rabbit

Oryctolagus cuniculus
(o-RICK-to-lay-gus kah-NICK-yoo-lus)

The European, or common, rabbit is the only species in the genus.

Other genera species:
Amami rabbit
Bunyoro rabbit
Volcano rabbit

Pikas

(twenty-one species)

Hares

(twenty-three species)

Lagomorphs

(Rabbits, hares, and pikas)

All illustrations Chris Turnball/Wildlife Art Agency

ANATOMY: THE RABBIT

The rabbit** (above center) **ranges in size from 10 to 11.5 in (25–29 cm) in the pygmy rabbit to 17–20 in (43–51 cm) in the Amami rabbit. Hares are larger** (top left) **and have bigger ears. Pikas** (top right) **are much smaller. The largest pika measures about 8 in (20 cm).

RABBIT'S TRACKS

When hopping or running, the hind feet fall almost level with the forefeet to give a uniform track pattern. When running, the European rabbit can reach speeds of 24 mph (39 km/h), which is about half the speed of a brown hare.

Simon Turvey/ Wildlife Art Agency

The structure of the skeleton shows how the curving spine and long hind feet enable the rabbit to propel its body forward, often using the two feet together.

The rabbit's hind legs are made for bounding. The long, flat feet give it a good grip on hard ground. On snow the feet act like snowshoes.

X-ray illustrations Elisabeth Smith

FACT FILE:

THE EUROPEAN RABBIT

CLASSIFICATION

GENUS: *ORYCTOLAGUS*

SPECIES: *CUNICULUS*

SIZE

LENGTH/MALE: UP TO 20 IN (51 CM)

WEIGHT/MALE: UP TO 6.6 LB (3 KG)

WEIGHT AT BIRTH: 1.4 OZ (40 G)

FEMALES ARE SMALLER THAN MALES, WITH NARROWER HEADS

COLORATION

GRAYISH WITH A BROWN TINGE ABOVE, PARTICULARLY AT NAPE; LIGHT GRAY BELOW

TAIL: BLACK ABOVE, WHITE BENEATH

DARK PATCHES AROUND EYES

LONG CLAWS FOR DIGGING

FEATURES

LONG, MOBILE EARS

HIGH-SET EYES ON SIDE OF HEAD

LONG HIND LEGS AND HOPPING GAIT

"POWDER-PUFF" TAIL FLASHES WHITE DURING FLIGHT

THE EARS

The rabbit's hearing is its most important sense. Its ears are fairly mobile and can turn toward sounds or lie back for running.

THE FUR

density varies between species and climate. The European rabbit has a dense winter coat.

HINDQUARTERS

are powerful and enable the rabbit to change direction rapidly when it is being chased by predators.

THE TAIL

is short, leaving nothing for a chasing, outstretched predator to grab while pursuing the rabbit.

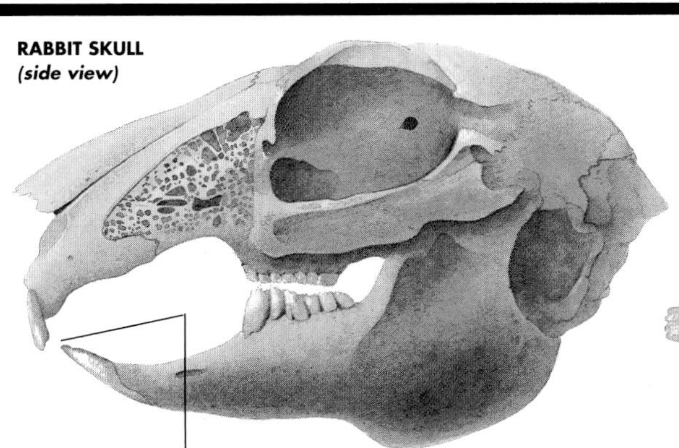

UNDERSIDE OF UPPER SKULLS

RABBIT *(below)* HARE *(right)*

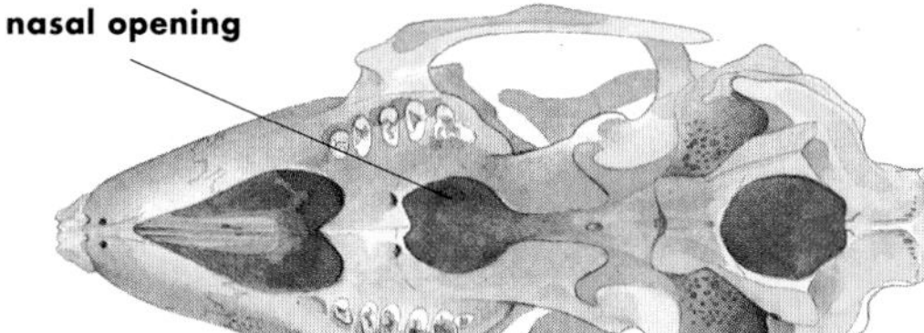

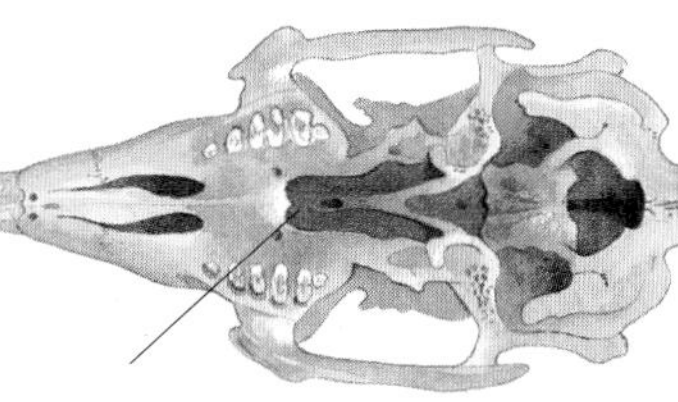

In the hare the rear nasal opening is much larger than the rabbit's. This is because the hare is a long-distance runner while the rabbit runs for short distances.

THE SHY SURVIVOR

TIMID AND VULNERABLE, THE RABBIT IS THE STAPLE PREY OF A HOST OF PREDATORS. IT MUST STAY CONSTANTLY ALERT TO SURVIVE

Head down, nibbling at the grass, a rabbit looks like an easy target for any predator. A fox, perhaps, padding softly through the shadows; a lynx crouched in the undergrowth; a buzzard circling overhead. There are hungry eyes everywhere, and the rabbit knows it; the awareness dominates its life. Food is easy to find—it grows all around; shelter is a quick sprint away. Social conflicts or sexual advances may distract it briefly, but a rabbit's main concern is staying alive.

Even with its head in the grass it is on the alert. Those long ears are not for show; they constantly monitor the tapestry of sound for approaching danger. Even if there is no hint of a threat, it will stop feeding at intervals and scan all around to make sure nothing is amiss. It cannot afford to take risks.

In gregarious species such as the European rabbit, one individual may briefly stand sentry for all; if it detects danger, it drums on the ground with its powerful hind legs to warn the others. Even if it

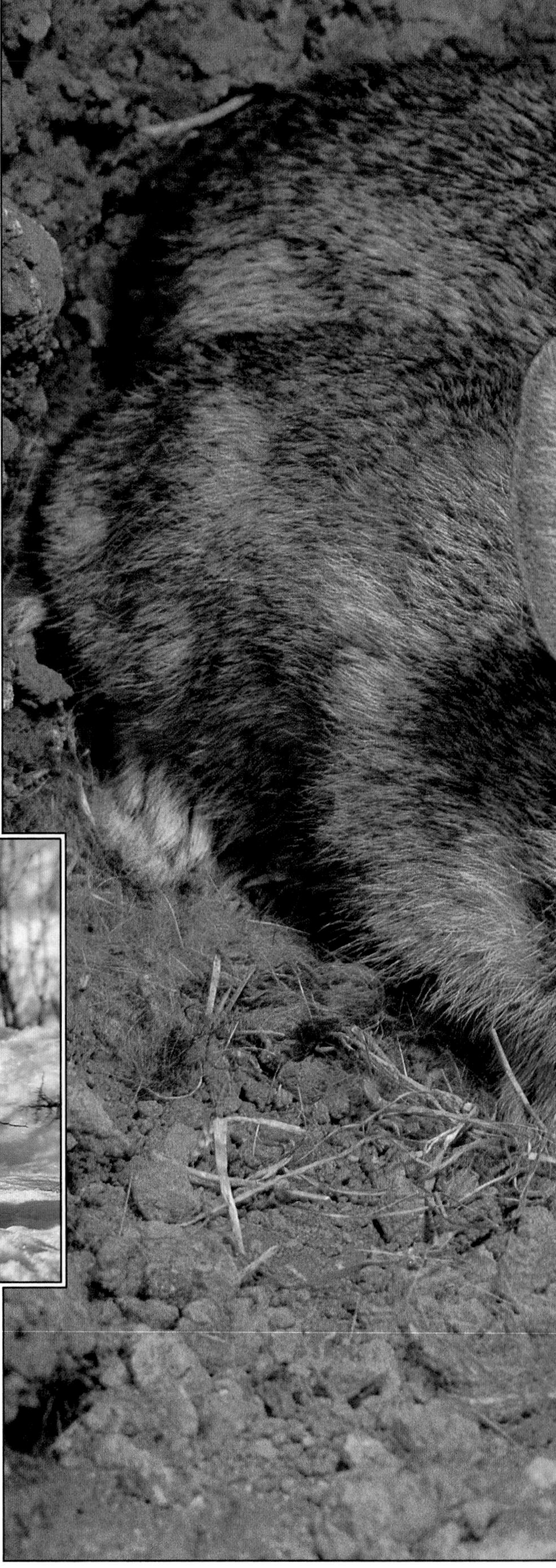

Once confined to a fairly small area of the world, the European rabbit (right) *has been widely introduced by humans to new areas, which it has successfully colonized.*

John Snow/NHPA

There are thirteen species of cottontails distributed in the United States. This one—the mountain cottontail (above)*—occurs in southwestern Canada and in the western United States.*

Michael Leach/NHPA

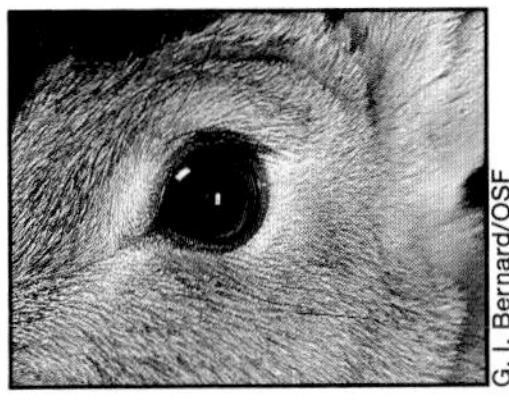
G. I. Bernard/OSF

The bright eyes of rabbits are situated on the sides of the head to give the widest possible field of vision.

Constantly twitching, a rabbit's nose is very sensitive and helps to alert it to danger.

G. I. Bernard/OSF

G. I. Bernard/OSF

The hind legs are longer than the front legs; strong muscles account for the rabbit's characteristic hop.

simply runs, its bobbing white tail flashes a warning—one which rabbits, with their wide field of vision, are well equipped to register even if they are facing the other way.

The risk of being eaten also determines a rabbit's daily routine. On some islands where they have few enemies they feed freely in broad daylight and people can approach them easily. Rabbits that have become naturalized in virtually predator-free countries such as New Zealand show the same boldness. But in areas where danger lurks behind every bush, they prefer to stay out of sight during the day, and only emerge to feed at dusk. In regions where they are at considerable risk, they may even avoid bright moonlight; the darker the night, the bolder they become.

THE SLIGHTEST NOISE TRIGGERS A RABBIT'S DEFENSIVE INSTINCT, CAUSING IT TO RUN FOR COVER INSTANTLY

Apart from its natural caution and acute senses, a rabbit's main defense against predation is its high breeding rate. In their native habitats few rabbits survive for long, but during their short lives they reproduce so rapidly that, even allowing for high infant mortality, there are always new recruits to replace the casualties. So although an individual rabbit may lose the battle for survival quite quickly, its genetic line may flourish for centuries. Ultimately this is what counts, and in this respect the timid, apparently defenseless rabbits are less vulnerable than awesome predators like tigers and wolves, which have no natural enemies at all. ■

HABITATS

Rabbits are normally associated with open grassland in mild areas where the soil is friable enough for easy burrowing, but they are found in a wide variety of habitats ranging from dense forests to deserts. The marsh rabbit, one of the cottontails of the Americas, lives in the coastal swamps of Florida, the Carolinas, and southern Virginia, and like the swamp rabbit of the central southern states, it is a strong swimmer. By contrast its close relative, the desert cottontail, has become adapted to life in the deserts of Utah, Nevada, California, and Mexico. The endangered Amami rabbit is restricted to dense forest on two of the Japanese Amami islands in the East China Sea, while the eastern cottontail is found in every kind of habitat over a vast range from Venezuela to Quebec.

The species with the largest range is the European rabbit. Originally a native of Spain, Portugal, and North Africa, it was adopted by the Romans, who found it excellent eating, and easy to maintain in captivity. Rabbits were kept in pens, where they formed breeding colonies, and wherever the Romans went, the rabbits went too.

In the Middle Ages the monks of northern Europe revived this idea, creating artificial warrens for imported rabbits on areas of light soil suitable for burrowing. Naturally, some rabbits managed to escape and breed in the wild, but the local predators and the rigors of the northern climate kept them in check. For an animal originally adapted to life under the Mediterranean sun, the cold, wet winters of northern Europe were a severe discouragement. Even today rabbits will stay in their burrows for days at a time during periods of heavy rain, strong winds, or falling snow.

Had the landscape remained in its medieval state, the European rabbit would probably never have flourished in the way that it has. For three hundred years after the breakdown of the warren system,

Frances Furlong/Survival Anglia

Ideally, rabbits like to dig their burrows in soft, light soils, often in a bank or on a slope.

KEY FACTS

- **Rabbits' teeth keep growing regardless of the rate of wear; if they do not grind against each other properly, they may grow faster than they wear down. Occasionally rabbits are found with front teeth that have grown into long, curved tusks; unable to feed properly, these unfortunates usually starve to death.**

- **European rabbits will occasionally eat worms, snails, and even insects if they get the chance.**

- **Rabbits prefer to graze short turf; lush vegetation makes their fur wet—which rabbits hate.**

BURROW

The European rabbit digs a complex warren with nest chambers, sleeping quarters, and escape routes.

Illustration Clive Pritchard/Wildlife Art Agency

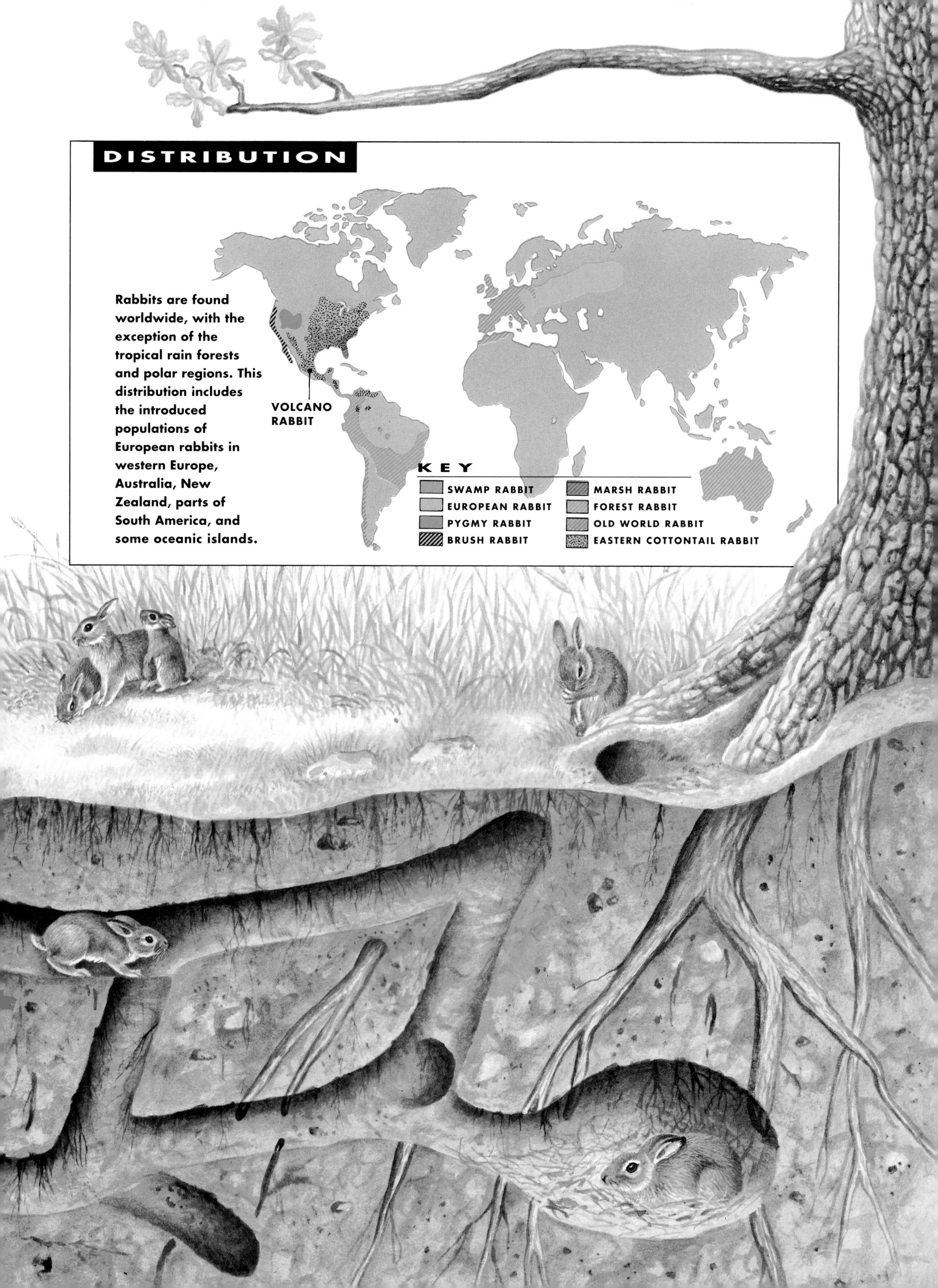
DISTRIBUTION
Rabbits are found worldwide, with the exception of the tropical rain forests and polar regions. This distribution includes the introduced populations of European rabbits in western Europe, Australia, New Zealand, parts of South America, and some oceanic islands.
VOLCANO RABBIT
KEY
SWAMP RABBIT
EUROPEAN RABBIT
PYGMY RABBIT
BRUSH RABBIT
MARSH RABBIT
FOREST RABBIT
OLD WORLD RABBIT
EASTERN COTTONTAIL RABBIT

rabbits were living wild on the grasslands of northern Europe, but they were never more than a picturesque addition to the wildlife. But the 18th century saw a dramatic increase in agricultural productivity, particularly in England, where farmers had begun to plant winter arable crops on their land instead of letting it lie fallow for several months. The sudden abundance of succulent winter food was exactly what the rabbits needed, and the result was a population explosion.

By the 1850s there were rabbits everywhere in Britain, and before long they had spread throughout Europe to southern Scandinavia, Poland, and the Ukraine. Meanwhile, the British colonists had introduced them to Australia, New Zealand, several oceanic islands—for the benefit of shipwrecked sailors—and Chile, in the belief that they would be an entertaining source of sport and meat. As a result, they overran many areas, particularly in Australia, where the climate suited them and they had no natural predators. They stripped the pastures, demolished young pine plantations, encouraged soil erosion, and undermined long sections of the transcontinental railway. The farming economies of Australia and New Zealand were crippled, and many farmers had to abandon sheep and try to earn a living from rabbits instead.

In the 1950s the world population of the European rabbit was virtually annihilated by myxomatosis—a killer virus deliberately introduced as a means of pest control. Very few survived, but since the initial epidemic the populations have acquired some immunity to the disease and have built up again, although not to the same level. Today the European rabbit is flourishing throughout its range and in many places its impact on the landscape is quite dramatic. They are, for example, largely responsible for the open landscapes of flower-rich turf found along many coastal clifftops. ■

FOCUS ON

THE WILTSHIRE DOWNS

The chalk downland of southern England is traditionally sheep country, and the sweeping expanses of springy turf that still survive are often assumed to be the result of centuries of sheep grazing. To some extent this is true, but the real landscape architects are the rabbits.

We know this because in the mid-1950s the downland rabbits were almost wiped out by the disease myxomatosis, and immediately the landscape started to change. Field margins and lanes became choked with long grass, and the hillsides burst into blossom as a host of wildflowers grew unchecked. Eventually the flowers gave way to bramble, gorse, and hawthorn, and the grassy downs began to turn into scrub woodland.

The process was eventually checked and even reversed by the revival of the rabbit, and today the downland is peppered with rabbit burrows surrounded by close-cropped turf, clumps of ragwort, and elder trees. Downland butterflies such as the common blue feed among the flowering spikes of orchids and the low-growing vetches and trefoils, while anthills provide living lookout posts for watchful rabbits, always alert for the foxes, stoats, and buzzards that constantly threaten to carry them away.

UPLAND REGENERATION

Years	
1	Introduction of Myxomatosis
2	
3	
4-5	
20-30	

Rabbits have shaped the landscape of much down country, nibbling down vegetation to such an extent that nothing remains but low grasses. The chart shows what happened to the downland after the introduction of myxomatosis. Some areas are now rabbit proof.

NEIGHBORS

The rabbit shares its rural habitat with a wide variety of well-known neighbors. As well as fast-moving mammals, the rabbit has to watch out for aerial predators, such as owls.

BADGER

Like the rabbit, the badger is mainly an animal of the night. It will prey on baby rabbits in their burrows.

BARN OWL

The beautiful barn owl is another nocturnal hunter. Small rodents are its principal victims.

Illustrations Kim Thompson

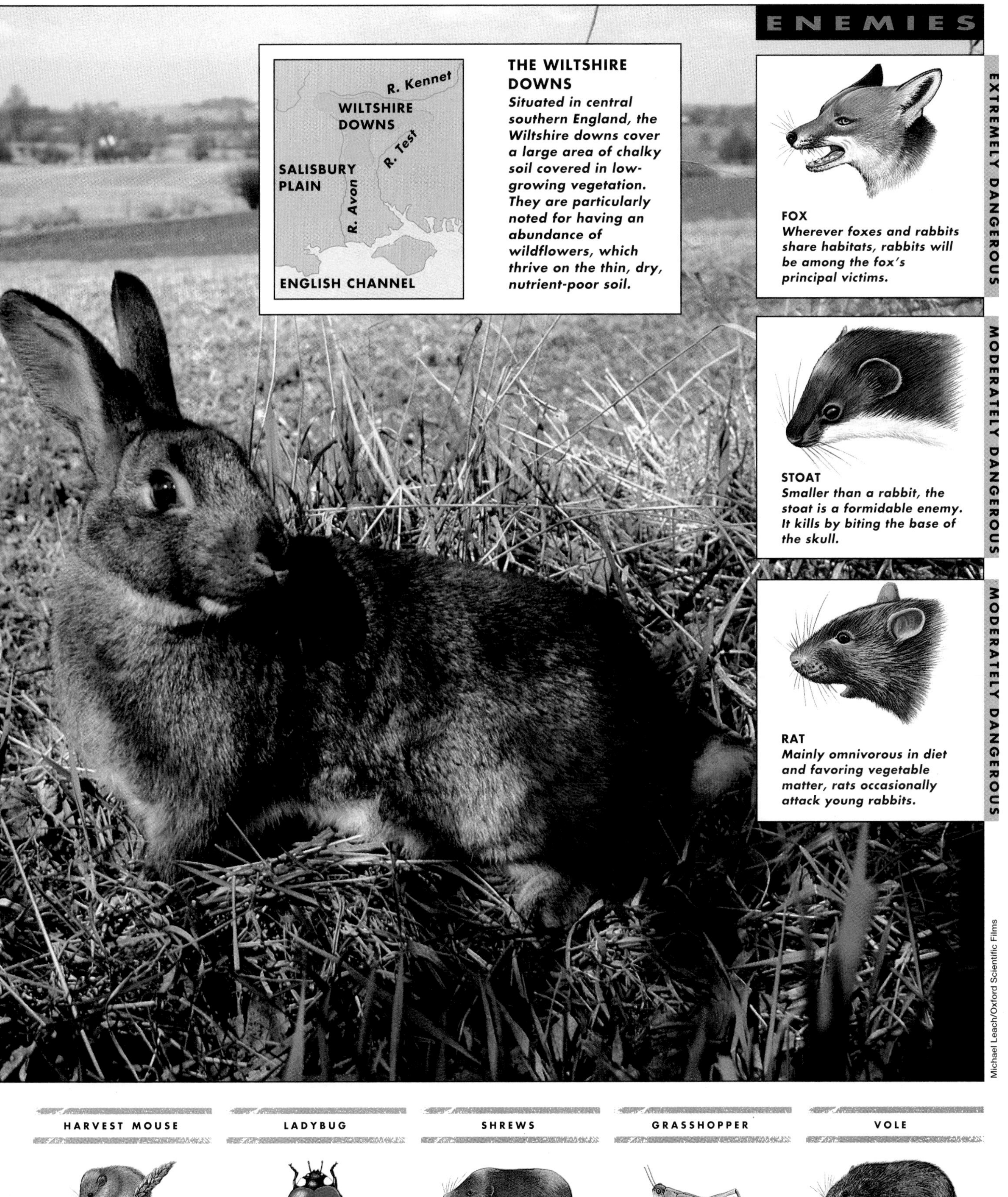

THE WILTSHIRE DOWNS

Situated in central southern England, the Wiltshire downs cover a large area of chalky soil covered in low-growing vegetation. They are particularly noted for having an abundance of wildflowers, which thrive on the thin, dry, nutrient-poor soil.

Michael Leach/Oxford Scientific Films

ENEMIES

EXTREMELY DANGEROUS

FOX
Wherever foxes and rabbits share habitats, rabbits will be among the fox's principal victims.

MODERATELY DANGEROUS

STOAT
Smaller than a rabbit, the stoat is a formidable enemy. It kills by biting the base of the skull.

MODERATELY DANGEROUS

RAT
Mainly omnivorous in diet and favoring vegetable matter, rats occasionally attack young rabbits.

HARVEST MOUSE

Roadside verges and grassy hedgerows are the habitats the harvest mouse and rabbit have in common.

LADYBUG

These brightly colored beetles are inhabitants of the temperate regions of Europe and North America.

SHREWS

Mouselike in appearance, shrews have much longer, more pointed noses. They are very nervous animals.

GRASSHOPPER

The grasshopper's rasping sound is one often associated with grassy areas—the rabbit's home.

VOLE

There are nearly seventy species of voles. They share many habitats with rabbits and are mainly active at night.

FOOD AND FEEDING

All rabbits are strict herbivores, equipped to deal with a wide variety of plant material, much of which is nutritionally useless to most animals. The process starts with the rabbit's teeth.

The main incisors are superbly adapted for the job of gnawing through tough vegetation, and grass in particular. Grass has an armor of silica spicules that acts like sandpaper on the teeth of any animal that eats it; in old age animals such as sheep may starve because their teeth have worn out. The front teeth of rabbits wear just as quickly, but they never wear out because they keep growing.

Each tooth is like a long, curved needle in a curved socket; as the sharp end is worn away, more tooth material is added at the other end, pushing the tooth out further to compensate for the wear. They also never get blunt, because the hard ena-mel on each tooth is thinner at the back and wears down faster than the front, leaving a chisel edge. In this way, the teeth are self-sharpening.

The more conventional cheek teeth are adequate for the job of pulping vegetation, readying it for the stomach juices to get to work on it. This is important; grass and foliage are composed of plant cells which resemble packets of protein encased in tough walls of woody cellulose; the rabbit has to crack through the cellulose to get at the protein.

Once the cell walls are crushed, the protein-rich contents can be digested relatively easily, but to survive on a strictly herbivorous diet, the rabbit must convert the cellulose itself—a very tough, complex carbohydrate—into energy-rich sugars. This is difficult, and other grazing animals such as cattle, sheep, and deer have evolved complex, capacious, multistage digestive systems to do the job. A rabbit's digestive system is relatively simple, so how does it manage?

A RABBIT SUPPLEMENTS ITS LEAFY DIET WITH SEEDS AND ROOTS THAT ARE RICH FOOD SOURCES

KEY FACTS

- **In winter, rabbits will strip the bark from trees, sometimes ringing their trunks and killing them. To prevent this, forestry workers protect the trunks of young trees with plastic sheaths.**
- **Foxes, buzzards, and many other predators rely heavily on rabbits for prey, and when rabbits are abundant, the predators tend to breed more successfully. When the European rabbit was almost wiped out by myxomatosis, many predators declined as well, since they had less food for their young.**

John Cox/Wildlife Art Agency

FOOD

Most rabbits are herbivores, but just occasionally some species include insects and invertebrates in their diet.

WORM

SNAIL

DANDELION

BARLEY

Prey illustrations Craig Robson/Wildlife Art Agency

Frances Furlong/Survival Anglia

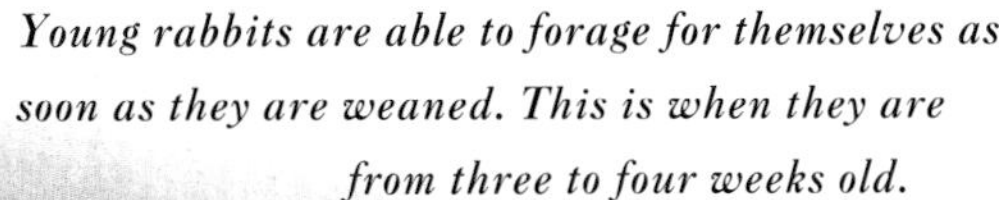

Young rabbits are able to forage for themselves as soon as they are weaned. This is when they are from three to four weeks old.

in SIGHT

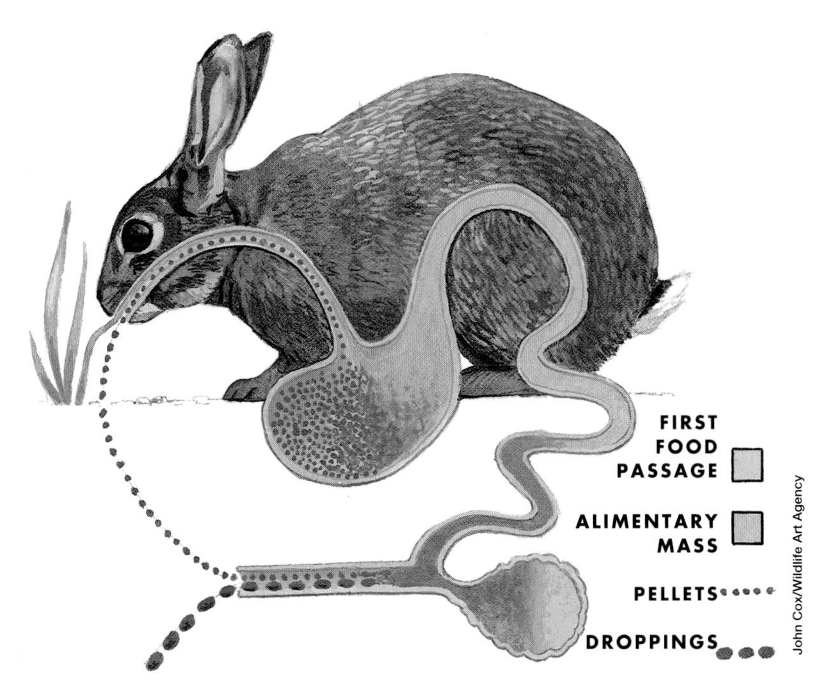

John Cox/Wildlife Art Agency

DOUBLE DIGESTION

The rabbit's habit of eating its own feces may seem revolting, but it makes sense. By the time the bacteria in the cecum have done their work on the rabbit's food, it is rich in vitamin B_{12} and other nutrients; however, it has already passed through the small intestine, which is specially adapted to absorb these nutrients.

The half-processed food emerges as moist, mucus-covered pellets, quite unlike the hard droppings found around the burrows. In nocturnal species the pellets emerge during the day and the rabbit eats them immediately. When all the food value has been extracted, the waste is ejected as hard droppings.

In rabbits, the appendix is enlarged into a stomachlike chamber called the cecum, containing bacteria that ferment the cellulose and break it down into sugars and other nutrients. Some of these can be absorbed directly through the cecum wall, but others pass on down the large intestine and emerge from the rabbit's anus. Rather than waste the nutrients, the rabbit eats them again—a practice known as refection. The nutrients pass into the small intestine, where they are absorbed.

Despite this "double digestion," a rabbit extracts relatively little food value from the plant foliage. It must eat a lot to get sufficient nutrients, so it spends most of its waking hours feeding. ■

EATING HABITS

Rabbits often scratch around in the soil looking for roots and bulbs to eat.

TERRITORY

A rabbit rarely has to forage far afield. Its main food, grass, grows all around. Because of the abundance, a rabbit is not particularly concerned with defending food resources against other rabbits; its main concern is the risk of becoming a food resource itself.

Even on the darkest night a European rabbit will rarely venture more than 650 ft (198 m) from its refuge. It normally stays much closer to home, nibbling its way across the turf in small arcs as it moves its head from side to side. At the slightest alarm, it bolts for cover, emerging, when it feels safe, to start grazing the nearest available patch of grass.

As a result, each rabbit's burrow is surrounded by a roughly circular grazed area, terrain permitting, and the rabbit rarely moves beyond it. Essentially this is the rabbit's home range: the term used to describe the area frequented by any individual animal on a regular basis. The rabbit feeds in this area, but in general it does not defend it against others.

Among rabbits, some species, such as the eastern cottontail, appear to be nonterritorial. Others,

DIGGING BURROWS

In soft soil new burrows are regularly dug but in hard soils the same burrows are used all the time. The different systems affect the behavior of the occupants.

Illustration Joanne Cowne

TYPES OF BURROW

The behavior of the European rabbit varies according to where it lives. In chalk the burrows are in clusters, and fights between females are common. Dune burrows are randomly distributed.

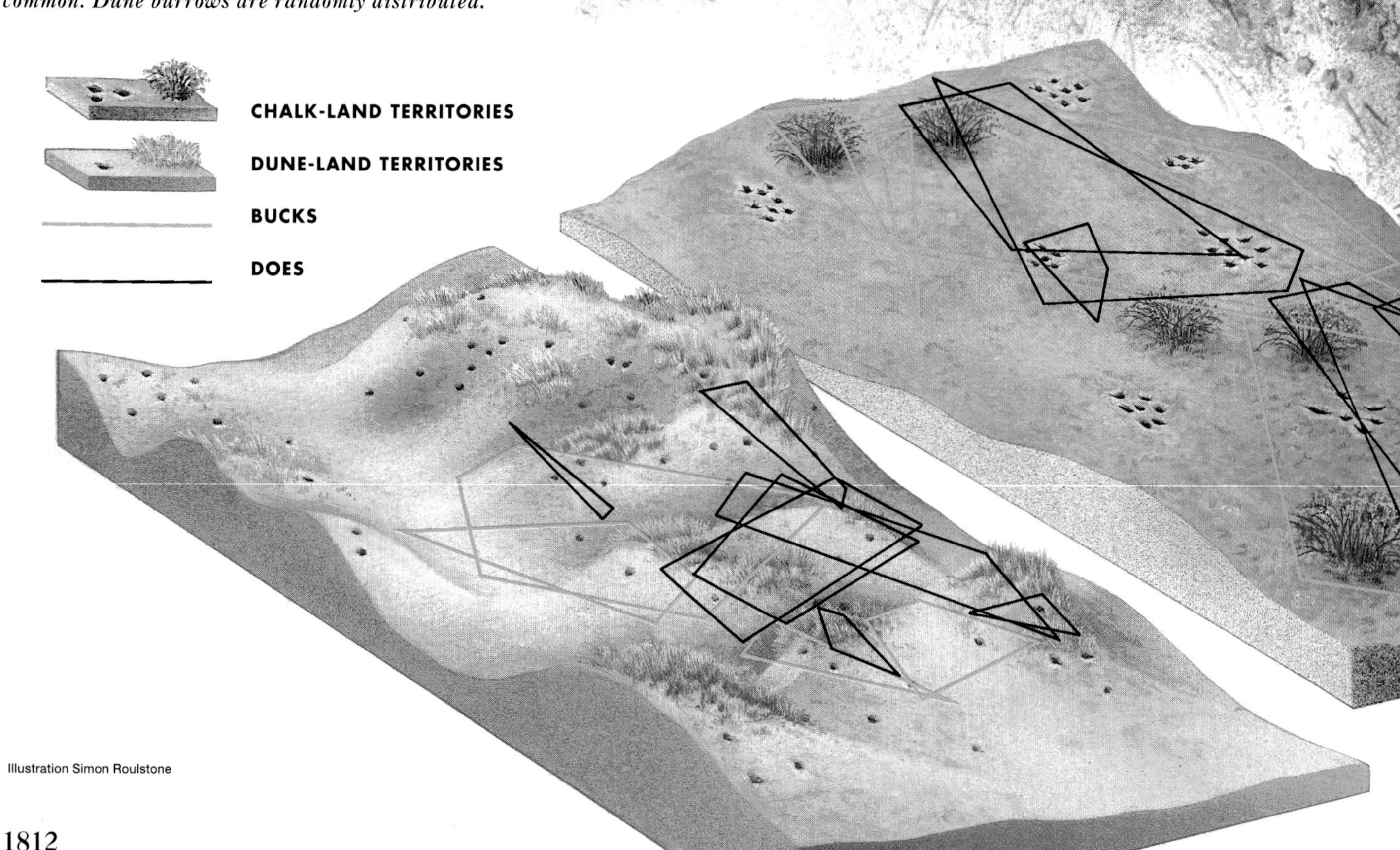

Illustration Simon Roulstone

Stefan Meyers/Ardea

Rabbits graze peacefully near their burrows but they are constantly alert to potential threats. At the first hint of trouble, they all run for cover.

in SIGHT

SCENTS AND SCRAPES

Rabbits mark their territory in several ways. A rabbit has a scent gland under its chin that it uses to mark vegetation—an action known as "chinning"—and it also has scent glands around its anus that perfume its droppings. As a result, it tends to leave its scent wherever it goes, and this may help it identify its home and also discourage trespassers. The droppings are often concentrated at particular points, such as the tops of anthills, and rabbits will also make scrapes in the ground that seem to function as territorial markers. The more dominant the rabbit, the more actively it marks its territory. However, most rabbits are not aggressively territorial; males may become more so in the breeding season.

such as the European rabbit, are highly territorial, but the nature of their territoriality is confusing and seems to vary with habitat.

The European rabbit is a gregarious animal, and until recently most naturalists agreed that it lived in social groups of six to ten adults and their young, occupying a communal burrow system which the rabbits defended as a group territory. On closer examination, however, rabbit society appears to be rather less harmonious.

In habitats where the soil is light and easy to burrow into, individuals tend to space themselves out. Their home ranges may overlap, but each female occupies her own burrow and uses it as a nursery for her young. If necessary she will dig a new burrow, and may even use several on a regular basis—but she will not share them with other females. Males also occupy their own burrows, and generally have larger ranges that may overlap those of several females.

In habitats where space is at a premium or the ground is particularly hard, however, studies have shown the situation to be different. It seems that burrows are excavated in tight, often interconnecting clusters and are the scene of constant low-key conflict. Dominant females occupy the best sites at the heart of the burrow system while their inferiors are often forced to dig short tunnels of their own in the thin, rocky soil. Their home ranges overlap to such an extent that they are virtually superimposed, and there is some territorial conflict near the burrows—yet the rabbits show little inclination to disperse more widely. ■

LIFE CYCLE

Rabbits are notoriously prolific breeders. According to popular mythology a few rabbits could generate enough descendants to overrun the landscape within a matter of months. Unlike most popular myths this is more or less true, but there are good reasons why.

A male rabbit can make no direct contribution to the care of his young. He cannot improve their chances of survival by, say, bringing them better food or teaching them where to graze. For both sexes, the only way they can guarantee the survival of their lineage is by generating a large number of offspring as quickly as possible. Male rabbits try to mate with as many females as possible. Females maximize their reproduction by producing large litters in rapid succession. Life is short and mortality rates are high.

The territory and home range of a male tends to overlap those of several females, and he is aggressive toward rival bucks that try to muscle in on his patch. Yet despite this he does not restrict his activities to an exclusive harem of females; he is a sexual opportunist, prepared to mate with any female that will have him. Studies of blood type among Australian populations of European rabbits have shown that, although a group of females may be dominated by one particular male, at least 16 percent of their young are sired by another.

Obviously this system is highly unstable, and the bucks are continually vying for dominance. They engage in spectacular combats in which they jump high off the ground and attempt to slash each other with their claws. The higher the male's social status, the better his chances of winning—and the better his chances with the females, who instinctively prefer to mate with a strong male because his strength is inherited by their young.

Female rabbits also compete for status, but for

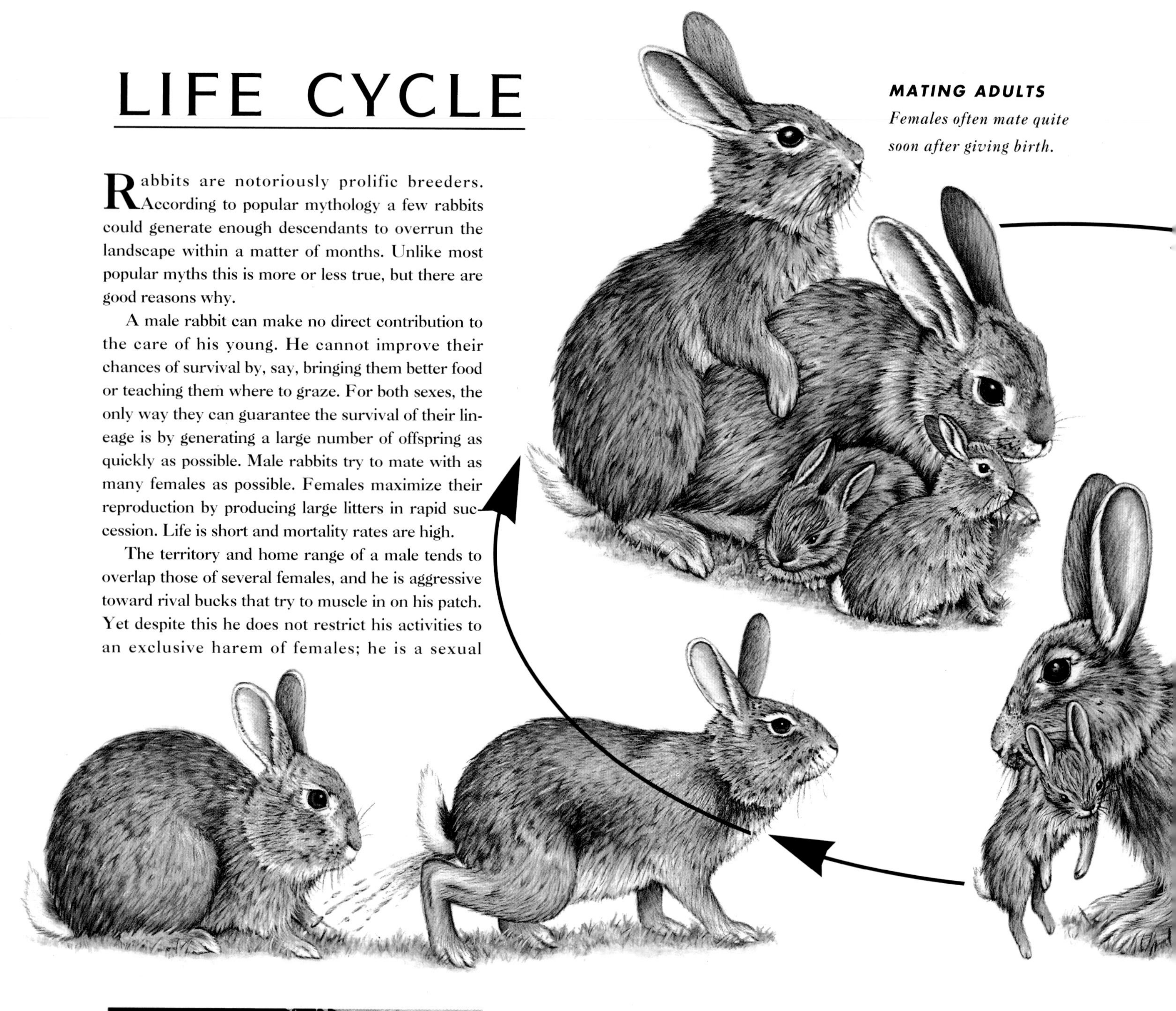

MATING ADULTS
Females often mate quite soon after giving birth.

MALE SPRAYING
Males often spray females with urine just before mating with them. This is done to warn other males to keep away.

AMAZING FACTS

NORTH AND SOUTH

Rabbits produce young at different stages of development, depending on their habitat. Among America's cottontails, the species that live in the north have large litters of relatively underdeveloped young after a short gestation to take maximum advantage of the short breeding season. Species that live in the southern latitudes bear smaller litters of relatively well-developed young after a longer gestation.

GROWING UP

The life of a young rabbit

NEWBORNS IN DEN

Rabbits are born blind, naked, and helpless, but they develop quickly. When they are left alone in the nursery burrow, the mother may cover the entrance.

CARRYING YOUNG

A doe will move her brood if she senses that danger threatens them.

Illustrations Angela Hargreaves/Wildlife Art Agency

William S. Paton/Planet Earth Pictures

FROM BIRTH TO DEATH

EUROPEAN RABBIT

GESTATION: 30 DAYS
LITTER SIZE: 3–7
BREEDING: LATE WINTER AND SPRING
WEIGHT AT BIRTH: 1.4 oz (40 g)
EYES OPEN: AT 10 DAYS
WEANING: 4–5 WEEKS
SEXUAL MATURITY: 5 MONTHS FOR MALES, 3 MONTHS FOR FEMALES
LONGEVITY: 1–2 YEARS; UP TO 10 YEARS IN CAPTIVITY

them the ultimate prize is the best breeding burrow. "Low-status" females often have to make do with short, blind tunnels—known as "stops." Infants born in these are less likely to survive.

Among European rabbits, females become sexually receptive for periods of between twelve and twenty-four hours every seventh day or so during the late winter and spring breeding season, and the males spend much of their time sniffing out receptive females. Having mated, the male makes off quickly to try his luck elsewhere.

Toward the end of her four-week gestation the female lines the nursery with grass and moss. Then about two days before the birth she plucks fur from her underside to make a soft nest for the young, which, in the European rabbit, are born blind, almost naked, and quite helpless. In this the rabbit is unlike its relative the hare, which bears well-developed, active, and alert young after a gestation of some six weeks. The difference reflects the difference in lifestyle: A hare is born in the open and needs to be able to fend for itself, whereas a rabbit is born in a protective burrow.

Despite their helplessness the young are left alone in the burrow for most of the time; indeed, the mother may seal the entrance to their nursery tunnel with earth while she is away feeding. She returns only once a night to suckle them, and then for only five minutes or so. But her milk is rich, and

in SIGHT

REABSORPTION

Bearing young is energy-intensive; if the risk of infant mortality is high, the energy invested in the young may be wasted. In stressful circumstances birth may occur prematurely, with little chance of survival. To prevent this, rabbits have evolved the ability to "resorb" embryos that are developing in the womb. They are broken down into their raw components, which are soaked up by the mother's tissues, so all the nutrients are recycled.

in SIGHT

HIGH-PLACED FRIENDS

During the 19th century, English landowners cursed the rabbit for destroying their crops, without realizing that they themselves were responsible for its proliferation. Besides planting the food it needed to survive the winter, they had almost eradicated the predators—weasels, foxes, stoats, and polecats—that would have held it in check.

the babies develop rapidly. Their eyes open at about ten days old, they are fully furred at two weeks, and they begin to explore the world outside their nursery within eighteen days. At three weeks they leave the nest and begin to sample plant foods.

THE NIBBLING HORDES

Sexual maturity comes early to rabbits. A female is capable of breeding at the age of about sixteen weeks, and since mating stimulates ovulation she is almost bound to conceive. She is quite likely to mate again immediately after giving birth, with the same results. If conditions are ideal she is capable of bearing six litters per year with an average of six young per litter. If only half of these are female, the following year could see the appearance of over six hundred baby rabbits all descended from one female—and if three hundred of these produce

G. I. Bernard/Oxford Scientific Films

At 18 days old, this baby rabbit (above) *is well on its way to becoming completely independent from its mother.*

E. R. Degginger/Oxford Scientific Films

These baby cottontail rabbits (left) *will be ready to leave their cozy nest at twelve to sixteen days old. There are usually about six babies in a litter.*

John Harris/Survival Anglia

Two species of South American rabbit. The Mexican cottontail (top) *is lighter in color than the volcano rabbit* (bottom).

another thirty-six each, there could be over ten thousand of them in all, nibbling at the grass.

But conditions are rarely ideal. Food is frequently short, the stress level is often high, and many litters are resorbed before they come to term. In practice, most female European rabbits bear about ten young per year, and if there is a healthy population of predators in the area, well over three-quarters of these will not survive their first summer.

In its original home in Spain and North Africa, the European rabbit was the staple diet of over forty different predators, including wolves, lynx, wildcats, and eagles, and most rabbit species in their native habitats are subject to a similar level of predation. Among the American cottontails the combination of predation, disease, and adverse climatic conditions accounts for 90 percent of the young born each year, so the legendary breeding potential of the rabbit begins to make sense. An animal that is simply a "walking lunch" for all the predators in its neighborhood must evolve the capacity to breed at a phenomenal rate—or face certain extinction.

But what if there are no predators? In 1859, the owner of Barwon Park in the Australian state of Victoria imported twenty-four wild European rabbits to brighten up the view from his veranda and provide a little sport. Presumably he was a bad shot because they flourished and multiplied. Since the climate was favorable, food was abundant, and there were virtually no native predators in Australia, the rabbits multiplied at something approaching their maximum potential rate: Within a few years their progeny had overrun two-thirds of the continent. The story was to be virtually repeated in New Zealand. ■

G. I. Bernard/Oxford Scientific Films

Rabbits take cover wherever they are when danger lurks. The one above is hiding in a cornfield.

Widely preyed upon by carnivores and birds of prey, the rabbit below has lost its life to a buzzard.

Michael Leach/NHPA

BACK FROM THE BRINK

DESPITE AN EPIDEMIC THAT NEARLY WIPED IT OFF THE FACE OF THE EARTH, THE EUROPEAN RABBIT NOW FLOURISHES IN HUGE NUMBERS, WHILE SOME SPECIES ARE IN DANGER OF EXTINCTION

Few animals know more about survival than the rabbits. For over thirty million years they have lived in the shadow of death, and the remorseless logic of natural selection has insured that all the rabbit species on earth today are superbly equipped to thrive in adversity. A rabbit's body plan, senses, and breeding habits have been defined by the daily threats it faces, with the result that most species are capable of surviving calamities that would annihilate most other animals.

Despite this some rabbit species are now endangered, mainly because they have become specialized for particular habitats that are currently under threat. Some of these are considered "relict" species: the sole surviving members of genera that have dwindled through the natural processes of evolution. Such species are often regarded as doomed to inevitable extinction, with or without the help of humans, but since they are all affected by human activity, this assertion cannot be tested. One thing is certain: A sole member of a genus is not necessarily a biological anachronism living on borrowed time. The sole member of the genus *Oryctolagus*—the European rabbit—is living, breeding proof to the contrary.

The meteoric success of the European rabbit in the 19th century was largely due to human intervention. European farmers created a winter food supply and tried to eradicate its enemies; elsewhere it was introduced to regions where food was already plentiful and predators unknown. In such circumstances the fast-breeding rabbit flourished as never before, and by the mid-20th century its population had reached plague proportions.

WHEN MYXOMATOSIS FIRST APPEARED IN AUSTRALIA, FARM PROFITS INCREASED BY $50 MILLION IN THE FIRST YEAR

But then the rabbits vanished, once again through human intervention. In the 1950s the world population was almost annihilated by myxomatosis, an insect-transmitted disease that is endemic among the forest rabbits of South America (*Sylvilagus brasiliensis*). To its original host species the myxoma virus is virtually harmless, rather like the common cold virus in Europe, but when it was introduced into Australia as a rabbit-control measure, it proved devastating, killing 99.8 percent of infected animals between 1950 and 1953.

Now a pest in Australia, rabbits are deliberately infected with myxomatosis (right). *Sometimes poisoned carrot bait is dropped by aircraft* (inset).

Inset J. W. Kiely/NHPA

A three-month-old volcano rabbit eating. But how long will it be before its habitat is destroyed?

John Harris/Survival Anglia

A.N.T./NHPA

THEN & NOW

This chart shows the possible rabbit population explosion in Australia over a five-year period.

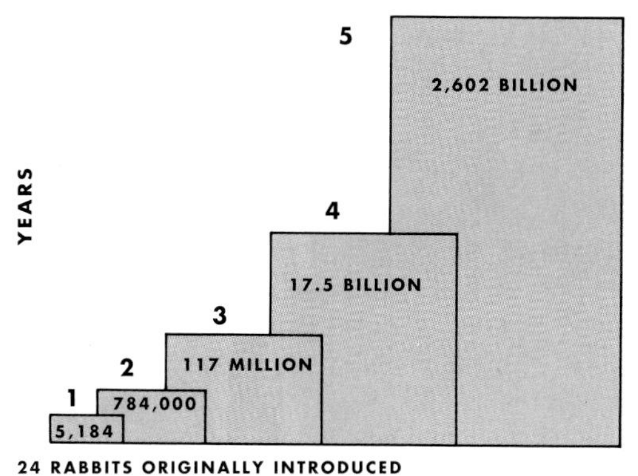

It is possible, under ideal conditions such as those found in Australia, for every female rabbit to produce six litters a year of six young each. Assuming that of the original 24 rabbits introduced into Australia, half were female, at the end of the first year there could be a total of 5,184 rabbits. At the end of year two this could have reached a total of 784,000 animals, and 117 million a year later, and so on.

As the introduced rabbits had no natural enemies, it is safe to assume that the figures above are a reasonable estimate. It is no wonder that the rabbit spread so rapidly across Australia and cost the farmers so much in lost sheep-grazing land.

Only one in five hundred survived. The disease swept rapidly across Australia, into New Zealand, and back to Europe, being deliberately introduced into France in 1952. In 1953 it appeared in Britain, and within five years the rabbits all but disappeared.

Yet the rabbit was not completely finished. The survivors had not escaped infection: They enjoyed a natural resistance to the virus that enabled them to defeat it and recover. They multiplied with their customary rapidity and passed on their resistance to their progeny, which multiplied in their turn.

Meanwhile, the most vulnerable strains died out, and by the early 1960s the mortality from myxomatosis had dropped to 90 percent. One in ten survived: reasonably good odds for a fast breeder. Gradually rabbit numbers started to creep up again.

Myxomatosis is still with us, but it is becoming less lethal each year; although new strains of the

John Daniels/Ardea

ALONGSIDE MAN

The European rabbit has been reared for at least 2,000 years, mainly for its meat. Selective breeding began during the late medieval period, apparently in France, and since then a vast number of breeds have been developed. Some of these have been bred for the pot, with the emphasis on meat production. The Flemish Giant, for example, can achieve a weight of 20 lb (9 kg)—six times the weight of a wild rabbit. Other breeds have been bred for their fur, and these include the Angora, whose long hair can be shorn off like the wool of a sheep and used to make yarn. Decorative pet breeds include the lop-eared and colored varieties.

Angora and chinchilla rabbits are bred for their fine fur.

Avril Ramage/Oxford Scientific Films

Lop-eared rabbits make popular pets and are often exhibited at pet shows.

virus have appeared, causing small epidemics, the rabbits rapidly become resistant to them as the survivors breed fast to fill the gaps in the population. In 1990 there were an estimated thirty million rabbits in Britain—a third of the 1930 peak before myxomatosis—and the population appears to be rising.

The situation is much the same throughout the world, and the European rabbit is once again classified as an agricultural pest: a remarkable achievement for a species that was on the edge of extinction forty years before. And unlike its original expansion, its recovery owed nothing to human intervention. Obviously the European rabbit has what it takes to survive in the modern world.

One of its main advantages is its enormous range. A small population could be wiped out without affecting the viability of the species as a whole. The rabbit species that are currently under threat are not so fortunate, since they occur in isolated, often fragmented pockets of habitat that are being rapidly eroded by human encroachment.

The volcano rabbit, for example, is restricted to two volcanic mountain ranges within easy reach of Mexico City. Active during the day, it is an easy target for casual gunmen and is threatened by habitat destruction. A similar problem afflicts the Amami rabbit, whose survival on two of the Japanese Amami islands is threatened by deforestation. Now reduced to about five thousand individuals, the species has been declared a "special natural monument" by the Japanese government. ■

David Thompson/Oxford Scientific Films

RABBITS IN DANGER

THE CHART BELOW SHOWS HOW THE INTERNATIONAL UNION FOR THE CONSERVATION OF NATURE (IUCN), OR THE WORLD CONSERVATION UNION CLASSIFIED THE CONSERVATISON STATUS OF CERTAIN RABBIT SPECIES. THE YEAR IN PARENTHESES IS THE DATE OF CLASSIFICATION:

VOLCANO RABBIT	ENDANGERED (1990)
AMAMI RABBIT	ENDANGERED (1990)

IN ADDITION TO THE ABOVE, TWO SPECIES OF RABBITLIKE HARES ARE ENDANGERED. THESE ARE THE BUSHMAN AND THE HISPID HARES. A THIRD SPECIES, THE SUMATRAN HARE, IS CITES LISTED.

ENDANGERED MEANS THAT THE ANIMAL'S SURVIVAL IS UNLIKELY UNLESS STEPS ARE TAKEN TO SAVE IT. *CITES* MEANS THAT THE SPECIES IS NOT CONSIDERED SUFFICIENTLY AT RISK TO BE ON THE DANGER LIST OF THE IUCN, BUT IT IS LISTED BY THE CONVENTION ON INTERNATIONAL TRADE IN ENDANGERED SPECIES (OF FLORA AND FAUNA).

INTO THE FUTURE

There can be little doubt that the European rabbit will be with us for a long time to come, regardless of what happens to the rest of the world's wildlife.

It has already demonstrated its ability to recover from catastrophe—an ability derived mainly from the remarkable breeding potential that has enabled it to survive a high rate of mortality throughout the millennia. It also enjoys a huge advantage over many other wild animals in that it has readily adapted to artificial landscapes, and so the more land that is cleared for agriculture, the more it will flourish. All attempts to control it by shooting, trapping, poisoning, gassing, and disease have failed, so there is no reason why such measures should threaten its survival in the future. The European rabbit is here to stay.

The same is true of other adaptable and widespread species such as the eastern cottontail, but most rabbits are much more restricted in their habitat and range. Many such species inhabit essentially wild environments which, by definition, are vulnerable to clearance, deforestation, drainage programs, or even urbanization—although species adapted to arid habitats, such as the desert cottontail, are probably safe enough.

For a rabbit, the two qualifications for survival in the future will be a high breeding rate and adaptability. All rabbits breed fast, but of the two rabbit species and other rabbitlike hare species currently under threat, at least three have become specialized for the conditions in their particular wild habitats and do not appear to flourish elsewhere. Specialization can be a route to success for animals that find themselves occupying improbable habitats, but in a changing world it is a route that often leads to a dead end. ■

THE COST OF RABBITS

Today it is estimated that rabbits cost farmers in the United Kingdom at least $150 million a year, partly through lost income and partly because of the costs of erecting rabbit-proof fencing, which has to extend at least 12 in (30 cm) underground to be effective.

UNDER THE VOLCANO

The volcano rabbit lives among the tussock grasses that grow beneath the pine forests on the slopes of Popocatepetl and nearby volcanoes around Mexico City. Its total range is tiny, so it is extremely vulnerable.

Such close proximity with humans creates all sorts of problems. The city is expanding fast, and the rabbit's habitat is being eroded by settlement and agriculture. The grasslands are frequently burned off to encourage young shoots to feed livestock and this destroys the cover that the rabbits need if they are to flourish. Until recently the total rabbit population was estimated at less than 1,000 animals—barely enough for long-term survival—so the species has been classified as endangered and is now strictly protected by the Mexican government. However, recent fieldwork indicates that the original estimates were pessimistic. At one of the main sites researchers found traces of 6,000 volcano rabbits, suggesting a much larger population.

STRIPED ENIGMA

As the only species of leporid with a striped coat, the rabbitlike Sumatran hare is uniquely intriguing to zoologists. The species is so rare, however, that virtually nothing is known about its habits and current conservation status. Its habitat—the mountain forests of western Sumatra—is so remote that only twenty definite sightings have been recorded, and it is hard to say whether it is extinct, reduced to remnant population, or simply very elusive. Most zoologists fear the worst. The forests are being cleared rapidly for cultivation and, according to local sources, the rabbits have vanished along with the trees. Some may survive, and if the forest clearances are stopped, the Sumatran hare may yet reappear.

Illustration Kim Thompson

RACCOONS

RELATIONS

The raccoons and their procyonid relatives are members of the order Carnivora, which also includes:

CATS

DOGS

BEARS

MONGOOSES

OTTERS

WEASELS

CIVETS

Carlo Dani/Natural Science Photos

Raccoons, together with their relatives the coatis, ringtail, cacomistle, olingos, and kinkajou, belong to the order Carnivora, even though they are omnivorous feeders. The red panda is a close relative, but it is classified in a separate subfamily.

ORDER

Carnivora

FAMILY

Procyonidae

SUBFAMILY

Procyoninae

GENERA

Procyon (raccoons—seven species)

Nasua (coatis—three species)

Nasuella (mountain coati)

Bassaricyon (olingos—two to five species)

Bassariscus (ringtail and cacomistle)

Potos (kinkajou)

MASKED BANDITS

WITH ITS CHARACTERISTIC BLACK MASK, THE RACCOON IS ONE OF AMERICA'S BEST-KNOWN ANIMALS. THERE ARE SOME SEVENTEEN MEMBERS OF ITS FAMILY SPREAD THROUGHOUT NORTH AND SOUTH AMERICA

In the dead of night on a sleeping street of a North American city, the streetlights pick out a furry figure shambling purposefully down the road. Stopping by a garbage can, it stands up on its hind legs, removes the lid with its forepaws, then deftly pulls the can over. Within seconds, the animal is rifling through the contents, turning them over in its dexterous paws, picking out and pushing into its mouth those that pass as remotely edible. Disturbed by a passing car, the animal lifts its head, and the motorist sees shining eyes surrounded by the dark "bandit" mask of a raccoon—one of the city's most successful animal opportunists and a raider of trash piles and garbage cans.

Native only to the Americas, to many people the raccoon is the best-known animal of the New World. In this instance, the raccoon referred to is the common raccoon, *Procyon lotor* (PRO-sie-on LO-tor), found from southern Canada south to

Mexico. However, there are five or six more raccoon species, occupying ranges from Mexico south to central South America. In addition, and found in many of the same areas, there are several more members of the same family, Procyonidae—namely, the coatis, olingos, ringtail, cacomistle, and kinkajou.

The earliest fossils of the raccoon family date from about twenty million years ago and were found in North America. They represent animals from the genus *Bassariscus*, which has two modern species—the ringtail and the cacomistle. During the Pliocene period (from five to two million years ago), the raccoon family spread farther into South America. Today the kinkajou and olingos are the South American representatives of the raccoon family.

Family features

All members of the raccoon family are comparatively small animals, generally about the build of a small to medium-sized dog, with a long body and long tail. Most are plantigrade—that is, they walk on the soles of their feet, like humans and bears. They have five toes on each foot, each bearing a nonretractile claw. The exception to this is the ringtail from western America, which is digitigrade (walks on its toes) and has semiretractile claws on its forefeet.

Most of these animals also have some kind of distinctive marking, the exception being the kinkajou, the coat of which is more or less uniformly olive-brown in color, fading slightly on the underparts. But the best-known markings are undoubtedly those of the common raccoon, its characteristic black face mask, which is outlined in white, helping to emphasize its reputation for having a somewhat

Martin Wendler/NHPA

Kenneth W. Fink/Ardea

The cacomistle (above) *and its relative the ringtail both have long, lithe bodies with long bushy tails.*

WHAT'S IN A NAME?

The raccoon—known colloquially in America as the coon—arrived at its name through the one given to it originally by North American Indians—*aroughcun* or *arakun*—which translates as "he who scratches with his hands." The genus name *Procyon* means "before dog," while the species name, *lotor*, means "washer" or "washing." All of these give indications about early observations of this animal.

Some people associate the raccoon with the bear family; the German name for it, for example, is *waschbaren*, meaning "wash bear." By complete contrast, the French refer to it as *raton laveur*, which means "little washing rat."

shifty character. Overall, the coat is usually a grizzled gray and there are between five and ten dark rings around the very bushy tail. All species of raccoons have the same basic markings, although the coat color varies.

The next best known of the species in the raccoon family, the coati, has as its most distinctive feature a long, tapered snout, which is remarkably mobile. The coat color varies from a reddish brown to gray and the long tail is ringed, usually quite indistinctly. The fur is fairly short on the head and legs, but much longer and stiffer on the body. The muzzle and chin are almost white, and there is a white or pale stripe that runs along the nose from the eyes. Often the eyes are ringed with white, and the chest is also white.

There are usually considered to be four species of coatis, contained in two genera. The best known is *Nasua nasua*, the ring-tailed coati, which, as its name suggests, has very distinct rings around its tail. The white-nosed coati, *N. narica*, is also named after its most distinctive feature—a startlingly white band around the end of its muzzle. The third member of this genus, *N. nelsoni*, is called the island coati, because it is found only on the Mexican island of Cozumel. The less well-known mountain coati, *Nasuella olivacea*, is similar to the other coatis, but with a smaller, more slender face, an olive-brown coat with a black muzzle, and dark circles around its eyes.

There are two species of ringtails, usually distinguished as the ringtail and the cacomistle. Their bodies are more slender than most of the other

A ring-tailed coati with its characteristic elongated, upturned, and highly mobile snout.

THE RACCOONS' FAMILY TREE

The raccoon family is divided into two clear subfamilies; one, the Procyoninae, contains the animals covered in this volume, and the other, the Ailurinae, contains the red panda. The giant panda was once included in the subfamily Ailurinae, although zoologists now classify it as a true bear in the family Ursidae.

OTHER SPECIES:
TRES MARIAS RACCOON
BARBADOS RACCOON
CRAB-EATING RACCOON
COZUMEL ISLAND RACCOON
GUADELOUPE RACCOON

COMMON RACCOON

Procyon lotor
(PRO-sie-on LO-tor)

The best known and most widely spread of all the animals in this family, the common raccoon is mainly nocturnal and solitary. It is distinguished by its "bandit" face mask, grizzled fur, arched back, and heavily ringed tail.

RINGTAIL

Bassariscus astutus
(bass-ah-RISS-kus a-STOO-tuss)

Overlapping with the raccoon in the southern parts of its range, the catlike ringtail is the only animal in the family to walk on its toes and to possess semiretractile claws. It is also the only procyonid that has retained a sharp cutting edge to its carnassial (cutting) teeth.

members of this family, but the most noticeable feature is the incredibly bushy and distinctively ringed tail, which is at least as long as the body.

Experts disagree on the number of species of olingos, genus *Bassaricyon*. Some say there are just two species, with various subspecies, while others consider there to be five separate species. Olingos have thick, soft hair that is usually quite a dark golden color, mixed with black on the upper parts. They are found from Central America south through Venezuela, Ecuador, Peru, and Brazil in South America. ■

SUBFAMILY AILURINAE

RED PANDA

B/W illustrations Ruth Grewcock

OLINGO

Bassaricyon

(bass-ah-rih-SIE-on)

Experts identify between two and five species of olingos. It is similar to the kinkajou in appearance but has a long-haired tail that is not prehensile. The Costa Rican and Panamanian olingos are thought to be subspecies of B. gabbi, and the British Guianan olingo a subspecies of B. alleni.

KINKAJOU

Potos flavus

(POT-oss FLAY-vuss)

Slightly stockier than the olingo, the kinkajou has bulging, dark, round eyes and a rounded head. Its coat is soft and velvety with a black line running down the back. Its most unusual feature is its tail; the kinkajou is the only New World carnivore to have a prehensile tail. Sometimes called a "honey bear," it uses its long extendable tongue to probe for nectar and honey.

COATI

Nasua nasua

(NASS-yoo-ah NASS-yoo-ah)

An animal of dense woodland, the coati is unusual for being mostly active by day; the females, too, are unusually sociable. Its most distinctive feature is its long, upturned, and highly mobile snout, which it uses to forage through the leaf litter for insects. It is also fond of fruit.

SUBFAMILY
PROCYONINAE

Color illustrations Nick Pike/Wildlife Art Agency

ANATOMY: THE RACCOON

The common raccoon (above left) *is as big as a medium-sized dog, although there is a marked size variation among individuals* (see Fact File). *The ring-tailed coati* (above center) *has a head-to-tail length of 32–50 in (81–127 cm), somewhat more than half being tail. The kinkajou* (above right) *has a head-and-body length of 16.5–22.5 in (42–57 cm); its prehensile tail measures 15.7–22 in (40–56 cm).*

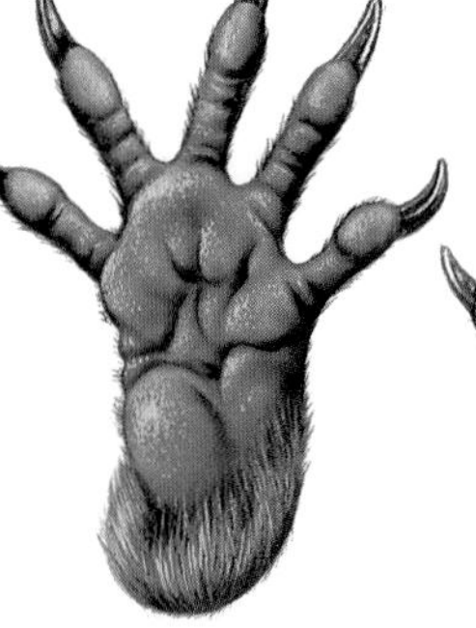

FOREFOOT

HIND FOOT

THE FUR

on the body is longer and more dense than on the face. It consists of a soft, woolly undercoat, with a top coat of longer, coarser hairs. Its denseness gives the raccoon an impression of robustness.

THE EARS

are comparatively small and rounded. They are usually tipped with white hairs. The inner surface of the ears is covered with longer but less dense, hair than on the outside.

THE EYES

are framed by the raccoon's most distinctive feature—the mask. Patches of black around each eye extend across the cheeks and are accentuated by a white line of fur above and below.

RACCOON FOOT FACTS

The common raccoon has highly dexterous forepaws, comparable to some of the primates. There are five toes on each foot; those on the forefeet are relatively long and can be spread widely. The soles are naked and planted on the ground as the animal walks, in the same way as bears and humans.

THE FACE

is somewhat foxlike in appearance; quite broad at the forehead, it tapers to a pointed muzzle. The nose is black and round.

X-RAY

SKELETON

Likened in size to a small to medium dog and in build to a stout cat, the common raccoon has a distinctly arched back. It also has a foxlike head, which is broad at the base but tapers to a pointed muzzle. The hind feet can grow up to 3 in (7.5 cm) long.

RACCOON SKELETON

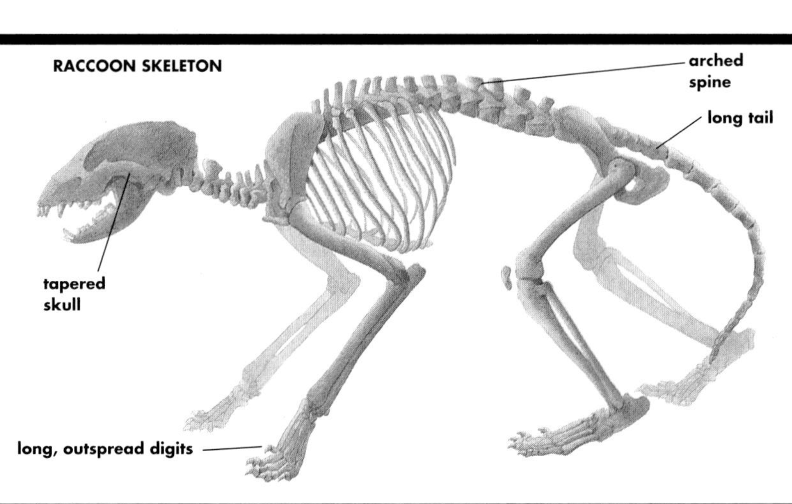

SKULLS

All procyonids have fairly robust, elongate skulls. The raccoon has forty teeth; this number varies slightly in the different species. In keeping with the omnivorous diet, the carnassials are adapted for cutting, rather than tearing, flesh.

X-ray illustrations Elisabeth Smith

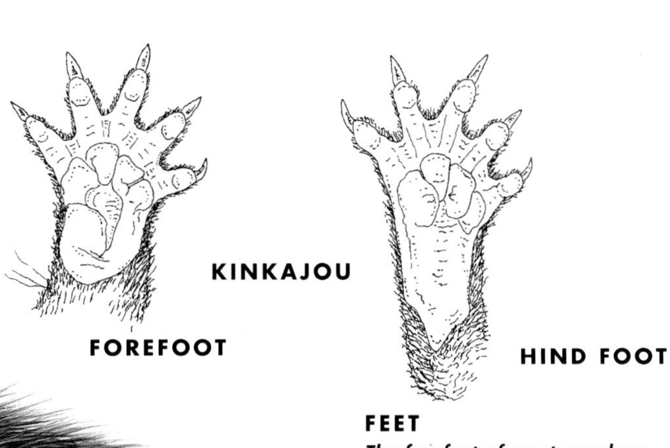

FEET

The forefeet of most members of this family are considerably shorter than the hind feet—with the exception of the ringtail, which has more catlike paws. The kinkajou, however, is unusual in having hairy soles on its feet. The toes of each foot are also joined by a weblike membrane that extends about a third of the way down.

THE LEGS

are fairly long, but tend not to look so because they are quite heavily furred at the top. The feet are characterized by long toes.

THE TAIL

is very bushy, with five to ten black or dark brown rings around it; the tip is always dark.

FACT FILE

COMMON RACCOON

CLASSIFICATION

GENUS: *PROCYON*

SPECIES: *LOTOR*

SIZE

HEAD–BODY LENGTH: 16–37 IN (41–94 CM)

TAIL LENGTH: 7.5–16 IN (19–41 CM)

WEIGHT: 11–46 LB (5–21 KG); MALES ARE LARGER THAN FEMALES

WEIGHT AT BIRTH: 2 OZ (56 G)

COLORATION

GENERALLY A GRIZZLED GRAY, VARYING FROM PALE TO QUITE DARK. OCCASIONALLY MORE REDDISH AND OFTEN WITH YELLOW-BROWN FUR AROUND NAPE OF NECK

FEATURES

THE FACE HAS A CHARACTERISTIC BLACK EYE MASK EDGED WITH WHITE, AND LONGER TUFTS OF HAIR BEHIND THE CHEEKS. THE EYES THEMSELVES ARE BLACK, ROUND, AND MEDIUM SIZED

THE TAIL IS BUSHY AND DISTINCTIVELY RINGED IN DARK AND PALE BANDS

FIVE TOES ON EACH FOOT, WITH PARTICULARLY LONG AND MANIPULATIVE DIGITS ON THE FOREPAWS. THE CLAWS ARE SHARP BUT CANNOT BE RETRACTED

ARCHED BACK

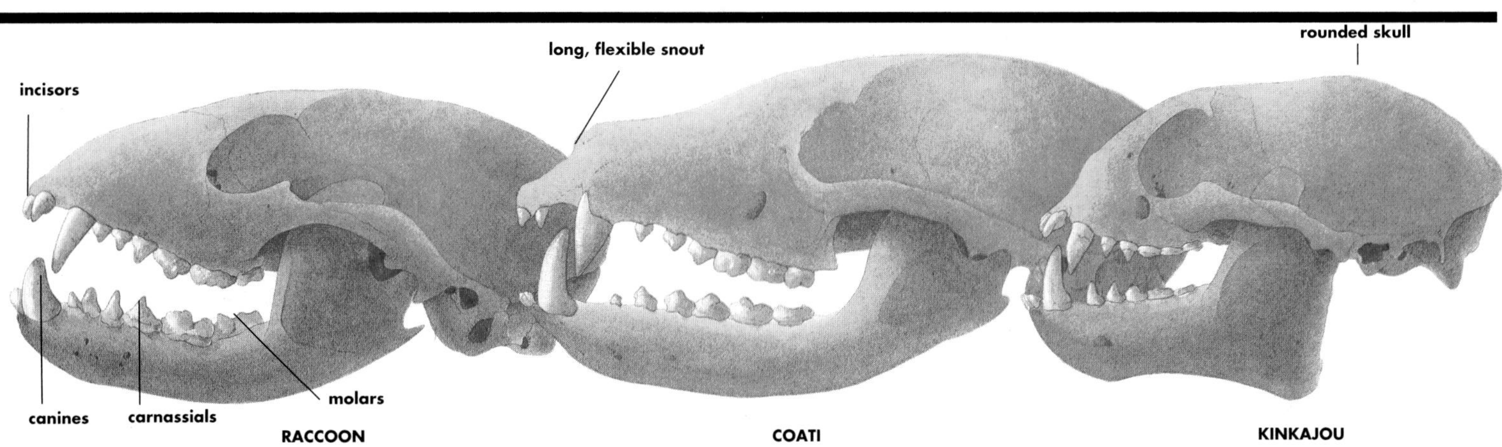

Illustrations Steve Kingston/B/W illustrations Ruth Grewcock

TAILS OF THE CITY

THE RACCOON WILL EAT ALMOST ANYTHING AND LIVE JUST ABOUT ANYWHERE. AS SUCH, IT HAS ACCESS TO A REMARKABLE SPREAD OF AMERICA, AND IT IS CONTINUING TO EXTEND ITS RANGE EVEN TODAY

Many of North America's mammals, including black bears, pumas, and the Virginia opossum, have adapted readily to the changing landscape that humans have created in the comparatively short time that they have shared it. Possibly the most adaptable of all is the common raccoon, once almost exclusively a woodland species, but now the most common of wild animals to be found also in urban environments.

Survival in what could be termed "human" territory is aided for the raccoon by the fact that it is mainly nocturnal. Indeed, the coati is the only member of the Procyonidae family that is generally most active by day. The coati breaks another of the usual characteristics of this family, too—that of being solitary, for female coatis, at least, tend to live in groups of up to about twenty-five animals, which include youngsters as well.

CLIMBING SKILLS

The raccoon is a good climber, although it spends less time in the trees than many other members of its family. When pushed—for example, if being chased by a coyote—a raccoon will often take to a tree as a means of defense. Coatis are mainly ground-foragers, but they do spend a fair amount of time up in the branches, where they rest and groom each other. A raccoon generally descends a tree trunk backward, except for the last few steps when it turns around. A coati, however, can reverse its ankle joints and come down headfirst from the tree crown. It can also drop from quite a height, although it can only leap about 3 ft (1 m) off the ground. Although its tail is not prehensile, like that of the kinkajou, the coati does use it to improve balance as it runs along branches, or as a brake when it is traveling down trees, curling it around small branches or vines during the descent.

The cacomistle spends more time in trees than does the ringtail—another that can rotate its feet through 180 degrees to permit headfirst descent down a tree. The ringtail is a most agile climber and has been observed ascending a crevice by keeping its four feet along one side and its back pressed hard against the other. Its partially retractile claws are so sharp that it can use them to get a grip on many almost-vertical surfaces. The kinkajou is perhaps the most arboreal of all members of this family, spending almost all its time in the branches. This is doubtless why it is the only member of this family to have a prehensile tail, which acts as a fifth limb, freeing its forepaws to gather fruit as it suspends itself from branches.

The sharp claws possessed by all the animals in this family are, in part, an adaptation to climbing trees. They help in getting a hold on the trunk

Claude Stedman/Survival Anglia

James Carmichael/NHPA

The olingo's large eyes help it to navigate by night through the canopy of tropical rain forests (above).

*in*SIGHT

RACCOON NOISES

By and large, members of the raccoon family avoid confrontation whenever possible. However, they do have a large range of vocalizations. These are said to include purrs, whimpers, snarls, growls, hisses, screams, and whinnies. The raccoon has been known to give a characteristic summer and early autumn call as dusk falls; this is said to be "as thrilling as the wail of the wolf" and similar to the hooting of a horned owl.

When trapped, the raccoon makes a pathetic, startled cry, which carries over a considerable distance and may act as a warning to other raccoons. Rage is indicated by an angry snarl, and the female makes a persistent sharp call during mating. Females keep in touch with their young with soft noises. The sociable female coati is generally even more vocal and also has a wide range of snorts, grunts, screams, whines, and chatters.

while ascending, for example; although once up in the heights, most of the animals tend to run along the branches using an innate balance rather than relying on their claws to act as hooks or their toes to grip the bark.

A NATURAL SWIMMER

Besides being an agile climber, the raccoon is also an adept swimmer. A quick jump into a lake or river is another way of escaping an enemy; or, alternatively, it may be a shortcut to a good foraging area. Certainly the raccoon is perfectly at home in water, and it does much of its feeding along streams and lakes, often fishing around in the shallows.

Touch and smell are the most highly developed of the raccoon's senses. If foraging on land, its nose is active all the time, investigating anything that might be considered food. Often the raccoon will then pick up the object with its paws, rolling it around and feeling it with its sensitive fingers. So dexterous and sensitive are the raccoon's long fingers that it will often hunt for food by feel, without having to look at what it is catching. The thumb and little finger on each forepaw are used to grasp edible matter. ■

Raccoons use tree holes extensively as nesting sites in woodland environments.

HABITATS

An expert's advice: "If men cut a raccoon's wood down to build a summer cottage, they can expect the animal to come and live in the fireplace chimney. Fill in the creek where raccoons catch shiners and chubs, and you will hear your garbage cans go rattling over at midnight. Pour concrete, and raccoons will make themselves at home in the culverts under the road. Raccoons take civilization in stride and grow fat where lampposts have replaced trees."

These words about the common raccoon appeared in *National Geographic* magazine in 1956; since then urbanization in the United States, as elsewhere, has spread even further. Today, the raccoon is even more successful and widespread, extending its range northward into southern Canada.

Although the raccoon has always been found in a wide variety of natural habitats, its favorite spot has consistently been wooded and brushy areas. It is particularly common near water—lakes, ponds, slow-flowing rivers, and streams. The most widespread of any animal in this family, it ranges from the southern edges of Canada south through most

Carol Farneti/Planet Earth Pictures

The kinkajou (right) *looks a lot like the olingo and lives in similar habitats.*

Hans Reinhard/Tony Stone Worldwide

of the United States into Central America. It is generally absent from the Rocky Mountains and parts of Nevada and Utah.

The common raccoon has also been introduced into parts of Europe and Asia, where it is extending its range with typical ease. Here, too, it has learned to live alongside humans—as a scavenger of waste and a plunderer of crops and livestock.

SOUTHERN RELATIVES

The various other species of raccoon, range from the southern United States down to the northern and central countries of South America. The crab-eating raccoon is found from Costa Rica south to northern Argentina, while at least three of the other species are confined to islands. The Tres Marías raccoon is an inhabitant of María Madre Island off the west coast of Mexico; the Cozumel Island raccoon, as its name suggests, inhabits Cozumel Island, which lies to the east of the Yucatán Peninsula in Mexico; and the Barbados raccoon is found on the island of the same name in the West Indies.

In northern regions, raccoons (left) *combat the cold of winter by growing longer, denser coats.*

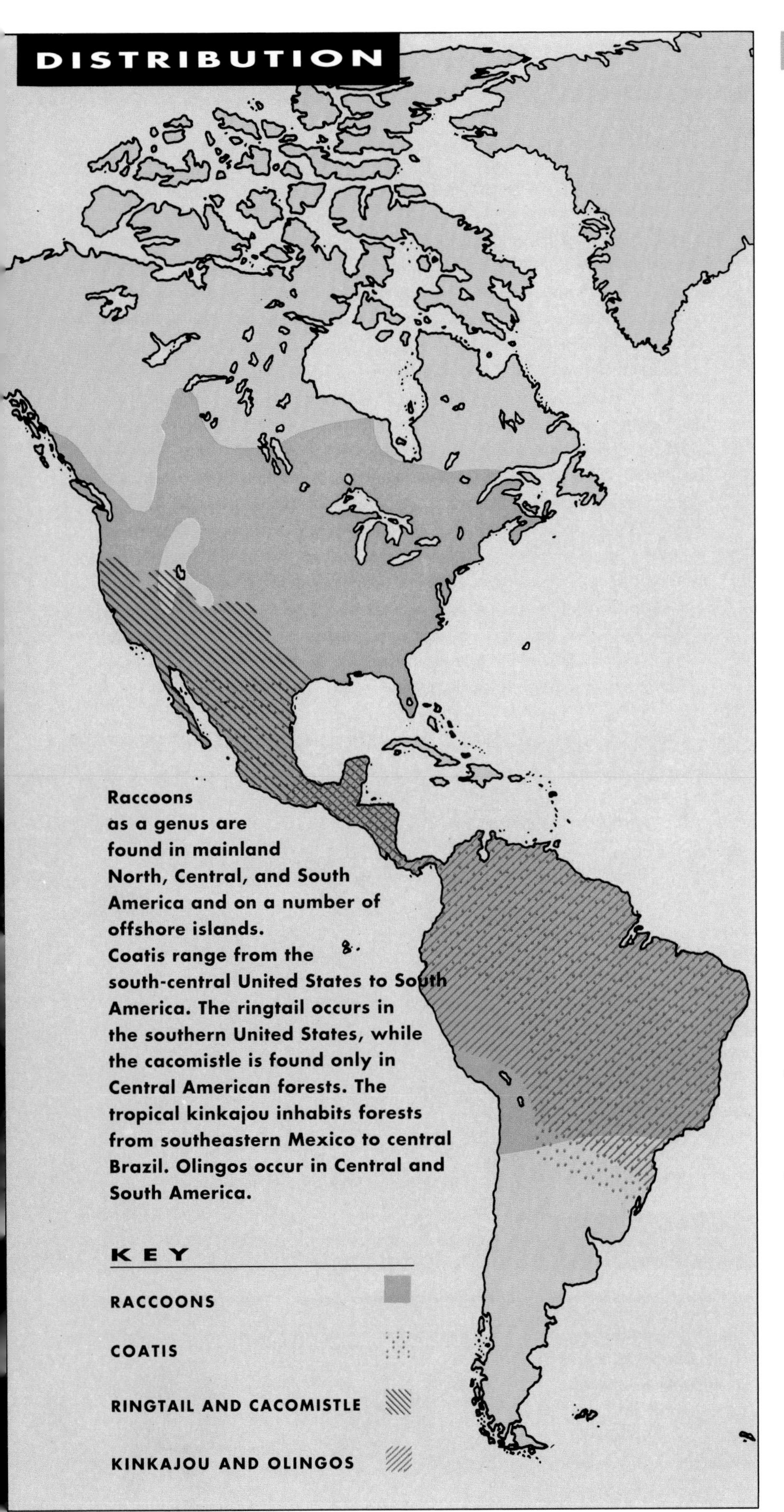

in SIGHT

ISLAND RACCOONS

Other than the common and crab-eating raccoons, all raccoon species live on islands in the Caribbean and off Mexico. They differ from the common raccoon mainly in the colors and lengths of their coats.

Many of these island species are threatened by the introduction of the common raccoon. The common species is far more adaptable and, should humans ever introduce it to these island refuges, it would almost certainly cause the downfall of these rare island raccoons through competition for food and territory.

One species, *Procyon maynardi*, from New Providence island in the Bahamas, is actually thought to be the common raccoon, introduced there much earlier by humans.

The coati, with its arboreal habits, is another that favors wooded areas, although these may be anything from the lowland forests of the Tropics to temperate deciduous forests, or even those at high altitudes. Across its range, which comprises the southern states of the United States south through northern and central South America, it may also be found in rocky, wooded canyons.

The most common of the coatis, the ring-tailed coati, is found from southeast Arizona through southwest New Mexico and southern Texas. Within this range it is most abundant in the mountainous areas of the extreme south of Arizona. The white-nosed coati is found from southeastern Arizona through Mexico and central America

WHEN LIVING SPACE IS SCARCE IN AN AREA, RACCOONS WILL READILY MOVE INTO ABANDONED FOX BURROWS

south to western Colombia and Ecuador. The island coati shares Cozumel Island with its native raccoon, while the mountain coati, about which very little is known, lives in the Andean forests of western Venezuela, Colombia, and Ecuador.

The stronghold of the ringtail is America's southern states—southwestern Oregon, California, southern Nevada, much of Utah, western Colorado, and southern Kansas down through Arizona, New Mexico, Oklahoma, and Texas. It is found in a variety of habitats, but it is most common where the landscape is rocky, favoring canyons and areas where there are lots of big boulders. This perhaps reflects the fact that it spends less time in the trees than many of its relatives, although it is still a skillful climber. Like the raccoon, it is seldom found far away from water. The cacomistle has a much smaller distribution and is found only in forested areas of Central America.

The kinkajou is found only in tropical forests; its range extends from southeastern Mexico to central Brazil. It spends almost all its time among the branches, feeding and sleeping by day in a hollow trunk or, occasionally, lying out on a branch. The olingo is found from Central America down through Venezuela, Ecuador, Peru, and Brazil. It is also an inhabitant of tropical forests, but may be found at altitudes from sea level up to about 6,500 ft (2,000 m). Nocturnal in habit as well, it is thought to make a rough nest of dry leaves in a hollow for its daytime slumbers.

LOCOMOTION

The raccoon usually moves around its home range at a sort of slow amble, with its head held low, its back characteristically arched, and its tail dangling behind it. If need be it can move quite fast, however—up to about 15 mph (24 km/h)—in a lumbering gallop by which it takes short bounds, bringing its hind feet down ahead of its forefeet. The coati, also a good swimmer, has a less pronouncedly arched back than the raccoon, so it appears to move a little less shamblingly on the ground, and it holds its tail almost vertically as it moves and forages. The kinkajou moves quickly in the tree branches, but it is generally a little more cautious as it travels over the ground from one tree to another. It tends to return to a particularly favorite tree each night. The olingo leaps from branch to branch with ease, making short work of gaps of 10 ft (3 m) or more. ■

FOCUS ON

WASHINGTON STATE

The most northwestern state in the United States, Washington has always proved excellent raccoon country. Although it is the smallest of the Pacific Coast states, it boasts three national parks—Mount Rainier, North Cascades, and Olympic—and nine national forests. It is known as the Evergreen State because of its richness of firs, hemlocks, pines, and other evergreen trees, and also because of its lush lowlands, which are typical of the western part of the state.

One of the most impressive areas is North Cascades, made a national park in the late 1960s. The Cascade mountains separate the western section of the state from the eastern section and are part of a long mountain range that stretches south from British Columbia into northern California. The range includes a number of volcanoes, including Mount St. Helens, which erupted in 1980. Many of the mountains have glaciers and permanent snowfields on their upper slopes, but lower down are the magnificent forests where the raccoons make their homes alongside beavers, martens, minks, muskrats, and western bobcats. American black bears, coyotes, cougars, and a subspecies of mule deer are all found in the Cascades, but it is thought that one-time residents grizzlies and wolves have long since disappeared.

Alan & Sandy Carey/Oxford Scientific Films

TEMPERATURE AND RAINFALL

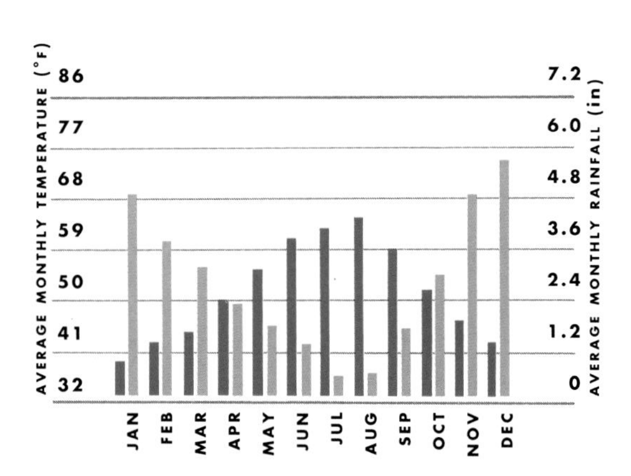

Western Washington State has a mild climate; the summers are pleasantly cool while the winters remain tolerable. But the winds from the Pacific Ocean are moist and bring a fair amount of rain to the west. The east has a considerably drier climate.

NEIGHBORS

The raccoon has a rich variety of neighbors, some of which it preys upon and others to which it is prey. With the decline of bears and wolves in many areas, the coyote is now its chief predator.

COYOTE

The best runners of the canids, coyotes have no problem in overtaking raccoons on the ground.

AMERICAN BLACK BEAR

The American black bear and common raccoon share many habitats—forested areas in particular.

Illustrations Peter Bull, Joanne Cowne, and Edwina Goldstone/Wildlife Art Agency

NORTH CASCADES NATIONAL PARK

Washington State borders Canada in the northwestern United States on the Pacific Coast. North Cascades National Park lies in the northwest of the state, between the cities of Seattle and Vancouver.

MUSTANG

The mustang usually lives on open grassland—a habitat that raccoons are slowly colonizing in some areas.

GOLDEN EAGLE

This majestic bird looks like a hawk but has a much larger wingspan. It preys on rabbits and rodents.

AMERICAN BULLFROG

This large frog takes its name from its bellowing call. Raccoons prey on several species of frogs.

RED-TAILED HAWK

One of North America's most impressive raptors, the red-tail has a soaring flight like that of an eagle.

CATTLE EGRET

This small heron is more often seen in Africa, but its range now includes the United States and even Canada.

FOOD AND FEEDING

Although classed as carnivores, most members of the raccoon family are more aptly termed omnivorous. The common raccoon, in particular, will eat anything. The most carnivorous in habit is the ringtail, and, it and the cacomistle, are the only members of this family to possess doglike teeth—reminders of these animals' ancestry as well as a reflection on their diet.

With a reputation for being a better mouser than a cat, the ringtail hunts by night, ambushing its prey, then pouncing on it like a fox does. It pins a victim to the ground with its forepaws and quickly bites into its neck to kill it. The ringtail then consumes the meal headfirst. Its diet of small mammals, reptiles, birds, and insects is supplemented by fruits such as persimmon, juniper, and mistletoe berries.

SEASONAL PICKINGS

The raccoon's diet is breathtaking in its variety, although it generally reflects what is seasonally available. As well as vegetables and fruit, it also eats grubs, crickets and grasshoppers, eggs and nestling birds, and small mammals from voles and mice to squirrels and muskrats. It preys on a huge variety of aquatic life, including frogs, crayfish, dragonfly larvae, oysters, clams, and small turtles.

Despite its varied diet, the raccoon is nevertheless a cautious feeder. Pushing its forepaws into crevices and turning over rocks in search of food, it first picks up an item in its fingers, then sniffs at it thoroughly to see if it is edible. After this thorough investigation, it will more often discard rather than consume the find. If the item is deemed edible, it is chewed thoroughly, not gulped down quickly. Small crabs are devoured whole, but larger ones are held against the ground with the forepaws and then eaten systematically. Usually the shell, pincers, and feet are discarded.

Unlike the other members of the raccoon family, the kinkajou feeds only on fruit and sugary foods.

Aldo Brando/Oxford Scientific Films

NOSING AROUND

Although insects and fruit are fvorites, the flexible-snouted coati (above) *won't pass up a young bird for its meal.*

A FRUIT DIET

The fruit-eating kinkajou (left) *spends the night among the branches, foraging for its favorite food. It uses its prehensile tail to cling to branches, while it probes the center of flowers for nectar with its long, extensible tongue.*

ANYTHING GOES

Lizards, spiders, scorpions, snakes, toads, and frogs all represent tasty morsels to the ringtail (below), *the most carnivorous of the raccoons. It will also make a meal of carrion.*

WASHING FOOD

Much has been made of the way raccoons often dip their food in water, apparently washing it. This habit accounts for its Latin species name, *lotor*, meaning "the washer." Studies have revealed, however, that a raccoon only dips food items in water when prevented from foraging naturally in streams or lakes—when in captivity, for example. It may be that the action of wetting the fingers enhances the sense of touch. Also, by holding the food in the water and handling it extensively, the raccoon is able to feel those parts that should be discarded. Raccoons scavenging food in urban conditions have been observed dipping items of food in birdbaths!

In spite of their ability to climb trees, raccoons rarely follow prey into trees. Instead, they search more methodically among the branches for young birds and eggs, or simply to gather nuts and berries.

Perhaps lacking the raccoon's extreme dexterity and sensitivity of touch with its forepaws, the coati has a different aid to foraging: its long, mobile snout. This it uses to investigate crevices and holes and to root in surface soil to find invertebrates, lizards, and grubs, as well as tubers. Having caught a lizard or invertebrate, the coati rolls it under its forefeet to remove scales and wings, as well as to avoid poisonous bites and stings.

Insects are undoubtedly the mainstay of the diet, but when fruit is abundant, the coati will turn its attention to this, shunning other food sources. ■

FINICKY FISHERMEN

The raccoon (left) *often forages in the shallows of a stream. Feeling with its sensitive paws, it fishes out delicacies and, after thorough investigation, pops them into its mouth.*

Illustration Kim Thompson

SOCIAL STRUCTURE

Most members of the raccoon family are solitary. Common raccoons often gather together, but generally they are only tolerating one another's company because they are clustered around a plentiful supply of food.

FRIENDLY FEMALES

The one animal in the group that breaks from the solitary rule is the coati, although it is only the adult females that are truly sociable; they form groups of up to about twenty-five individuals. The band forages together during the day, usually spread out loosely across the ground, the young ones in the middle protected by the older animals on the outside. They cover the ground carefully and systematically, rooting with their long snouts into the ground cover and uncovering stones, or using their long claws to dig small holes, which they then sniff out thoroughly.

Young coatis are playful and tend to spend a good deal of time chasing each other up and down trees and making a lot of noise. They may suckle from females in the group other than their mothers. Juvenile males, up to two years old, are included in the female band, but the only time an older male is tolerated within the group is during the mating season, and even then he remains fully subordinate to the females.

FEMALE COATIS FIERCELY DEFEND THEIR YOUNG, SCARING OFF INTRUDERS WITH LOUD HISSES AND SCREAMS

HOMES ON THE RANGE

The extent of a group's range is approximately 85–110 acres (35–45 ha), although the members usually restrict themselves to a fairly small core area within this. They are not territorial and other groups' ranges will overlap. Male coatis usually wander over a larger area, but, again, although they may stand their ground in an encounter with another male, they are not aggressively territorial.

The home range of the solitary, generally somewhat sedentary, common raccoon varies enormously with the location, population density, and abundance of food. Several may be found in 2.5 acres (1 ha), or it has been known for a single animal to have a year-round range of 12,350 acres (5,000 ha). A more usual size for a home range is 12–123 acres (5–50 ha). While males' territories will overlap with those of females, they rarely infringe upon

GROOMING

Coatis break up their foraging bouts and siestas with grooming sessions (right). *Standing head to tail, they take turns investigating each other's fur.*

HANDS ON

The coati uses its teeth to comb carefully through its fur (center). *It scratches gently with its claws to help the grooming process.*

B/W illustration Ruth Grewcock

Color illustrations Robin Budden/Wildlife Art Agency

those of other males. In any event, a raccoon's philosophy is to keep itself to itself, and it seems to adopt an active policy to avoid other individuals. If two do meet, they generally challenge one another by growling, lowering their heads, baring their teeth, and making themselves look bigger by bristling up the fur on their hackles.

Usually more aggressive in encounters with a relative is the ringtail, which, besides screaming, also emits a foul-smelling fluid from its anal glands.

Although it does not defend its home range in an aggressive manner, it does scent mark it by urinating at key places. Its closest relative, the cacomistle, which spends more time among the branches of trees than the ringtail, occupies a home range of a similar size, but it does not appear to scent mark.

The kinkajou scent marks its territory, rubbing the scent glands on its chest and belly along tree branches. It is not territorial, though scent marking might be a way of advertising sexuality. Kinkajous are often found foraging in pairs, occasionally alongside olingos, which are also seen in pairs. Olingos scent mark, too, but with urine rather than secretions from scent glands. ■

REST AND WORK

After resting in a tree for a few midday hours over (above), *a coati returns to the task of foraging among the leaf litter for insects* (below).

In northern regions, the raccoon may spend the winter in a cozy den. It is not a true hibernator, since its metabolic rate and body temperature remain stable and it is easily woken. But it does live off its body fat at such a time, and a raccoon can easily weigh 50 percent less at the end of the winter. To prepare for this, many will feed heavily in autumn on rich, fattening food.

LIFE IN THE CITY

HIGH-RISE HOME

In the search for a secure home for its kits, a raccoon will normally head for the nearest hollow tree. But in town, these are in short supply. Not surprisingly, it will make do with the next best thing: the warm, snug shelter of a chimney flue.

Ever since humans invaded raccoon territory, these naturally shy animals have learned to exploit the intrusion. In vacation cabins in remote woodland areas, raccoons quickly turned their dexterous paws to opening doors—first to get into the dwelling and then to get into the cupboards. They even learned to open refrigerator doors. As usual, such raids would be done at night when the raccoons could reasonably hope to be undisturbed by human owners.

Not only did raccoons quickly grasp the fact that such human dwellings provided easy pickings, but they learned, too, that they provided safe, dry shelter. Barns and outbuildings erected by farmers as they settled and began cultivating land across America provided ideal shelters for raccoons, while the boldest of animals would make their homes in the chimney or seldom-visited attics of a main farmhouse.

CITY SLICKERS

Where raccoons have perhaps most successfully exploited the march of civilization, however, is in the heart of busy cities. One example where raccoons apparently thrive in large numbers is the capital—Washington, D.C.

Raccoons in Washington were subjected to an extensive study in the 1980s. The study was centered on an area of natural park situated in the confines of metropolitan Washington. The study revealed that the city raccoons live longer than raccoons in the surrounding rural area, partly because there is no hunting and trapping allowed in the city park and partly because there is less competition for food.

Although raccoons in an urban environment make their homes in different places from those used by their more rural cousins, their habits have not changed that much. Indeed, they have been so successful in cities because their natural habits are ideally adapted to the demands of such an environment. They are no more tolerant of humans than they would be if encountered in the wild;

KEY FACTS

- **Providing a raccoon can survive its first winter, it has a longer life expectancy in the city than in a more rural habitat—up to eight years, as opposed to five.**
- **Urban raccoons are generally smaller than their woodland cousins.**
- **Where unusual noises in a wood send raccoons scuttling to safety, in the city they have learned to ignore the noise of cars and their horns, as well as other unfamiliar sounds.**
- **The most unusual home known to have been frequented by an urban raccoon was under the hood of an abandoned car.**

Illustrations Robin Bouttell/Wildlife Art Agency

they simply attempt to avoid them by operating at night and by using the quietest, most out-of-the-way routes. For example, they are very secretive and will remain in the tunnels of the sewer system for as long as possible, sometimes traveling up to half a mile (0.8 km) underground rather than taking to the more exposed routes above ground. Perhaps above all, their omnivorous diet allows them to survive on both the natural and artificial foods that humans regularly discard.

Handy as ever

They have, however, exploited their manual dexterity to the full within the urban situation. Their manipulative fingers have not only become adept at removing lids of garbage cans and opening doors, but have even mastered screw-top jars and the removal of corks from wine bottles. A garbage can lid removed, the raccoon behaves as it would if searching for food in the wild; the contents are riffled through with its fingers and anything seemingly edible is subjected to the usual "scratch and sniff" investigation. The diet changes just a little; grasshoppers and crickets are exchanged for leftover hamburgers and discarded sandwiches!

Raccoons in an urban environment run a different gamut of dangers—hostile humans who object to the mess left behind by these raiding "vandals," domestic dogs, high fences, fast cars, and so on. Those that live in the cities tend to do so throughout their entire life, breeding and bringing up a family in these conditions. The young animals are educated in the ways of city life by their mothers, just as they would be in the laws of the wild if they lived in uninhabited woodland.

Authorities in some cities have learned that they have to fight back. Special garbage cans, called raccoon busters, are used. There is also a recognized job for a "raccoon-remover"; when these animals invade the attic or chimney, the raccoon-remover who comes to take them away and introduces them to a "more rustic lifestyle"! ■

Zig Leszczynski/Oxford Scientific Films

Some raccoons, having learned that humans can be softhearted, have taken to roadside begging (above).

CAN CAPERS

Raccoons are actually tidy scroungers, rarely leaving more mess than they find. But an overturned garbage can is never easy to ignore!

LIFE CYCLE

The mating season for the common raccoon is at its height in February and March, although activity may occur beyond this time. Raccoons in southern climes have been known to begin mating in December. A male may stay with a mate for a week or so before wandering off to find another.

Gestation lasts about sixty-three days, during which time the female makes a nest of leaves in a hollow tree, a fallen log, or a rocky crevice. Up to seven young—called cubs or kits—are born, with three to four being the usual number. Their eyes open at about three weeks old—by then, their ears are already open. At ten weeks old, they are making short trips with their mother, and a week or two later they join her on all her forays. Weaning takes about four months; males are mature at about two years old, but females may become pregnant at only a year old.

COATIS AND RINGTAILS

Between February and March, a male coati wins his way into a group of females by grooming them submissively. Soon after mating, the females chase him away again. Although coatis are generally active by day, mating usually occurs at night.

Gestation is about seventy-seven days, and a few weeks before the birth, each female leaves the group to build a lone nest in a tree. She stays with her litter of four to six young, leaving them only briefly to forage, until they are active at about five weeks old. By then they have at least trebled their weight to about 17 oz (500 g), and are ready to join the group.

COMPETITION

Females generally accept only one mate per season. In their quest for a partner, males (above) *may travel far from their usual home range and can be unusually fierce toward rivals.*

INDEPENDENCE

Some young leave the mother and go off to find a home range of their own in the late autumn (above). *Others will stay with her through the winter, sharing her den, before dispersing at the beginning of spring, by which time the mother is usually busy preparing for a new litter.*

A kinkajou (below) *weighs up to 7 oz (200 g) at birth. It may open its eyes after just a week.*

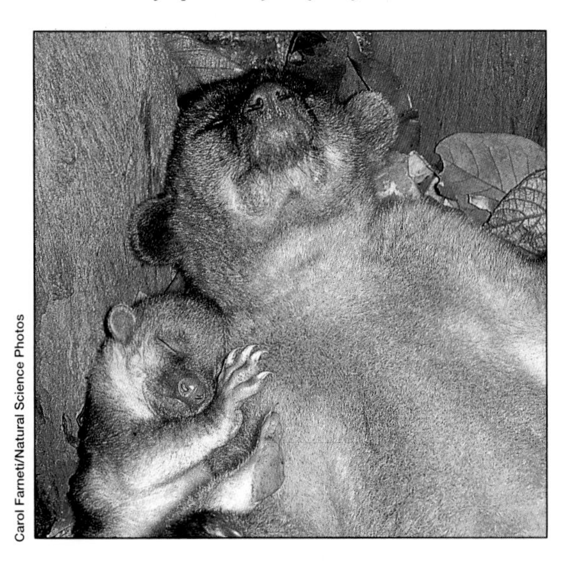

Carol Farneti/Natural Science Photos

Ringtails mate between February and May, giving birth in April to July. There are usually two to four in a litter. Born in a cozy den, the 1-oz (28-g) newborns have fuzzy white hair and stubby tails. Their eyes open at about five weeks; by this time they are taking solid food and have begun to grow an adult coat. The males help rear the young, bringing solid food to the den. At two months old, the young begin to forage with their parents, and at four months they can hunt independently. They usually disperse by the onset of winter.

KINKAJOUS AND OLINGOS

In their more tropical environment, both kinkajous and olingos can give birth at any time of the year. The kinkajou's gestation lasts up to 118 days—the

GROWING UP

The life of a young raccoon

MATING

The act of mating (above) *induces ovulation in the female.*

TUCKERED OUT

The female becomes increasingly lethargic during her gestation; she gives birth between April and June. The kits are blind and helpless at birth, but they develop quickly.

NIGHT SCHOOL

By the time they are twelve weeks old, the kits accompany their mother wherever she goes, learning the skills they will need for survival by watching and imitating her.

longest of any procyonid—while that of the olingo is about seventy-three days. Both of these animals usually give birth to a single offspring. By the time the young kinkajou is seven weeks old, its tail has become prehensile. Unlike the raccoon, the males become sexually mature first, at eighteen months old, while the females do not begin to breed until they are over two years old.

The olingo's single young weighs 2 oz (55 g) at birth and does not open its eyes until it is nearly four weeks old. Both sexes reach sexual maturity a little before they are two years old. ■

FROM BIRTH TO DEATH

COMMON RACCOON

MATING SEASON: FEBRUARY TO MARCH, SOMETIMES LATER
GESTATION: AVERAGE 63 DAYS
NO. OF YOUNG: 2–7, USUALLY 3–4
WEANED: BY 4 MONTHS
SEXUAL MATURITY: FEMALE 1 YEAR, MALE 2 YEARS
LONGEVITY: OFTEN NO MORE THAN 5 YEARS IN THE WILD; UP TO 20 IN CAPTIVITY

COATI

MATING SEASON: FEBRUARY TO MARCH
GESTATION: AVERAGE 77 DAYS
NO. OF YOUNG: 4–6
WEANED: APPROXIMATELY 4 MONTHS
SEXUAL MATURITY: FEMALE 2 YEARS, MALE 3 YEARS
LONGEVITY: 15 YEARS OR MORE IN CAPTIVITY; LESS IN THE WILD

Illustrations Simon Turvey/Wildlife Art Agency

MAN'S PEST FRIEND

THE COMMON RACCOON'S ADAPTABILITY HAS ALLOWED IT TO EXTEND ITS RANGE WELL BEYOND ITS ORIGINAL BOUNDARIES. THE FUTURE OF SOME OF ITS CLOSEST RELATIVES, HOWEVER, SEEMS LESS SECURE

Almost more than any other animal in America, the common raccoon has captured people's imagination, with its apparently curious and mischievous nature and its ability to take civilization in stride, even turning the intrusion of humans to its advantage. In the 1830s–1840s, the Whig party took the raccoon as its emblem. It has also been the hero, or perhaps antihero, of folklore where, as might be imagined, it is portrayed as the smart character that outdoes the others.

THE FUR TRADE

Before settlers arrived in the New World, the Native Americans had hunted the raccoon just as they did the other wild animals that shared the land. The raccoon yielded warm and particularly hard-wearing furs that protected from the cold, as well as good-tasting meat.

Soon after the arrival of the settlers, the value of the raccoon's pelt was realized by the fur trade. Although it probably reached its height during the 19th century and the beginning of the 20th, efforts were being made as early as the 17th century to impose taxes and bans on the export of raccoon pelts in order to keep some check on the slaughter. Quite early on, it was estimated that over a million raccoons were killed each year to satisfy the lust for the thick, long, durable fur. The fact that the raccoon survived such a level—and indeed even higher levels later—of persecution says a lot for the animal as a breed.

Early on, raccoon pelts were used as hard currency. One story states that when the frontiersmen of Tennessee set up the State of Franklin, the secretary to the governor received five hundred raccoon skins a year, while each member of the assembly received three a day. Early settlers traded pelts for everyday commodities such as flour and sugar, while the Native Americans would use them as currency in exchange for guns or other such items.

COON HUNTS

Raccoon hunting is a popular sport in much of the United States. The recognized season is the late autumn, when the animals are fattening up to prepare for winter. Hunting takes place at night when the raccoons are active.

The raccoon is hunted by a pack of dogs, which generally chase it up a tree. Sometimes the followers will shake the tree to dislodge the quarry or

Raccoons may be an urban nuisance, but they have undeniable charm (right).

L. Lee Rue/Frank Lane Picture Agency

The coonskin hat (above) *is a potent symbol of North America's rugged frontiersmen.*

Kenneth W. Fink/Ardea

THEN & NOW

This map shows the areas of western and central Europe into which the raccoon has been introduced in the latter half of this century.

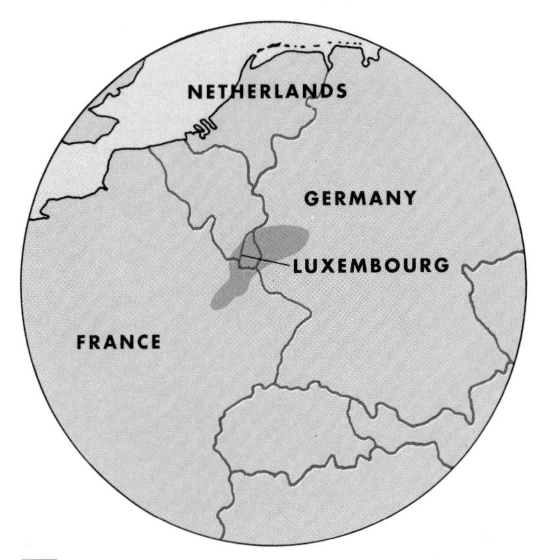

RACCOONS IN EUROPE

Native only to the United States, the common raccoon was recently introduced into Europe—initially Germany—in an attempt to capitalize on the value of its fur. The idea was to establish raccoon farms. Some sources claim that the project failed and that two pairs were released into the wild, while others say that numbers simply escaped and took off for a life of freedom. Either way, as might be expected with this adaptable animal, it flourished and there is now a thriving feral population emanating from the Eifel district of western Germany and spreading into the Mosel Valley, as well as in France, the Netherlands, and Luxembourg. It has also been introduced into parts of the former Soviet Union, where it has thrived in some areas.

The raccoon's success in Eurasia has sometimes been attributed to the fact that one of Europe's native carnivores, the bear, which is also mainly omnivorous, has now disappeared from much of its former habitat, leaving a niche to be filled. In many of its newly inhabited areas, with the decline of the commercial value of its fur, the raccoon is regarded as a pest.

Mark Newman/Frank Lane Picture Agency

A coati displays the bold, opportunistic habits typical of its cousin, the raccoon.

even shoot it down from the branches. If it is young or small, it is usually spared. A raccoon can be a tough adversary in such a hunt, however; if one of the hounds gets a grip on its tail, say, the raccoon will fight back with teeth and claws as viciously as any cornered or captured animal.

Raccoons as pests

In many areas, farmers wage continual war on raccoons for the damage they do to their cornfields. Fresh corn is a favorite among raccoons, and at nighttime they enter the cornfields, often with a litter of young, to pull over the stalks with their forepaws and tear off the husks from the ears. In addition, they steal into chicken houses and kill hens. As the demand for pelts became less, and as some states sought to protect raccoons from the overzealous hunters with their hounds, farmers in many areas were persecuting these animals, which they saw as real threats to their livelihoods. In the 1950s, some states offered bounties for raccoon hides in an attempt to control numbers.

Raccoons are also a potential threat in that they carry rabies. However, there are few, if any, reports of humans catching rabies from raccoons. ■

ALONGSIDE MAN

CLEVER PLAYMATES

Of all America's wild animals, the common raccoon probably makes the best and most popular pet. If caught and handled while still young, they are said to make affectionate pets and will quickly learn to tolerate other domestic animals, such as cats and dogs. Indeed, they are forever inciting these poor animals to play, for their nature, particularly when young, is curious and playful. As they get older, however, they have been known to turn vicious—biting and scratching—when angered.

Many people consider raccoons to be intelligent animals, and raccoons have proved themselves able to learn and be trained to some extent. There are stories of raccoons learning how to secure food by pulling on a baited rope, for example, which would then open a door leading to food. The association made, the raccoon would pull on the rope even when it was not baited. One report tells of a female raccoon trying to show her cubs this trick some two years later. Another story tells of a raccoon trained to put a coin in a vending machine to receive food. Given the coin, the raccoon would first turn this over and over in its hands to see if it felt like food!

RACCOONS IN DANGER

The International Union for the Conservation of Nature (IUCN), or the World Conservation Union, lists the following procyonids in its *Red Data Book*:

Barbados raccoon	Extinct?
Olingo	Insufficiently known
Cacomistle	Vulnerable
Cozumel Island coati	Indeterminate
Mountain coati	Insufficiently known

In addition, four subspecies of raccoons are listed, either as indeterminate or insufficiently known.

INTO THE FUTURE

Although it is estimated that there are over four million raccoons killed in the United States each year—through hunting and trapping—the numbers of this cunning, resourceful animal seem to increase rather than decrease, and certainly it has carved a niche for itself among the urban wildlife. Indeed, because of its partiality to the by-products of human settlement—food-filled garbage cans and cozy chimney-pot nesting sites—it is widely viewed as a pest. Some of the other members of its family, however, are apparently looking forward to a less rosy future.

The most threatened of all the raccoon species appears to be the Barbados raccoon, which is known only on Barbados and may already be extinct. All other raccoon species, with the exception of the common and crab-eating raccoon, are vulnerable to a certain extent, largely because they live in restricted habitats. Pressures from hunting or from competition with the more successful common raccoon, which has been introduced in many areas, could seriously affect any one of these other species.

Of the other members of the procyonid family, two species of olingos are also facing an uncertain future. These are the Chiriqui olingo, *Bassaricyon pauli*, and Harris's olingo, *B. lasius*. The first is known only from Cerro Pando in western Panama, and the second only from Cartago in central Costa Rica. Debate rages as to whether they are both subspecies of the more widespread *B. gabbi*, or whether they are species in their own right.

The Cozumel Island coati is another that, by nature of its restricted environment—the Mexican island of Cozumel, off the Yucatán Peninsula—lives under some threat, as does its neighbor the Cozumel Island raccoon. While in no danger as a species, there is a colony of white-nosed coatis in Costa Rica that faces possible devastation—the devil in the piece being, for once, not man but another wild animal (see The Nancite Coatis). ■

PREDICTION

THREATENED SUBSPECIES

The raccoon as a species is assured a future, although some of its subspecies will probably die out in the long term. Those particularly threatened are the island-dwellers, which are sensitive to the slightest change in their ecosystem.

THE NANCITE COATIS

The Nancite beach of Costa Rica is included in the Santa Rosa National Park, an area of secondary-growth forest that is gradually maturing to provide a rich habitat for a number of wild animals. One inhabitant is the white-nosed coati. The coatis at Nancite are spoiled with food, since the beach is an important nesting ground for turtles, whose eggs provide a rich source of nutrients. In the turtles' peak nesting season of August–September, there may be as many as 40,000 turtles laying their eggs at any one time. To the coatis' misfortune, however, they share the idyllic spot with some small monkeys: white-faced capuchins.

Owing to the ideal conditions, the white-faced capuchins have been gradually colonizing the area for the last ten years—and it seems that they have a penchant for eating baby coatis. And just about the only time that the coatis are vulnerable is when they are very young, for this is the time when the female coatis leave the protection of the group and make a solitary nest. The monkeys seem to know exactly where the mothering coatis have made their nests, as well as when they are nursing young, and they check around the nests every day. Although the female coati is fierce in the protection of her young, she is no match for a group of persistent, hungry monkeys. It has been estimated that over the last two years, only five out of at least a hundred newborn coatis have survived the carnage wreaked by these white-faced capuchins.

Illustration Evi Antoniou

INDEX

Published by Marshall Cavendish Corporation
99 White Plains Road
Tarrytown, New York 10591-9001

The material in this series was first published in the English language by Marshall Cavendish Limited, of 119 Wardour Street, London W1V 3TD, England.

Library of Congress Cataloging-in-Publication Data

Encyclopedia of mammals.
p. cm.
Includes index.
ISBN 0-7614-0575-5 (set) ISBN 0-7614-0587-9 (v. 12)

Summary: Detailed articles cover the history, anatomy, feeding habits, social structure, reproduction, territory, and current status of ninety-five mammals around the world.
1. Mammals—Encyclopedias, Juvenile. [1. Mammals—Encyclopedias.] I. Marshall Cavendish Corporation.
QL706.2.E54 1996
599'.003—dc20 96-17736
CIP
AC

Printed in Malaysia
Bound in U.S.A.